TRANQUEBAR PRESS

INGA

Poile Sengupta was born in Ernakulam, Kerala, and began writing while in school in Delhi. Her work includes fiction, poetry and drama for adults, as well as for children. Her collection of six plays was published by Routledge, in 2010, as *Women Centre Stage: The Dramatist and the Play*. Her recent writing for children includes *Role Call* and *Role Call Again* by Rupa, and *Vikram and Vetal, Vikramaditya's Throne* and *Good Heavens! One Act Plays for Children* by Puffin. Her short fiction for children has been extensively anthologised.

Poile Sengupta is a well known theatre person in Bangalore, which is now her home.

This is her first novel.

INGA

Poile Sengupta

TRANQUEBAR

TRANQUEBAR PRESS
An imprint of westland ltd

61, Silverline Building, 2nd Floor, Alapakkam Main Road, Maduravoyal, Chennai 600095
93, 1st Floor, Sham Lal Road, Daryaganj, New Delhi 110002

First published in India in TRANQUEBAR by westland ltd 2014

10 9 8 7 6 5 4 3 2 1

ISBN: 978-93-84030-64-3

Typeset in Goudy Old Style by SÜRYA, New Delhi

For my son Aditya, a long promised birthday gift,
with all my love and respect
for who he is

A NOTE

This book, the memoirs of my dearly beloved wife Rapa, has been a torment for me for the last forty years. I found the journal under her hospital mattress, an hour after she had died, a notebook in a large, brown envelope which also held a book of jottings, a set of her explorations in writing, a collection of letters and a few newspaper cuttings. She had written her account, in long hand with a fountain pen, during her last weeks in hospital. I put it away then, and kept it hidden all these years, taking it out at times, only for my own reading. However my ordeal is not over. My anguish remains.

Did I do wrong in concealing Rapa's work all these years? You will understand, when you read this, why I did so. But then, why did Rapa write this journal at all, in the last weeks of her life? What had she wanted me to do with it? Had she wanted the world to know? She told me once that an autobiography was too easy a storytelling, and unimportant to anyone but the writer. Then why this record? I have no answer to these questions and will never get one.

I am certain, however, that Rapa would have taken the literary world by storm had she not died so young. She would have written books that reflected her immense talent.

She would have been on your bookshelf, with Byatt and Murakami and Gordimer.

Why do I publish this now? Perhaps, it is my last chance to fulfil Rapa's wish, her intense desire to be an author. Late last year, I fell ill and suddenly felt my seventy years. When I recovered, I resolved to approach a publisher with the manuscript I had locked away for so long. He was excited, his response immediate.

With the help of the editor, despite my limited skills with the computer, I have been able to divide Rapa's dateless journal into chapters. I have also inserted, hopefully in the right places, her pieces of creative writing, and the letters and newspaper cuttings she had preserved.

And so, here is Rapa's book, my tribute to her, my one true friend, my love.

1

Now when I think of it, my life started that summer when I first told Inga I was going to write a book. She was about eleven years old then, and I had just entered my fourteenth year. I was in Komala Nivas for the summer holidays and far away from Delhi where my father lived in all the vainglory of being a Member of Parliament. I was unleashed from his savage controlling, his viciousness.

We were in our secret place that day, Inga and I, eating raw green mangoes that we had stolen from the storeroom, where they had been heaped to be sliced, salted and pickled. Mangoes are such egotistical fruit. They demand your complete attention, whether they are ripe or green. My mango was small, the size of a pebble, but it burned my tongue and lips, the salt I held in my palm had become wet and rough. It was hot, my chin itched. I knew we could not be seen by the eyes of the house but I was not sure of the ears. So I leaned close to Inga and whispered, 'I'm going to write a book. About Sister-in-law Too.' Inga laughed.

If anyone could transform laughter to light, she did, Inga. Radiance upon radiance of laughter, chime upon bell chime of light sparkled and shone everywhere. It was as if the sky showered tiny star grains that scattered, glinting, on the hay heap we were cocooned in; they sparkled on the leaves of the jackfruit tree above and dusted my arms with gold. Who could resist such a dance of light . . .? I couldn't, I never could. Almost never.

There was a sudden scramble of sound from the far side of the cowshed and I saw Sister-in-law Too shoot out and run towards the house, tripping and falling in her hurry. She turned for a second to look at us laughing, my eyes collided with hers, and then she was off, buttoning her blouse and trying to gather up her sari at the same time. I watched her go, hoping she would fall headlong; sadly, she did not. I hated Sister-in-law Too. She was the wife of Brother Two, who, at the time, was away studying in Madras or so it was assumed. Sister-in-law Too considered herself a nonpareil, always smiling at her reflection in the mirror and sniffing into her armpits. Once, I asked her why she did that, smelt herself, and she whipped around and said she was not an ugly black rat like me, she was a goddess, as fair as milk, as graceful as a deer, she was a raashaati, a royal princess. I hated her from then. I vowed to take revenge. 'Like Draupadi?' Inga asked. I did not know who Draupadi was but I said yes, like her.

I kept watch on Sister-in-law Too whenever I could, sometimes with Inga, usually without. Inga was not a good detective. She giggled too much, or she laughed, she did not even know how to shadow anyone properly; and I would tell her she could never have been in the Secret Seven. Of course I had to explain to her who the Secret Seven were and she giggled again. The only time she tried to be secretive, was when we had to go to the storeroom to get green mangoes. She did giggle a little and tripped once or twice in her excitement but no more than that. She remembered to walk tiptoe and to keep her tongue stuck to the back of her upper teeth, the way I had taught her to do.

Sister-in-law Too was a sly one. She often disappeared when I was being oiled before the long Friday bath, or when my hair was being combed and braided in the early evenings. But I remember very clearly the two times I did catch her. One was that time at the cowshed, the other was earlier. It was a hot afternoon, everyone seemed to be dozing. Inga and I had slipped into the dark storeroom to get mangoes. We found Sister-in-law Too there. She was rolling about on the floor, with her sari drawn up, her hand between her legs, making moaning sounds. Her eyes were shut. Inga whispered loudly that Sister-in-law Too seemed to have got a stomach ache maybe because she had eaten too many green mangoes. Sister-in-law Too abruptly changed the moaning into pain sounds. 'Ayyo! My stomach is paining so much! Ayyo! Ayyo! What pain!' She turned away from us, managed to pull the sari down, still crying, 'Ayyo! I cannot bear this pain. Ayyo! Ayyo!' The liar. The self-titled bloody raashaati. The storeroom smelt overwhelmingly of earth, ripe jackfruit and animal. I grabbed a few mangoes, took Inga by the arm and dragged her away. Sister-in-law Too was our enemy.

She was so very sly, Sister-in-law Too. When we, the women and children, sat together for the noon meal, she would say, 'Of course Inga will marry one Collector, that I am sure, she is so pretty like one doll. But I am telling you, Rapa is black it is true, but she has good features if you go to see.' I knew what she was actually saying; did she think she could fool me? She was calling me a piece of dirty coal, an ugly black rat ... I used to stick my tongue out at her whenever she said this, or make a face, and my mother, without even seeming to notice, would say, 'Rapa! That will do! Remember, she is your sister-in-law too.'

Sister-in-law Too! There she sat mincing at her food, gleefully listening to my mother rebuke me, and admiring her own hands and fingers, as if they were exquisite pieces of something or the other, jewellery perhaps. From her mat in the corner, Sister-in-law One, in her tired, waxen way, would then tell my mother, 'Rapa is only a child, Amma. She never shows a face like that to me.' Sister-in-law One was boring. There was something wrong with her legs, so she had to be helped to go to the bathroom and to bathe and dress. At other times, she dragged herself around on her buttocks, using her arms for steering. I never knew why Brother One married her. Those days, before Goblin came to Komala Nivas, he hardly spoke to her when he came in to eat. He would speak briefly to my mother or to Rukku Paati as they brought the food out, and then only to ask for more of this and some more of that. But Sister-in-law One always made sure she sat near him and served him his meal, searching his face anxiously all the while. He never would look at her.

Letter from Inga

Dear Rapa,
I am writing this letter to Komala Nivas because you are there now. Do not ask how I am knowing this.

This is a very late letter. You may have been so angry when you came from your school and you saw Mother and I were not there. No, we did not at all go off suddenly. We were thinking to go for a long time. You must have seen that there was always fighting in the house, between your mother and my mother. It became very, very bad. I wanted to tell you but both your mother and my mother stopped me. It was only that one time they agreed about anything.

Anyway, we have settled down here now. I am going to school and after finishing school final, then I will join shorthand typing classes. After that I will try to get small office work. Mother is giving tuition to some girls in mathematics and also teaching light music. We are managing somehow, so we are quite all right.

Mother does not want you to know our house address, so I am giving you post box number. You can write to me c/o that. Please do not mistake this.

Inga

Journal

Inga and I were never actually caught in the act of eating green mangoes. When we got a stomach ache, everyone knew anyway. Then we were thoroughly humiliated. We were forced to drink loathsomely bitter omum water and were laughed at, mostly by Great Aunt Kuppai. She was the worst. 'Today, it is mangoes,' she would say. 'Tomorrow when some rascal will fill your belly, you can hide it you think? A swollen belly? Like jackfruit hanging? Listen to me you corpses! You are all cursed. All of you with breasts and a hole! That whore Kunti made sure a woman can hide nothing! Her tongue or her belly will talk! Here drink this, shanishwari! Shut your mouth and swallow it.'

After the day I saw her running out of the cowshed, Sister-in-law Too tried to make up with me. She began to oil me for the Friday bath, even though earlier she would stop after oiling Inga, saying her arms were aching, and then she would disappear. I realized much later that she probably rushed to the cowshed. Paru would have been sent to get cow feed; she was always out on Friday mornings. But at the time, before I knew all this, I only felt furious. What did she think, the bloody raashaati, the slimy princess! That some of my blackness would rub off on her? That she would get soot on her lily white palms?

But now, all of a sudden, here she was, insisting on oiling me all over, even tickling me under my armpits, like a giddy girl. The sickening hypocrite! Inga used to laugh her merry laugh when she was tickled. I never did. In the evenings too, Sister-in-law Too began to comb and plait my hair and actually spared some of her jasmine strings for me, all in public view. Great Aunt Kuppai said grumpily to my mother, 'So, finally your second daughter-in-law is learning how how to behave in her in-laws' house, is it? Does she even think about her husband for one minute? Poor boy. So far away, studying so hard. Eating some lodge food! Cooked by what shudra hands I do not want to think!'

I knew what Sister-in-law Too was doing and why. I enjoyed knowing it. She knew I knew, and she was too cunning, far too sly to ask me not to say anything to anybody. But, however much I spied on her, however cleverly I kept watch, I could not catch her again.

I did not need to.

Begat! What a satisfying word it is! It scorns. It despises. It spits. Summarily it dismisses all that bleating nonsense about love and romance, moonlight and motherhood. Begat! My father begat me. And he begat my brothers. And he begat several other offspring of (off?) unacknowledged women. . . . Begat! My father! No handsome seducer he, not a Wickham or a Steerforth. Just a very rich man, dark, with a rolling belly and an ugly triangle of skin under his chin. A begetter!

Begetter! Inga would not have approved of such words and it would have shown on her face. She had a curious way of showing her disapproval, Inga. She flattened down her nose so that the delicate white skin creased into tiny lines like the markings on a butterfly. Yes, Inga would have disapproved. She disliked – too strong a word – she moved tremulously away from the stink of the barnyard, from stained mattresses and misshapen pillows and the dark, smelly, secret things that make up our inner lives. Mine, certainly. Definitely my father's. And yet . . . I knew not.

Letter from Inga

Dear Rapa,

Why you have so much of interest about our Indian stories so suddenly? You never asked like this before. When you were reading that drama by William Shakespeare – I think its name was As You Like It *– you went almost mad. You were shouting that Shakespeare was the best writer in this whole world. You also told that people in that drama are like us only. Your name was Rosalind and I was the other girl, her cousin, who had a name starting with 's'. The bad people in the drama you told are like Sister-in-law Too and Great Aunt Kuppai, etc. My God, how you used to be able to say so many* lines from that book. You were knowing that whole thing by heart or what?

Anyway, about that question you are asking. Kunti was a queen in Mahabharata. Her husband's name was Pandu and she had five sons called five Pandava brothers. But not any of the Pandavas was by Pandu. You see Pandu had curse that he will die there and then, in case he slept with his wife. But he had to have a son, he was king you see. So his poor wife used one secret mantra that she had earlier got from sage Durvasa. Maybe that sage knew that she will need it. Anyway, by saying that secret mantra, Kunti called whatever god she wanted and get a son from him. So Kunti got three boys called Yudhishthira or Dharmaputra, son of Dharma, Bhima, son of Vayu, wind god, then Arjuna, son of Indra, sky god. Then because she was kind lady, Kunti told that mantra to Pandu's second wife Madri, who got twins, Nakula and Sahadeva, sons of Ashwini Kumaras, sons of sun god. Madri was so clever. She got two sons in one go itself!

But Kunti did one stupid thing. Before she got married even, she wanted to test that mantra, so she called sun god. Of course he came and she got pregnant. So actually she got four sons but that first son she had to hide. She put him inside a basket and put it in the river. He was saved by some poor people. Karna was the name of this son of Kunti. He suffered all his life. On the day he died, Kunti cried over his body and then everyone got to know.

Before this all happened, nobody was able to make out if a lady was pregnant. They looked same as always. But after Kunti's action, ladies are not able to hide that they are pregnant. That is why, our elders like Great Aunt Kuppai used to say that all because of Kunti, ladies are cursed.

Inga

2

Journal

The next big thing that happened that summer was Sister-in-law Too's mysterious illness. She sat in a corner, in the back verandah, smelling horribly of old, stagnant water and some stinky medicine. She did not seem to be having baths or even changing her clothes, and once when she got up, I saw a large, round patch of blood on her buttocks. It was like looking at the back of a red-bottomed Rhesus monkey. She stopped eating as well. My mother got frightened and wanted to call the doctor, but Great Aunt Kuppai said, 'You want to put coal on your face? Call her father mother.'

Sister-in-law Too's parents arrived three days later. By that time, Sister-in-law Too had recovered enough to have a bath and come away from the back verandah. But as soon as she heard a car stop at the front gate, she started moaning, 'O! My head! It is going round and round!' Then she slumped to the floor and stretched out limp. For once, I wished my father had been there. He had little patience with this sort of playacting; he would have snapped at her and made her jump to attention. But the only male in the house was Brother One and he was already on the front steps ushering in the visitors, while my mother, agitated, waited in the

main hall. Great Aunt Kuppai was sitting with us in the
inner room by the door, fanning herself. She did not move
nor speak when Sister-in-law Too collapsed on the floor. It
was Sister-in-law One who took charge of the drama. She
dragged herself to the still figure, called loudly towards the
kitchen for water, and when it came, slapped fistfuls of it
onto the face of Sister-in-law Too and, in spite of fiercely
muttered protests from the prone figure, pushed her into
sitting up.

We could hear Sister-in-law Too's mother, Meenakshi
Athai, the fish-eyed one, talking loudly, unceasingly, outside.
She was my father's cousin and had the voice of a woman
who triumphed at bargaining. 'The second we got the wire,
I said they are worrying for nothing. My girl has health. She
runs and runs doing work. If she has stomach pain during
her untouchable time, so what is there? Her husband is not
with her no? Healthy girls need a healthy husband. Then all
this stomach pain will go. I said to her father, whatever it is,
we are going to her in-laws' house, we cannot go with empty
hands. This is my maternal house, true, but that is another
matter. We must always see what is correct. So I told that
snacks maami, that old murukku maami you know, to come
and make. I know Rukku Maami also makes but still . . .
Two tins she made. She made some ladoos also. My girl likes
ladoo.'

I saw FishEyes step into the inner room, grandly, like a
decorated elephant, still talking. 'So this black girl is
Thangam's daughter? And this other girl is? O I know! I
know! Fatherless girls should never have such good colour
and curly hair. So where is my golden child? My flower bud?'

FishEyes had several yards of jasmine coiled around her

hair bun, and whatever part of her was visible glinted with diamonds – her earlobes, both nostrils, her podgy neck, her arms from wrist to elbow. As she walked further in, the flower bud, propped up against the wall, her face and the top of her sari dripping wet, began to make a sound that was a moaning and a wailing and much else beside. FishEyes took one look at the bud and screamed. 'O my treasure girl! My child of gold! You have cried so much? This who who have done to you?'

That was when the fight started.

Letter from Inga

Dear Rapa,
Yes, Great Aunt Kuppai and Sister-in-law Too's mother were related even before the marriage of Brother Two. Meenakshi Athai is a niece of your grandfather and also of Great Aunt Kuppai. She is the daughter of their sister Ammini who married Great Uncle Kunjappa. Great Aunt Ammini died two days after delivering Meenakshi Athai in her in-law's house only. Meenakshi Athai was brought up by her father's mother. Great Uncle Kunjappa did not marry again and died after Athai was married off to Dorai Athimbiar who comes from a very rich family. You don't know all this Rapa?
Inga

Journal

When FishEyes began screaming accusations, Great Aunt threw a look of flame at her, and the words exploded like mustard seeds in hot oil, 'Yedeeye Meenu! Watch your mouth and talk!'

FishEyes paid no attention. She pulled her daughter's face to her silk-bloused bosom, and rocked to and fro, wailing loudly, her words a dirge. 'O my golden child! What have they done to you? They have looted your beauty. They have destroyed your lustre! I brought you here as a lotus bud! I brought you up like a princess! Look at you now! O, my honey face. O pearl of my eyes!'

Great Aunt Kuppai snorted. 'So why,' she asked sharply, 'did you dress your lotus bud in one old sari for her marriage? The sari you bought for that previous alliance which broke! Because this was only Kittu's son? Is that why?'

FishEyes turned around furiously. 'Who said it was that old sari?' she screamed. 'You of all people are saying this Kuppaathai? Everything I got new new for my child! You think I am telling lies?'

Great Aunt Kuppai's fanning became faster; her old hand fan crackled with the fury of the activity. 'Whose granddaughter are you?' she snarled. 'That grandmother of yours, your sapless father's mother, was she a woman or a raakshasi?' Great Aunt's eyes darted to my mother who was still standing at the doorway, quite silent. 'Thangam, do you know how that raakshasi treated my poor sister, my Ammini? They did not even give her food to eat. Such a big house, such a big kitchen, so many eversilver vessels and my poor sister starved! And when she was pregnant with this thankless girl, do you know what that woman did? She made my poor sister to clean sacks and sacks of tamarind. With all those hundreds of servants, she could not make them to do it? She made my sister to do it. Why? So that my sister's belly is heated up, her womb is washed out! In the end, between this girl and that woman, they killed Ammini!'

FishEyes shrieked. 'You dare take my grandmother's name like that? I know how she was treated in this house! She was the mother of this house's son-in-law or not? But when she came, what respect she got from you? She slept on a torn mat! Even the rasam was cold! And I know how you kick all other people to one corner! I know very well that.'

Great Aunt Kuppai flung down her fan, got up with a small grunt, and went close to FishEyes. 'Shut your mouth,' she hissed. 'You think I want the whole world to hear about your daughter's shame? Ask her what what she has been doing. Ask! In the temple and the pond-side, they are talking. Do you know what they are saying about her? A girl from this house, this family?'

My mother cut in, suddenly. Unexpectedly. 'Rapa! Inga! Why are you two sitting here? Go and ask Dorai Athimbiar if he wants coffee. Go!'

'Coffee?' Meenakshi Athai screamed. 'You think I will touch anything in this house? Even amritham if you give me, even nectar, I will not have, it will be poison for me.'

She pushed away her daughter and got up, her bosom heaving. 'I will take my poor tortured child and go. I will not sleep with my head facing in the direction of this house. I have no more a mother's house! Come my champaka poo, my poor flower bud. Let us go.'

Great Aunt Kuppai picked up her fan and sat down again, settling her back against the wall. 'Yes, go!' she said, as if she was tired of it all. 'And take those smelly tins of murukku also. Even our cows won't eat that. Rukku had to throw all your marriage eatables to the backyard crows.'

FishEyes did not answer. She pushed past us, pulling her champaka flower by the arm and asking her in a dangerously level voice where her 'clothes and all' were. My mother tried to calm her down, muttered some words of peace, but Great Aunt Kuppai said sharply, 'Thangam! Bring me a mouthful of buttermilk. My tongue is dry.'

In a very short time they were done and FishEyes swept out with her pearl ruby child, carrying three heavily pregnant cloth bags, a tall, silver lamp, hastily cleaned of its oil, and a glittering steel trunk. Brother One and Dorai Athimbiar were still sitting uncomfortably on the only two chairs in the house. They had obviously heard the quarrel, but discretion as an ornament has been finely wrought by Brahmin males. They said nothing. 'Why are you sitting there like a doll?' FishEyes screamed, storming past her husband on her way out of the house. 'Do you know how she humiliated me? Insulted me? Listen, you all! My feet will not cross this doorstep again! Guruvayurappa, you are witness. Come on, call that driver! Where is he, the rascal? I will not stand here one minute more!'

Dorai Athimbiar got up hurriedly, patted Brother One on the shoulder, incoherently muttering words of leave-taking, and followed his wife and daughter out to the shining black car. As the car door was opened for her, Sister-in-law Too lifted her head and looked straight into the face of Brother One who was standing on the verandah. He cleared his throat and slid his eyes away.

There seemed very little to do in Komala Nivas with Sister-in-law Too gone. No more shadowing. No more spying. She had left nothing behind, not even a bottle of hair oil or a tin of that heavily-scented talcum powder she used. It was as if she had never lived in the house. My mother did not speak about her. She seemed to spend most of the day in the kitchen with Rukku Paati, the cook, shouting words to her, because Paati was deaf. It was now Paru who oiled Inga; nothing much else changed. But Great Aunt Kuppai pulled my hair and pushed my head more furiously than earlier and kept muttering under her breath as she oiled me for a bath. 'Like mother! Like daughter! Can't keep their legs shut. You Coal Face! Sit still! Someone as black as you, only a blind man will marry. My poor Kittan! Why was he cursed with a devil like you? A black devil!' Then she said something scornful about my mother and her inability to produce a son, a statement I neither understood nor paid much attention to, at the time.

Would it have made any difference if I had? I don't know. All through my growing up years, I had considered Brother One and Brother Two my own brothers, my mother's sons. Why would I have thought otherwise? I saw her giving them so much of her indulgence, such lengths of time, without the constant irritability she showed me. Her step-motherliness was never towards them.

Letters from Inga

You did not know this for so many years? Yes, I knew that Brother One and Brother Two are not born from your mother. Their real mother's name was Komalam and she died when Brother Two came. But why you are so angry about it? They are still your brothers only, your father is same.

Inga

Dear Rapa,
No, nobody told me. Not like that anyway. I just got to know.

There was so much of talking in Komala Nivas. All the different different athais and chittis and periammas, that big mouth wife of Milk Pappachu, then that old Sethu Paati who used to come just to sleep at night, they talked so much, they knew things about everybody. You used to see them also, talking near the well, in the storeroom, the kitchen, in the corner of the back verandah, where they sat at least one time in one month. The only place where they did not go to talk, was near the cowshed, I don't know why.

It is so funny, they never thought that children have such big ears so they talked even in front of us. It is true I stayed for a longer time in that house than you. But when you came with your mother for the holidays, it was the same thing. The talking became even more. It is just that you were so busy doing I spy with Sister-in-law Too and reading your books, you did not notice. In any case, what matters now? Those who have to suffer, are.

Inga

Journal

About ten or fifteen days after Sister-in-law Too left, Inga and I were suddenly sent to our grandmother – the mother of my mother and hers. I did not want to go; I felt that something was about to happen in Komala Nivas. My father was expected from Delhi and Great Aunt Kuppai had a shut face. But I also wanted to be with Inga. We went by bus, a hot, smelly bus full of sweaty people. I refused to sit on anyone's knees, so I kept standing, but Inga was passed from one capacious lap to another and exclaimed over. I was wild with her for being so accommodating, but she refused to notice my head shakings and my glaring. I whispered to

Mikhale to get her to stand near us but he said very loudly that she was doing no harm and everybody loved her for her sweet face.

Mikhale was the family's greying errand boy, 'my Man Friday' my father used to call him. Boastfully. At first I thought he was supposed to be on duty on Fridays alone. But I found he was there all through, from Monday to Sunday; he never seemed to go to a home of his own. Later, when I read *Robinson Crusoe*, I understood the reference, just another grand term for a slave. How my father loved a slave and how the poor idiot adored him. He . . . But I digress. On that bus journey, I found out something else about Mikhale. The bus had emptied, and we were the only three passengers, when the bus driver called out to Mikhale. 'Eda,' he shouted over the noise of the bus, 'You were very right about my sister. The wedding date is fixed. Next month it is.'

The bus conductor, who was tallying the fare money, looked up and asked whether Mikhale was an astrologer. The driver laughed and said, 'He has no need for charts and calculations and fuss like that. He just reads your face and tells your future.' Mikhale looked embarrassed. 'Sometimes what I say comes right,' he mumbled. 'Nothing big. Just what is written on foreheads.'

'Then tell me about me!' demanded the conductor and turned his face towards Mikhale. But we had reached the lane to Grandmother's house and we got off with 'another time' from Mikhale. I did not let go though. 'What is written on my face?' I stopped and asked, as we entered the dusty alley. Mikhale put down our bags, wiped his forehead and said, 'You do not worry. You will marry a big man, ICS officer. You will become famous!'

'And me?' asked Inga, turning her petal face up to him. He studied her for a long moment but did not speak. There came over his face, a look of tremendous sadness. He picked up the bags and said, 'You are still too small, my little sparrow. I cannot see. Come, let us run. It is going to rain.'

Letter from Inga

> Oh Rapa, you are really strange! Chiyaam Maama was just a big man who never became more than eight years old. He really never wanted to cause hurt to anybody or make anyone afraid. He had such a pure heart you know. Whatever money he got he used to give it to the temple.
>
> Inga

Journal

Grandmother lived in an old ramshackle house near the temple. I don't remember my grandfather, I think he died when I was about a year old. My grandfather had been a priest; the family was always quite poor, even I knew that. Chiyaam Maama was the only son, brother to my mother and Inga's. He was a large, hairy man, and if it wasn't for his being as fair-complexioned as my mother and aunt, he may as well have been a chimpanzee. He certainly behaved very unlike a maama and someone older than my mother. He was always asking for money, especially from me, and shouted if I said I did not have any. 'You English-speaking girl,' he would yell. 'Chiyaam is not believing you. Your father is such a R-I-C-H man. He cannot give poor Chiyaam two coins?' Once when I was quite little, he took my mother and me for a boat ride down the river. I still remember how frightened I was when he stopped the boat midstream, and said he would not take us back until he got money. I think my mother gave him four annas. She laughed a lot too, I remember.

Strangely, Chiyaam Maama did not ask Inga for money. He would kiss her heavily on top of her head and bring her crushed flowers every evening from the temple. And Grandmother was very calm about it all, unnaturally so, I thought. 'Don't answer him little one,' she would tell me. 'Just eat well. Do you want more sugar with that idli?'

Long afterwards I asked my mother why they had not locked him up in some asylum. She looked at me sharply and said, 'Why? What harm he did to anybody, poor boy? He was so innocent, like a one-day baby he was. A tender, green baby. When he was hungry, he had food, when he was tired, he went to sleep. In between time, he was in the temple. That was his life.'

Everything in Grandmother's house smelt of the temple, especially the food. And there was not much of that. It was not like in Komala Nivas. No mounds of green mangoes to be pickled, no heavy smelling jackfruit jam being cooked in an enormous tureen, no tall tins of murukku and banana chips stacked in the storeroom.

'My god is poor,' Chiyaam Maama would roar every now and then. 'He is not like that rascal Kalla Krishnan, that thief. That one has all neta people under his armpit, so clever he is. My poor Rama. He is one simple fellow, one paavam god.'

In Grandmother's house, we got up at dawn to the chanting from the temple, where I could clearly distinguish my uncle's loud voice in perfect accord with the priests; we ate by the temple's meal timings and went to sleep by twilight. The only excitement was when Mikhale arrived once every four days or so, and came up to the front courtyard with sacks of rice and pulses, jaggery and tamarind, and a bunch of long, ripe Kerala bananas. He always said that it was all given to him by a relative and since he himself did not have a home 'as such', he had brought it for Grandmother. I knew even then that this was a piece of fiction, that Mikhale had no generous relative, that he had brought it from Komala Nivas, but obviously, this was the only way Grandmother would accept help from a married daughter.

~

THE MYSTERY OF THULASI INN
Chapter One
(Written when I was twelve)

Rapa and Inga left the caravan at the bottom of the lane and walked up to the quaint tumbledown cottage they had seen from the road. Miss Pappada said anxiously, 'I do hope we are not on a wild goose chase. My word, what a curious place this is. Are you certain it is Thulasi Inn?'

'I vote we find out,' Rapa said cheerfully. She ran up the steep path quickly and banged the old brass knocker on the sturdy wooden door. The door flung open and an old lady with white hair and bright eyes, stepped out and said in her lilting Tamizh voice, 'My dears. I have been waiting for you from dawn. Ohoh! It looks like rain. Quickly, come in, come in.'

The cottage was as neat as its owner, with its old stone

walls and a huge fireplace. 'This house was built by the British people,' the talkative old lady explained, pointing to the fireplace. 'They had all these things. But why do we need it? If there is a cold wind, we close off all the windows.' She cackled with laughter and then asked, 'You want to go to the bathroom?'

'I am feeling awfully empty,' Inga said, looking hungrily around the tiny parlour.

'Ohoh!' exclaimed the old lady, slapping herself on the forehead. 'Stupid woman I am! Here, my little parrots, I have made everything ready for you. From dawn I have been cooking and cooking.' She pointed to a bench that stood against the wall, and which was loaded with shiny steel dishes. What a spread it was! There was a mountain of snow-white idli and crisp brown vadai, next to a bowl filled with creamy coconut chutney. There were layers of crisp, paper-like dosai to be had with steaming hot sambar and mashed potato curry, and there was a deep dish of rava halva decorated with fried cashew nuts and raisins. In a corner were baskets lined with banana leaves and heaped with cut jackfruit, golden-red mangoes and bunches of bananas.

'This is smashing,' whispered Inga as she sat on the floor and heaped the plantain leaf in front of her, with a generous helping of idli and chutney. Rapa and Miss Pappada sat next to her and tucked into the delicious food.

'I have never eaten a vada that is so crisp and soft at the same time,' declared Miss Pappada. She turned to the beaming hostess and asked, 'Do you do all the cooking yourself?'

But before the old lady could answer, a ferocious growl

came from the open door. An enormous man, with long, hairy arms, stood there shutting out the daylight. 'Oh ho hum,' he growled. 'I smell the blood of English-speaking people!'

The old lady turned pale. 'There is nobody here,' she squeaked. 'Nobody here.' She tottered to the door and shut it firmly, turning the key in the lock. Miss Pappada and the girls looked wonderingly at each other. Who was this man? Why was the old lady so afraid of him? Rapa felt a familiar tingling in her veins. This was a Mystery, she was sure of it. 'O goody!' she thought. 'It is not going to be a boring old holiday after all!'

3

Journal

It rained the whole time during that month we spent in Grandmother's house. We had to go to the temple with Grandmother twice every day: after our morning bath and then again, after the evening bath. Each time, we got wet all over again, because the one umbrella there was did not do for the three of us. Apart from that, there was nothing. I remember how boring the afternoons were. Inga sat unmoving on the black stone platform that ran along the outer wall of the house and stared at the rain. She never left off watching, it was as if she was at a performance where dancers swayed and whirled and dropped to the ground as the rainbeat rose and fell. Sometimes the rain pelted down, it blew into our faces, at other times it was so silent that I imagined it had stopped. But there, in the small front courtyard marked out by slimy green bricks, I could see the flattened red mud pitted with rain, where it dripped off the roof tiles. Everywhere, there was a smell of earth and leaf and damp clothes. No one came calling, there was nothing to do.

I read my Enid Blytons over and over again, and backwards and forwards, then I tried to read them out aloud to Inga.

But when I was halfway through the first chapter of one of the mysteries, she asked, 'They don't have a bath before going out? What dirty children, I don't want to hear about them.' She flattened her nose so that her delicate skin creased into a thousand little lines. It was no use.

It then occurred to me that I could start writing a book, not the one about Sister-in-law Too, but another one, a mystery story that Inga might like, where the children had baths. It would be good practice, anyway. But when I asked for paper, there was none to be had. I looked wherever I was told to look, there was not a scrap, not even a postage stamp worth. Finally, after some muttered grumbling, Grandmother set down the bamboo tray of rice grains into which she had been peering, and pulled out something from under her; she had been sitting on it. It was a ledger of some sort, longish, with a frayed red cloth cover; and it seemed to have been used to keep accounts. Grandmother put her finger into the middle of it, carefully tugged out a blank, yellowing page and asked if it would do. One sheet of paper for a whole mystery book? I said I would try to make it do.

I had written only the first chapter when Mikhale suddenly arrived late one evening in a car saying we were to leave at once, so that we would be at Komala Nivas before daybreak. The rain stopped abruptly.

I did not know why we were travelling through the night, and I didn't bother to ask. Who would give me an answer anyway? When we reached, it was still dark, and Komala Nivas was bursting with people. There were hurricane lanterns here and there and all the electric lights were on. There was a huge, thatched awning over the front courtyard so that the house looked different, and, in the half light, secretive. I could hear my father's loud voice, talking, it seemed, to his usual band of lackeys. They would be standing around him, their waists bent, heads lowered, their hands held, palms upward, just above the navel, the posture of the eternal supplicant. It did not take long for Mikhale to join them, just as soon as he deposited Inga and me on the front verandah with our bags, and shouted into the house that we had arrived. Nobody seemed particularly concerned. Inga ran in calling out to her mother, I went in more slowly, dragging the bags. The house smelt of jasmine and sweat and talcum powder, of hot oil, pickles, sour curds and cooking. The inner rooms were full of women and girls dressed in silks, and with strings of flowers in their hair. Some of them were shaking out saris, others were folding towels or petticoats, one or two were dressing their hair. And all of them were talking without pause, some in shrill tones, some whispering in tight groups.

'. . . the boy is in Madras studying they say . . . more than two years since the marriage . . . yes, yes that is right because my son's marriage was same muhurtam and my grandson is now already one-and-a-half years you should see how he . . . chhe nothing wrong with the girl . . . like a goddess she is . . . such good colour . . . does the boy have . . .?'

Then they saw me and all the voices dropped. 'Thangam's daughter . . . could she not look like her mother . . . what is there, her father has money . . .'

One of the girls detached herself from the whisperers and danced up to me, swinging her two long oily pigtails that were twined very tightly with flowers. She was about my age and was dressed in a long red skirt and a purple blouse with swollen sleeves. She looked deeply knowing.

'I am your sister-in-law's younger sister,' she announced, then switched from Tamizh to English. 'My name is Ambuja but you call me Ambu, all right? See I am knowing very much English like you itself. We can be jolly friends no? Come, you are wanting to wear bangles like me no?' She jangled the many, multicoloured glass bangles up and down her arms. 'I will show.' She pushed my bags to a corner and dragged me to the side verandah. Here, where Inga and I usually played hopscotch, there were flaring lamps and another noisy crowd of chattering women. At the far end, an old man sat with a cloth cradle filled with ropes of glass bangles. In the middle of the crowd was Sister-in-law Too, wearing a black sari and lots of jewellery. She looked quite sick. She saw me and gave me a beaming false smile. 'Come Rapa, come my child,' she screamed. 'You must wear many bangles. Show your hands, show.'

'Show no,' commanded Pigtails. 'It is all right. Bangle-seller can take your right hand, that is rule. Any other man takes right hand means,' she giggled, 'means, marriage only.'

The bangle-seller's touch was light, an expert's. He smoothed the purple and red glass rings over my knuckles and my wrist as if bangle and hand were soft moist clay. It was done in an instant and then I was free. Pigtails had taken her eyes off me and was examining one of her sister's necklaces. It was a good time to flee back into the house but I found the door blocked by FishEyes. 'My little girl,' she was saying loudly, 'she never at all knew. She is saying even now when the monthly got stopped she is not knowing. You see what happened, after Deepavali, I kept my child with me for two three more days. Just like that. She should also be in her mother's house no? At that time, my son-in-law, my maapillai also came to my house. It was more than one year after marriage no? Poor boy, leave also he does not get. But that time, somehow he managed. That time only this happened. And my silly paavam girl did not at all make out. Why because monthlies also she was getting, little, little . . . Anyway, I said we must have all ceremonies for my flower bud. So . . .'

I heard a hoarse giggle in my ear and a rope of hair grazed my elbow. 'So funny!' Pigtails whispered. 'Your brother never came. Akka cried and cried. But he did not at all came.' She giggled again into my ear.

I pulled myself out of her affection, and ran towards the cowshed, away from her, away from FishEyes, away from them all. The moon was bright and yet, in my hurry, I almost fell. 'Inga,' I shouted as I neared our secret place. 'Inga! Are you there?' She was not, nor was she up her favourite mango tree. 'Inga,' I called again. 'Inga!'

Then from the cowshed, Paru yelled, 'She and her mother are gone.'

Gone?

But before I could find out anything more, I saw my mother rush out through the back door. She was screaming for me. 'Rapa, you are there I know. Come here now. Ippo! Don't you know your father is wanting? Calling and calling you?'

Even now, I remember so clearly all that happened, almost every word that was spoken that day, when I answered my father's summons.

My father was sitting in the shadowed front courtyard, on one of the wooden chairs, fanning himself. On the other chair, was a fair-skinned, balding man, with thick glasses.

Brother One was standing behind them, arms folded, face sullen. My father seemed to be in one of his rare good moods. 'No, no!' he was saying. 'All this is for and by women only.' Then, in English, he added, 'The initial contribution alone is the man's.' He laughed loudly and then went on. 'I think the boy is to come for the religious function later. Anyway, I am leaving all this nonsense for them to look after inside. I simply thought since I am here, I might as well give a small meal to my party workers. Must keep them happy you know.' He bellowed again. Then he caught sight of me and said pleasantly, 'You have come at last is it? Where were you? Why are you wearing those stupid bangles? Ask your mother to take them off. Not now fool. After I finish.' He turned to the bald man and said, 'She speaks only English you know. I am sending her to the best convent school in Delhi. My two sons are no good except in spending their father's money. But she is doing very well, very well. Dee Rapa! Do you know who this is? He is a big English professor from Madras. Forget your Shakespeare! We have our very own Seshappa Aiyar here. Say something you have learnt in school to him. Some English piece you fool! . . . How do I know what? Use your brains.' He turned to the bald man and said, 'Sesha! I have to attend to some work, I will just come.' My father got up, belching, and walked towards the house with Brother One following him, four steps behind. I stared at the bald man. My father shouted, 'Why are you standing there like a urinal wall? Start talking something!' I started reciting my favourite poem. 'Daffodils by William Wordsworth,' I began.

When I came to the line, '. . . they flash upon that inward eye, which is the bliss of solitude . . .' the bald man said it with me and we finished the poem together. Then without a pause, he began, "'Make me a willow cabin at your gate, And call upon my soul within the house; Write loyal cantons of contemned love And sing them loud even in the dead of night; Halloo your name to the reverberate hills And make the babbling gossip of the air Cry out. . . .'"

Everything around me dissolved – my father's loud peremptory voice, the shouts of the men in the make-do kitchen behind me, the shrill chattering of the women inside the house. I forgot even Inga as I watched him, his head thrown back, his eyes closed, his voice, music. I was scooped up high; I soared, face tingling, rosy, free, across streaming skies, the wind ran like rivulets through my hair, my arms silver-frosted, my head crowned with stars.

He paused, when he spoke again, his voice was a whisper, a coaxing, almost a teasing. "'Shall I compare thee to a summer's day? Thou art more lovely and more temperate Rough winds do shake the darling buds of May . . .'"

Then my father returned and the dancing flowers and the gentle green meadows of England disappeared.

My mother dragged me to the outer bathroom with the copper boilers and wrenched off the bangles. It hurt. She made me bathe in horribly hot water, then ordered me to dress in the long skirt and silk blouse that she had brought. But she refused to tell me where Inga was and rushed back into the house even before I was ready. I followed her, rubbing my wrists and hands and flopping back my wet hair, and saw her scurrying about, carrying huge, silver plates heaped with flowers and coconuts, small sugar crystals, bananas and sweets. Great Aunt Kuppai sat splendidly alone on the big swing in the inner hall, fanning herself vigorously, her lips slammed shut. And in her usual corner, was Sister-in-law One. She was crying.

Who was there to tell me where Inga had gone? Paru? But before I could turn and run back to the cowshed, I was trapped by Pigtails and another girl, who, I was told, was 'my bestest coussin'. They closed around me, one to the left, the other to my right, and in sickening friendliness carried me to the long side room where the women had gathered, with Sister-in-law Too installed in the middle on a colourful mat. Some of the women were singing a song which made the others laugh and look slyly at Sister-in-law Too. 'Very dirty song,' whispered Pigtails, 'about things man does to woman, exetra exetra.' Then she climbed further into my ear and said, 'I am talking English only, so my coussin is not understanding.' The 'coussin' pulled me to her side and asked in Tamizh, 'Why you are so black? You are not Brahmin girl?'

The songs went on and on. Some of the women got up and went round Sister-in-law Too, bending and clapping their hands in a sort of dance, my mother among them. The room was filling up with the stench of dying flowers, blackened bananas and too many sweaty women who had used talcum powder. The singing stopped and some sort of an announcement was made by FishEyes. There were loud giggles and two or three women slunk out of the room; the others watched them go and nudged each other vulgarly. Pigtails said in my ear, 'They are all having swollen up stomachs. So they have to go away so they should not put bad eye on my sister.'

I was then startled by my mother calling my name sharply. 'You have to put the first bangle,' she said in a tone that would not tolerate a refusal. Or a hesitation. She made me sit on the mat, facing Sister-in-law Too and picked up a trayful of bangles – silver, gold and glass – which she thrust towards me. 'Put the kaapu,' my mother said, pointing to the gold ones. 'Two two on one one hand,' came a scream from FishEyes. 'All this thing you must know, this is not your England.' There was a wave of sniggering, my mother wiped her face with her sari end. Sister-in-law Too held out her arms to me, she had small hands, soft and white and the bangles slipped over them like hoops of sunlight. Even now, I don't know why, when I touched her, why, in that hot room, I suddenly felt so cold.

I couldn't get away. I was not needed anymore I could see, but Pigtails and her cousin pulled me back into their sticky web of friendship and there I stood between them, forced to watch what seemed to be some strange, heathen rite. The arms of Sister-in-law Too were now crammed with bangles, mostly of glass, which the other women had taken turns in putting on. Every time she moved, even a little, the bangles jangled and sparkled. The crowd then began chanting the words, 'aanpillai, penpillai, aanpillai, penpillai', as two hefty women thumped Sister-in-law Too's back from the neck downwards.

'They are saying,' came the hoarse whisper in my left ear, 'aanpillai means boy and penpillai means girl. When they stop beating Akka, we will see what word comes.'

The chanting picked up speed and grew louder. Just as the thumpers reached the waist, everyone, including my gaolers, shouted 'aanpillai'. Such contrivance. My eardrums had almost burst.

The ceremony now seemed to be over. The women got

up, tightening their saris across bosom and behind. Suddenly, there was a loud, angry shout from the courtyard, 'Thangam.' My father, who else? My mother dropped the plate she was holding and hurried towards the front of the house. In the general confusion, my gaolers having slackened in their watch, I slipped away and went into the quiet emptiness of the kitchen. There was enough food there for several picnic baskets and no guard: Rukku Paati was in the other room. I made a cradle of my skirt and filled it with idli, vadai, ladoo and a few bananas, enough for two. Surely Inga was now in our secret place.

I was in the deserted back verandah, and turning towards the cowshed, when I heard Brother One call my name. I froze. Now what? 'That Professor Seshan asked me to give you this,' he shouted from inside the house. 'Here, take it. As if I do not have a hundred and one other things to do! I also have to run behind my stupid sister! Here!' Something slid across the floor and stopped against the threshold. It was a book, old, much thumbed, with the professor's name written in tiny letters on the first page at the top. The book was *Alice in Wonderland*.

4

Letters from Inga

Dear Rapa,
That day was a very very bad day. Please do not ask me to remember.
  Inga

Dear Rapa,
Why your mother is telling you all these wrong things? We did not at all go to that postmaster's house. Mother was very angry. She just made me walk and walk that full day. I do not know where we were going. We had no food with us, not even water. I was so tired and so hungry, I kept falling down. When the sky was almost fully dark, my mother suddenly picked me up and started to run. She was saying, 'This is what I should have done then itself. Then itself I should have done it.' There was a pond nearby and that postmaster was walking up from the steps, wiping his face. He saw us and took us to the bus stop. He gave me some bananas and then brought us to Komala Nivas. That is all.
  Inga

Journal

I waited for Inga all day, sitting in our secret place. The waiting would have been tedious if I hadn't had Alice and the food for company. I absorbed the one and relished the other, and finished both. Inga did not appear. I heard Paru washing the cowshed, that meant it was getting to the evening bath time and I had better go back to the house before somebody came looking for me. As I crossed the cowshed, Paru called out, 'What child? Your sister is not come back no?' I wanted to make it clear to her that Inga was my cousin, not my sister but I did not know the Malayalam word for 'cousin' so I let it go.

The back door was shut, unusually enough, but not latched and the house was starkly silent. The crowds had disappeared, the room had been cleaned thoroughly, only the smell of crushed flowers and betel leaves lingered. Rukku Paati was fast asleep, curled across the doorway to the kitchen. In the long, inner hall, Great Aunt Kuppai's swing moved gently, creaking a little, as if she had got up from it violently sometime ago, and it was only now coming to a stop. I looked for Sister-in-law One, she was not in her corner either. Then I noticed a crumpled bit of pink paper on the floor; it was a telegram from Brother Two and the pasted words read, 'regret unable attend ceremony'. I left the crumple on the floor, even though it was evidence, and crept towards the front hall. I heard a murmur of voices in the side room where Great Aunt Kuppai and FishEyes had had their big fight. This time, the door was shut tight, but even more strange, I could hear men's voices inside, my father's and one other. I didn't remember ever seeing a man in that room before. I went quietly up to the door and listened. This had something to do with Sister-in-law Too I was sure, and I had to listen to it as much as I could and remember it all so I could tell Inga.

The voices were low at first, it was difficult to understand what was being discussed. I heard my father tell my mother to shut up and stop snivelling. I heard the other male voice murmur something, presumably to calm him down. Then my father spoke louder, 'Look what he has done, Seshu!' So the other man in the room was the professor! My father was shouting now, 'How I can look people straight after this? He has poured cow dung on my head, Seshu. He has heaped dung on my head.'

Nobody else said anything for a while, I could hear my mother still sobbing. My father groaned, 'Ishwara! Guruvayurappa! Why did you give me such a son? He has smeared coal on my face. What will my party workers say now? They will laugh at me only!'

Great Aunt Kuppai spoke up suddenly. 'Enough!' she snapped. 'It is enough what you say about that poor boy. He has not come, so he has not come. So what?'

'Kuppaathai,' my father said in an anguished way. 'You did not hear what all that woman screamed and screamed? What filth came from her mouth?'

'Yes I heard,' retorted Great Aunt. 'But my mouth was shut because all your party people were there. Now, I can also ask, what did her daughter do? Why did that prostitute try to wash out her belly?'

'What!'

Great Aunt Kuppai snorted. 'You think I did not know?' she said. 'That girl was ready to go to anyone, even to a shudran she will go. Who has filled her belly? Ask her. Ask her loud voice mother! Ask! I am barren, my thali is cut but I have eyes. I have ears. My boy has not touched her, not touched that white slut.'

'What are you saying Kuppaathai?' my father asked. His voice was trembling. 'What are you saying?'

Great Aunt did not reply. My father waited, then he spoke to my mother, 'Thangam. You tell me what all has happened in this house when I was not here. You were not seeing or what?'

Great Aunt Kuppai snorted again. 'Where does your wife have time?' she asked. 'She is only looking after her own sister and her sister's calf.'

My mother burst into loud sobs. 'What all I can do I am doing,' she said through her tears. 'What less is it I have done? You ask everyone. Your son and daughter-in-law are sitting here, you ask them.' She paused, then said, very emphatically, 'Kuppaathai, I did not call my sister to stay here. She is here because of your nephew's wish only.'

'For my poor nephew, all that is white, is milk,' snapped Great Aunt Kuppai. 'Kittan just has to see a woman with wet eyes, and he . . .'

My father interrupted her. 'To come back to the point,' he said in English, 'what are we to do now, Seshu?'

'Nothing has to be done,' said Great Aunt Kuppai flatly, in Tamizh. I was surprised at how much English she understood. 'What has happened has happened. Whatever it is, who has to give answers will only tell lies. Whether mother or daughter.'

'What do we do, Seshu?' my father asked again, clinging to English as if to a raft. 'I do not know what to do.'

'Do nothing,' said the professor. 'Do nothing. Say nothing. All this is a nine-day wonder, Kitta, believe me. Memories are short.'

Great Aunt Kuppai snorted or so it seemed. I heard the chairs creak and Great Aunt Kuppai heaving herself up. I ran back quickly towards the kitchen, calling for my mother as if I had just come in.

I did not know when Inga and her mother returned. Paru told me the next morning that they had come back late. I did not see them at all during the next two days that I was in Komala Nivas, before we left for Delhi.

The news came a fortnight after we reached Delhi. Sister-in-law Too had given birth to a daughter and then died. That was the end of Sister-in-law Too.

≈

ADVICE FROM A PIGTAIL
(Written when I was fourteen)

Rapa opened her eyes and found she had fallen upon a heap of soft, damp leaves. She was not hurt a bit, and she jumped to her feet and looked about her. She was in a strange garden full of giant flowers and fruits that lay scattered all over the ground. 'The first thing I should do,' said Rapa to herself, as she wandered around, 'is to be the right colour. And then I should find Inga.'

It seemed a very good plan and excellently arranged; the only question was, how was she to set about it? She was peering around anxiously among the giant jackfruit and the green mangoes, when she heard a voice calling out to her. It seemed to come from a large coconut that stood near her and was as tall as herself. She searched under it and all around it and behind it and when she did not find anything, she said, 'Come! Come! I have often met a face without a voice, but a voice without a face! It's the queerest thing I ever heard.'

It then occurred to her that she should look at the top of the coconut. She stood on tiptoe and peeped, and found herself looking into the eyes of a long black Pigtail that was coiled on top of the coconut, sucking at a jasmine stalk. The Pigtail and Rapa stared at each other, then the Pigtail took the stalk out of its mouth and spoke to her in a sharp voice. 'What is your caste?' said the Pigtail.

This did not seem an encouraging beginning to a conversation. 'I . . . I don't quite know, Miss,' replied Rapa shyly. 'I thought I was a different colour this morning, but now I seem to have changed again.'

'What do you mean by that?' said the Pigtail. 'Explain.'

'I'm afraid, Miss, I can hardly explain that,' said Rapa, 'because I don't quite know what this is all about, you see.'

'I don't see,' said the Pigtail.

Rapa was a little annoyed at the Pigtail's sharp tone and very short remarks, and she drew herself up and said, 'I think you should tell me what your caste is, first.'

'Why?' said the Pigtail.

This was a rather puzzling question, and as Rapa could not think of any good answer, and as the Pigtail seemed to be in a very unfriendly state, she turned away.

'Wait,' the Pigtail called out. 'Come back and recite the five times table.'

Rapa did not want to offend the Pigtail and as she had nothing else to do, she folded her hands, and began:

'Five one's are live,

'Five two's are men,

'Five three's are very mean,

'Five four's are fun,

'Five five's are . . .'

'Stop. That is not right,' said the Pigtail.

'It is not quite right,' said Rapa in a timid voice, 'some of the words seem to have changed.'

'It is wrong from start to finish,' said the Pigtail decidedly.

There was silence for a few minutes. The Pigtail was the first to speak.

'Are you satisfied with your colour now?' it asked.

'I should like my face to be a little fairer, if you don't mind,' said Rapa. 'Black as coal is such a wretched colour to be.'

'It is a very good colour indeed,' said the Pigtail rearing up angrily as it spoke (it was exactly the colour of coal).

'But I'm not used to it,' said poor Rapa in a pleading tone. And to herself she said, 'I wish the creature would not be angered so easily.'

'You will get used to it,' remarked the Pigtail, as it crawled off the coconut, saying as it went, 'One side will make you fairer, the other side will make you darker.'

'Of what?' thought Rapa. 'One side and the other side of what?'

'Of the broken coconut,' said the Pigtail, just as if Rapa had spoken the question aloud, and the next moment, it was gone out of sight.

Rapa looked at a half coconut that stood next to her like a huge bowl, wondering which its two sides were, and, as the rim was perfectly round, this was a difficult question to answer. At last, she put her arms round the coconut as far as they would stretch, and broke off a bit with each hand.

'Now which will do what?' she asked herself and took a little bite of the piece in her right hand. The next instant, her arms and legs had become the colour of charred paper. This frightened her a good deal, and she hastily nibbled at the bit of coconut in her other hand. Her arms and legs grew fairer and she set to work determinedly eating the coconut piece in her left hand, till she turned as fair as an English girl with golden ringlets to match.

Journal

My father did not attend Sister-in-law Too's last rites; nor did he allow my mother to go. Of course, he did not expressly forbid her, did not say the words out aloud but he made his disapproval very clear. My father had a remarkable talent for not saying anything but declaring much. If asked an uncomfortable question, he either closed his eyes and hummed a classical raga as if in deep musical meditation, or he hurriedly picked up a newspaper, crackled open the political news page and plunged into it. If neither was a good enough tactic, he left the room. This time, unusually, my mother followed him through the door. I heard her pleading with him, saying, rather loudly for her, as he moved from room to room in the sprawling MP's bungalow we lived in, that after all it was his son's wife, a daughter-in-law of the house, and if she did not go what would everyone say? My father did not speak; I heard him bumping into the edges and thrusts of chairs and stools and tables, as he tried to escape, then I heard them in the inner verandah, and then, suddenly, they were both in my room, where I was reading an Enid Blyton.

My father immediately flew into a rage, another of his extraordinary talents. He called me a gutterful of names, most of which I did not understand then because they were Tamizh Malayalam words. Since then, I have educated myself in this area. The gist of my father's explosive speech was that I was a disgrace to him, a wastrel, I would come to no good just like his two sons, and that he would go bankrupt trying to get me a husband because I was dark, ugly, a brainless fool, and my mouth stank.

Many years later, when I was better Tamizhised, I realized that he had also said that I would end up as a slut, a prostitute and my brothers, pimps.

How wrong the man was.

Letter from Inga

Dear Rapa,

Only Great Aunt Kuppai went, she took Paru. She went and came back the same day in a car. I think your father told his party people to get the car for her. She came back very late in the night, I was sleeping by that time. In the morning, I heard Paru telling my mother that Brother Two did everything and went away after he finished his bath because he has urgent work in Madras. Sister-in-law Too's family members thought the baby will also die. But of course, she did not, I don't know why.

Inga

Journal

It was a week or ten days later, that news of the Big Scandal reached us. It was a Sunday and a very hot Delhi day. My father was at his weekly oiling ritual in the inner verandah, just outside my room, so that he could 'supervise' me. My mother had brought in the ornate twin metal bowls with the single handle; one bowl with cooling oil for the head and the other containing an evil-smelling green concoction for the rest of him. She had heated this, she said, to near steaming and she was cautioning my father about its high heat, when the phone rang. This was most unusual for a Sunday. I heard the supplicant in the office chamber pick up the phone, shout that it was a trunk call and saw him running into the verandah, cradling the instrument as if it were a baby, the long wire uncoiling behind. He gave the receiver to my father with the usual sickly bow and stood to attention, holding the base of the telephone, now turned to a royal crown, in the palm of his hand.

My father had, by then, ignoring my mother's warning, plunged his hand into the steaming green glue. At the first words he heard over the telephone, he yelled, 'Ayyo! What are you saying?' and lifted his arm towards the top of his head. The Supplicant leapt forward and, in a gesture worthy of any Tamizh film hero, held my father's hand before it unfisted. My father's bald head was saved from a nasty scald. But that was all that was saved on that occasion. The trunk call was from Prof. Seshu to say that Brother Two had eloped with a low-caste girl, and was nowhere to be found.

Letter from Inga

Dear Rapa,

We got the news about Brother Two because of a letter from Venki Maama from Madras. It came late in the night. Brother One was talking to Great Aunt Kuppai in the hall, about the death ceremonies that they had to do. It is true that Mother and I were in the back room but I remember what was in the letter because Brother One read it out loudly. I heard everything but at that time, I did not understand everything.

Venki Maama said in the letter that Brother Two was not doing his studies properly and he was going to a 'bad' house. Venki Maama, it seemed, had gone many times to see Brother Two and ordered him to stop going to that house. But Brother Two said he was going to marry the girl from that house and the whole world cannot stop him. He also said, it seems, that he was like Gandhi and did not believe in rubbish like caste system.

When he came to this part, Brother One got very angry. He started shouting that because Great Aunt Kuppai and your mother carried Brother Two on top of their heads, the rascal thought he can do anything. Great Aunt shouted back that it was Venki Maama who took the poor boy to that house when he used to visit the girl's mother and it all is his fault. After more shouting, Great Aunt Kuppai told Brother One to give that man some money and wire to your father. After that, I heard her tell Paru to lock the door.

I heard the full story many years afterwards.

Inga

I call Venki Maama, Venki Maama, because he is my mother's second cousin. That way, if you go to see, he is your

*maama also. But he is also your father's first cousin so that is
why you have to call him Chitappa. If he was older than your
father, you will call him Periappa.*

Inga

Journal

My father left for Komala Nivas the next day; my mother
could not go because of me of course. But for once he was
generous with money; I suspect he was trying to bribe the
Hand of Fate so that this latest family crisis did not smear
cow dung on his spotless reputation as the Great Leader of
Men, never defeated yet at the polls. Who would have
thought the old man was so highly superstitious. Obviously,
he would be. He was both a bully and a coward; most men
are.

It was always easy to deal with my mother when she was
not in Komala Nivas. I would only have to discover her in
tears, pester her with questions and she would give me
money and ask one of the supplicants to escort me to a
bookshop. She did not care to supervise my homework
either. So as soon as I got home from school, I was free to
eat eclairs with Fatty, explore a smuggler's cove with the
Famous Five, and run wild like William. I also had long
arguments with Alice's Humpty Dumpty. I could not think
of him as an egg though, because eggs never entered our
house; he was Kuzhakkattai, the white ball of rice flour,
speckled with coconut flakes and mustard seeds that we ate
for tiffin sometimes.

KUZHAKKATTAI
(written when I was fourteen-and-a-half)

It was sitting on a mat of banana leaf which lay on the kitchen ledge. As Rapa came within a few feet of it, she saw that it was much the largest kuzhakkattai she had ever seen besides being the most curious. 'Why!' exclaimed Rapa to herself, 'it has eyes, a nose and a mouth and it's wearing a mundu so I can't see its legs. I do wish I knew if it had any legs at all. To run away with.' She tried to imagine her father chasing a kuzhakkattai that had run away from him, when she found herself being addressed.

'Don't stand there laughing to yourself,' said Kuzhakkattai, looking at a tree some distance away. 'What is your family name?'

'I'm not certain of my family name, Sir,' said Rapa timidly, 'but my name is . . .'

'It is very provoking,' Kuzhakkattai said, 'to be called "Sir" when I have not been knighted – yet.' Rapa didn't know what to say to this so she stood and thought of how the Queen would say, 'I dub thee knight. Rise Sir Kuzha . . .'

'For,' she said aloud, 'Her Majesty would find his name most difficult to pronounce.'

'It is a distinguished family name with great meaning,' Kuzhakkattai cried. 'It means the shape I am – and a handsome shape it is too. Besides, only a Brahmin can pronounce my name as it should be.'

'What nonsense!' Rapa said indignantly. 'What has a word, or a name,' she added hastily, 'to do with who says it?'

'It has a great deal to do with it,' replied the other. 'For instance, do you consider me your father's brother or your mother's?'

'I really wouldn't know.'

'Precisely,' said Kuzhakkattai. 'Here's another question for you. Do you think I'm older than your father and mother or younger?'

Rapa was much too puzzled to venture an answer, so after a minute, Kuzhakkattai spoke again. 'If I was older than your father, you would have to address me with a certain name, but if I was younger, you would have to use a different title. Likewise if I was related to your mother.'

Rapa considered a little. 'Mayhap,' she said at last, rather timidly, 'I could just call you uncle.'

'Uncle!' Kuzhakkattai raised his voice almost to a scream as he repeated the word. 'Uncle!'

Evidently, he was thoroughly offended though he did not say anything more for a minute or two. When he spoke again, it was in a low growl. 'It is most provoking,' he said, 'to be addressed in a foreign tongue.'

'I do beg your pardon,' Rapa said in a humble tone. 'I know it's ignorant of me but I thought English was not . . .'

'They have a temper, some of them words,' Kuzhakkattai interrupted. 'Particularly the ones from the father's line. They are very proud. And that's because they mean what they mean – neither more nor less. The question is who is to be master, that's all. Goodbye.'

This was quite sudden, but since Kuzhakkattai had by then shut his eyes, Rapa felt it would not be civil to stay. 'Goodbye,' she said, and getting no reply, she walked away quietly. She had not gone far when she heard a loud scream behind her and a large crow flew past with what looked very much like Kuzhakkattai's neck and his chest with the sacred thread dangling from its beak.

Journal

I could not find out, till much later, what happened to Brother Two. My father returned after four or five weeks, with a contingent of party workers who had to be fed and housed till the finger of winter touched Delhi, when they fled, squawking. If my father did speak to my mother about Brother Two then, I was not able to find out, and she would not tell. It is so difficult, sometimes, to accept that it is the end of a trail, or even to realize that it is the end. I wish now, that. . . .

Anyway, a few months later, on a chill day in January, there came a letter from Dorai Athimbiar. My father began shouting much before he finished reading it. 'This letter is not from Dorai,' he screamed, shaking the single sheet of notepaper violently. 'It is that woman's. The fool of a husband has only written what she has dictated. She thinks I am also a fool. I can't make out? Every word is hers, it is all her doing.'

'What is in the letter?' I heard my mother ask.

'You have also gone deaf is it?' he yelled at her. 'I told you. That . . . that just-born calf, he is sending to Komala Nivas. We are supposed to look after your daughter-in-law's leavings. God knows which rogue's it is. And now I have to feed its mouth? Is it my responsibility? Am I supposed to look after my country or that prostitute's droppings?'

It took about a fortnight for Brother One to reply to the telegram that my father sent him. My esteemed parent had ranted all that intervening time, about his lucklessness in his children, the woeful lack of telephones in the country, Brother One's laziness, drunkenness and his parsimony; my mother's idiocy was also thrown in for good measure. 'What has fate done to me?' he shouted every night. 'Why should my life be so bitter? I cannot even go there now! O Guruvayurappa! Republic Day is coming. And then Gandhi's death day. Can I leave now? Has anybody in my family thought of that?'

The letter from Brother One was also a short one. I heard my father read it out aloud to my mother. It was of course written in English, since it was about important matters. I kept the letter in my diary for a long time, after he had flung it away. 'Dear Father,' Brother One had written. 'I beg your forgiveness for the late reply. I was not in the house when . . .'

'What does he mean, the idiot!' my father roared. 'What does he mean, not in the house! Is he some menstruating harlot? Not in the house! This is the English he has learnt?'

My mother made no answer. My father waited, then decided to go on with the letter. 'I was not in the house when the child came. Nobody told me also. So I got to know only after three days.'

My father bellowed again. 'He must have been tumbling with some slut. Or drunk and weaving about on the road.'

'Anyway, since the child is already here, sent with a servant girl,' the letter went on, 'what should I do? With respects, Yours . . .'

That was not the end though; there was more to the letter, a postscript from Great Aunt Kuppai. In Tamizh. 'Kitta you have to come here and decide about many things. Is this house some post office? Or one railway station? People can just send off unwanted things here or what? Bring your wife also.'

But the month was January, and nothing, not even Great

Aunt Kuppai's command, could stem my father's patriotism or his great love for Gandhi. He went shivering on that bleak 26th January morning, to salute the tricolour as it fluttered against the sunless sky, and to applaud as the proud parade marched past. He did not care to take my mother and me; he never did, except once. That was when I was eight-and-a-half years old. I remember I was made to sit on a carpet at the edge of a wide, empty road, which I later realized was Rajpath, down which the parade would pass. It was very cold and the grass was wet. There were lots of screaming children and fussy parents around me but, apart for pinning a shawl over my cardigan and giving me a packet of biscuits, my mother had left me there on the damp carpet, alone. Then I noticed a fair handsome man walking down the road, he was smiling and waving to the crowd. He stopped in front of me and asked how old I was. I remember how suddenly everyone grew quiet. I told the man my age. He stepped across the grass, bent low, cupped my face between his palms and placed a gentle kiss on my cheek. The man was Pandit Nehru.

By the time my father realized what had happened, Panditji had walked on, greeting other children. But I remember my father, and a few minutes later my mother, hugging me awkwardly, making sure everyone knew I was their child. 'My youngest,' my father announced proudly to nobody in particular. 'Only seven years.' He did not even get my age right.

For many days after that, I was known in school as the girl who was kissed by Chacha Nehru. I suppose my father had told Mother Superior about it. Several teachers and girls came to look curiously at me and to ask me what I felt.

Someone asked whether I had stopped washing the cheek
which he had kissed. I did not understand, then, what all
the fuss was about; the event became significant later when
it occurred to me that as far as I could remember, I had
never been kissed before.

I don't think the kiss made much of an impression in
Komala Nivas though, and I'm not sure how my father used
it to strengthen his own party position. But he did not take
my mother and me to the parade again. Many years later, on
a particularly bitter day in Komala Nivas, my mother told
me that as I grew older, I became uglier, and so my father no
longer wished to claim me as his daughter in public.

My father used other devices to make himself feel superior.
In the four days between the 26th and 30th of January, he
practised Gandhi's favourite hymns and, presumably, lent
his unmusical voice to the solemn ceremony at Rajghat on
Martyrs' Day.

Patriotism! What a ridiculous notion it is! What is this so-
called love for our birth nation about? Is it a love for our
rivers, mountains and deserts? And does the emotion cover
our country's history of war and pillage, of killing and
destruction? Does patriotism also include love for our leaders?
Leaders like my father who professed Gandhism, because it
took them closer to seats of power; my father could, when
required, produce tears at the mention of Gandhi's death.
He claimed loudly and often, that as a college student, he
had met Gandhi, been swept off his feet and decided that,
at his wedding, he would insist on wearing khadi and not
silk. I never knew the truth of that.

As I write this, I remember, with a wrench in my stomach,

the day I surprised Inga staring intently at a calendar in one of the inside rooms of Komala Nivas. When she saw me, she half giggled and ran off before I could stop her. The calendar hung on a nail on the wall and was a single sheet showing all the twelve months of the year. It was greasy and outdated. But it carried a picture of Gandhi's face with his ears sticking out, his mouth open in a wide, toothless laugh.

5

Journal

We went to Komala Nivas in the February of that year, two months before my school closed for the summer. My father charmed Mother Superior into believing that a brother of mine in Kerala, who was dying of a mysterious family curse, wanted to see his baby sister before he closed his eyes and was harvested by our Heavenly Father. I remember standing in the stuffy school parlour with its strange food smells, watching Mother Superior's face. It was the face of the white race listening to an outlandish heathen tale; she looked disbelieving, horrified, concerned, anxious. My father hastened to assure her that the illness was not infectious in the least and that it affected only the third male offspring in every sixth generation.

'The Sisters shall say a special rosary for your poor brave son,' she said in her Irish burr. 'God's will be done.'

My father's will was certainly done and so with months of class work and homework written into the school diary and my textbooks packed in a separate box, we travelled southward. This was the first time I would see Inga and Komala Nivas at this time of the year, and the first time I would stay for so long.

It was hot when we reached, hot and dusty. At the station platform, my father walked into the embrace of his party workers, and ordered us to go on to the house with Mikhale; he said he would come later. The car that took us home smelt of searing tin and petrol. My mother sat grim and silent all through the ride, as she had in the train. As we went up the steps of Komala Nivas, we heard the sudden wail of a baby, loud, angry, unending. Great Aunt Kuppai darkened the entrance; she uttered no word of greeting but moved to give us way. Inga was nowhere to be seen.

I look at what I've just written and find it reads like a paragraph from a novel of suspense, the small details, the smell of the car, Great Aunt Kuppai at the doorway, Inga's absence. Why do I remember it like this? It was only a baby after all, crying rather loudly and long. Yet, even at that moment, it sounded unwholesome. Inauspicious. Far from welcoming.

My mother went in with her bags; I heard Great Aunt Kuppai asking Mikhale about my father. She gave a snort at his reply and walked towards her swing. I followed her. The inner hall smelt like a bathroom that had not been cleaned. Sister-in-law One's corner was cluttered with rubber sheets, shreds of cloth and bottles shaped like half moons, one filled with water, another with what looked like milk. In the middle of all this, and cradling a screaming bundle in her arms, was Sister-in-law One, her face glowing. She held the baby out to my mother and said, 'Amma, see! Goddess Laxmi has come to our house. See Rapa! See Kutti Paapa!'

I peered over my mother's shoulder.

Hush! A sight to beware of, not to tell

Jesu Marie guard me well.

Goddess Laxmi, my little niece, was a goblin. Its head was huge, with two strands of sand-coloured hair across the middle. Its eyes were screwed shut because it was still yelling, but it had almost no eyebrows and its skin was red and wrinkled like the outside of a ripe mango gone bad. I was still looking at Goblin, when I heard running footsteps at the back door, they were Inga's; she had obviously been at school. Before I could call out to her, she was in the hall, rushing towards Goblin, saying, 'Kutti Paapa! Kutti Paapa! Don't cry. I have come home. See!' At the sound of her voice, Goblin stopped screaming and turned its face towards her. Inga sat down cross-legged next to Sister-in-law One and held her arms out to my mother. She said, 'Give her Periamma! Give Kutti Paapa to me!' Then, with the baby bundle on her lap, she turned to Sister-in-law One and asked anxiously, 'Did Kutti Paapa drink milk? Why she is crying so much?'

'Becauth thee wanthed to play with you!' said Sister-in-law One in baby Tamizh. 'Thee hath thopped crying now, thee!' They both laughed, my mother sat down and joined them; Goblin made a strange sound and they all laughed again.

There was not a word for me from Inga.

Letter from Inga

Dear Rapa,
I did not say anything to you? How can that be? But actually I don't remember about that time. We were all so busy with kutti paapa I mean Laxmi. It is true what elders say that one baby in the house means the work of four adults. Anyway,

why are you thinking about all this after so many years? All your letters now are angry letters about past things. What is the use? Those days are gone, they will never come back.

   Inga

POEM
(Written I do not remember when)

The letters of the alphabet met one day
Each had many secrets they say,
They pulled each other by the hand,
And had a meeting in language land.
The A's, E's, I's, the O's and the U's
Rushed into the hall, breaking queues,
They spread themselves everywhere
And shouted loudly, 'We don't care.'
The J's and S's were more sedate,
They walked in with a stately gait,
They sat gravely in their appointed place
Like judges and sages from an ancient race.
Q came in all pale and white
A queen in a quiver of fright,
The vowels took up a jeering chant
The U's loudest with, 'We shan't, we shan't.'
The judges rapped for silence to no avail
The vowels' chant had the force of a gale,
The consonants in fear to each other said,
'Without the vowels, we'll all be dead.'
The Y's saw their advantage
They joined the jeer, added their rage,

The chanting rose to an almighty roar
The consonants howled, 'No more! No more!'
Dignity gone, they dropped to their knees
In abrupt silence, said, 'Ask what you please,
'We in number are more, that's quite true
'But dear vowels, we cannot live without you.'
The vowels yelled, 'We've won the poll,
'We are now in total control.'
They clapped and made hideous noise,
When Q stood up, returned to poise.
'I must remind you,' she quietly said,
'Without us, you five are dead.
'Which of you alone can make a word?
'Correctly spelt, clearly heard?'
I stood up looking very proud,
And said, 'I am a word,' bold and loud,
'I have great meaning unlike A and O
'Unlike U and E, I need no one in tow.'
Stunned, the other vowels looked away,
They did not speak, what could they say?
But some K's, G's and P's in the back row
Sobbed mutely, their voices robbed long ago.

Journal

It got worse. Somebody, I later realized it was Brother One,
called an astrologer to take a look at Goblin. Was it to cast
her horoscope? As far as I knew, all the births in our family
were recorded by the family astrologer, who only needed the

exact time of the birth and did not ask to see the 'native', the person whose horoscope was being written. I later learnt that the family astrologer, perhaps prompted by Great Aunt Kuppai, had refused to cast the horoscope of a baby whose parentage was obscure.

Anyway, a couple of days after we arrived, a tall man with eyes like the ancient mariner's, was escorted fussily into the front hall. He carried a cloth bundle containing, I suppose, his palm leaf references and his cowrie shells. He did not allow anyone to touch the bag. Nor, as a matter of fact, did he open it himself. Instead, he did something strange. When he saw Goblin, who had been brought out and was in Inga's lap in the front hall, he stood still for a long time, looking. Then, very slowly, he tucked the cloth bundle under his arm, took a step back, put his palms together and made a deep bow. Without saying a word to anyone, he turned and left the house.

The report of this event spread as far as crows fly and as loudly as crows can caw. My father, who was in the arms of either his party workers or his latest conquest when he heard the news, sprung up and hurried home. Like all bullies, he was intensely credulous; what he called himself, though, was God-fearing. He came as quickly as he could, picking up confirmation along the way, from those running to or rushing out of Komala Nivas. He plunged into the house, panting, sweaty, and made his way directly to the corner, which as far as I know, he had never glanced at in all his adult life. He threw himself at the feet of Inga, who was cleaning Goblin's bottom. 'Devi! Bhagavati!' my father cried and knocked his head on the floor several times. He sat up, his face streamed with tears, and held out his arms to receive a now clean but still naked Goblin, touched her toes to his forehead and cried again, 'You have blessed me! Devi you have blessed me! You have blessed this humble house!' The crowd thronging the inner hall joined him at different pitches in a paean of thanks to the goddess. Goblin wriggled in my father's arms and bawled. The stage was set.

Letter from Inga

Rapa,
What has happened to you? What all is your mother saying? I was holding Kutti Paapa when that astrologer came because who else was there? Sister-in-law One could not come out, you know that. Kutti Paapa used to cry if other people took her. You and your mother know that also. My mother was in her usual place in the back verandah all the time that day. She never told me what to do or what to say. Why should she?
Inga

Journal

Before the sun set that day, my father had sent off his party workers to hunt down the astrologer. They could not find him. They told my father in tones of dutiful virtue that the man had no family, he lived in lodgings, and the woman who cooked and cleaned for him, could only say that he often disappeared like this for many months at a time. The room he stayed in gave nothing away, they said, there was just a spare set of clothes on a wall shelf. My father then began more extensive investigations but, for a brutish man like him, his directions lacked the usual force. Even when he found out that it was Brother One who had sent for the astrologer, there was no eruption of searing lava. It took me a while to realize why. Komala Nivas was besieged, my father's attention was craved for, he was now truly a Leader. Every kind of acquaintance was heading to the house; neighbours of course, and relatives, infirm-of-purpose relatives, ailing relatives, aged and young relatives, relatives of relatives, strangers claiming to be relatives, long-lost found-again relatives and of course, members of the Party and their relatives. The local big head, the district bigger head, the state's biggest head, they all came calling. To see Goblin snoozing in Inga's lap. Or waving her arms and legs fitfully. Or just lolling.

Who was bigger, Mister Bigger or Baby Bigger? My father's expanse was enormous. He strutted about in the front courtyard, now almost permanently under an awning, and supervised the stream of visitors. The earlier cascade he had demoniacally regulated according to Inga's school timings; the stream was allowed to flow only between seven-thirty and eight in the morning and an extra half an hour on Sundays, not a moment more. Pilgrims of the right caste alone were allowed into the house. The rest stood in the courtyard and had to be content with staring at Goblin as she was held aloft by Brother One at the upper half of a window in the front hall. My father had employed party workers to throw out those who overstayed or were otherwise unwelcome, whatever their age, sex and condition. Most of the relatives who had come to squat, were also evicted similarly. Of course, members of the Party could come whenever they wanted; there was one who arrived in full regalia at two in the morning. We were all rudely woken up and forced to stay awake without yawning, and Goblin howled the whole time. My father kept complaining of a backache, no surprise that, bowing as low and as often as he did. But when did a mere backache matter? There were rumours that he was to be made minister, chief minister of the state, cabinet minister at Delhi, maybe even a governor. None of this happened though; whatever Goblin was, she obviously could not influence political machinations. But my father's circle of power expanded, he certainly and steadily grew more wealthy, his name was engraved on college plaques and on temple paving stones; an irrigation canal that was half dug was named after him, it was later abandoned and turned into an informal urinal. My father began to hobnob with small-time former royals and aristocratic jewellers, feasted with district collectors and judges; he slept with their mistresses, but he managed to remember my mother and gifted her a diamond set soon after the Goblin Fair began. Superstitious fear again? He also installed a water pipe connection with a pump, from the well to the kitchen and the bathrooms in Komala Nivas.

This last alone pleased Great Aunt Kuppai, she was heavily disapproving of everything else that was going on. She and I were the only ones who stayed away from the Fair. Great Aunt had the long swing removed from the inner hall, which was now all Goblin's, and put up in another room, further recessed, stuffier, darker. There we sat, she and I, she with her hand fan on the creaking swing, I with my books on the floor. All the while, the pilgrims came, paused and departed. We hardly spoke to each other, except when she ordered me to bring her a drink of water or coffee or milk, and when she wanted me to fetch my mother. Once, abruptly, she asked me what I was reading but before I could tell her, she said the only book worth reading was the *Mahabharata*; everything that happened in the world was in it and there was nothing that happened in the world that was not in it.

She did not speak to my mother either, beyond giving directions about what was to be cooked and how the larder was to be managed. Her silence was as sharp and final as the serrated edge of a knife; she spoke nothing, she said everything. It was an excellent strategy and my mother was rendered weaponless, in spite of the stones that sparkled around her neck and wrists, and in her ears.

It was the strangest time I have ever known, witching time. Everyone in Komala Nivas, except Aunt Kuppai, had become someone else. My mother laughed and giggled most of the time with Sister-in-law One; they were like a pair of giddy girls. Brother One hardly went out of the house. He was at the Goblin stall all day long; once, outside visiting hours and when nobody was about, I caught him with his hand inside Sister-in-law One's blouse, he did not even take it away when he saw me. 'Why? You are my wife,' I heard him tell her. Paru in the cowshed had an enraptured audience around her every time I went there, listening to her tales of the wonders Goblin was performing. Apparently, Paru herself had got rid of a long-time itch which, she had been told by big doctors, was incurable. Many years later, my mother told me that Paru's 'itch' had been her unemployed drunken husband who suddenly disappeared around that time.

Komala Nivas itself changed. It took on the tawdry glamour of a cinema house, the open-mouthed abandon of an unwalled well. And Inga was lost to me.

Letter from Inga

Dear Rapa,

How was I supposed to stop anything? Don't you at all remember my age at that time? I simply did what all they told me. Yes. I heard a lot of people who came, saying that so and so, and so and so had got a son or got money or got married. It seems that some boy near Madras who was nearly dead became all right after his aunty came to see Kutti Paapa. His aunty only told my mother in the temple. At that time, I used to believe everything, now I know that such stories are also made up many times.

Inga

Journal

About two or three weeks after the Goblin Fair started, we had a visitation. It was a blazing hot afternoon, Inga was at school and the rest of the house was asleep, Goblin between Brother One and Sister-in-law One. My father had supervised the morning visitors, eaten and gone out. I had freed myself from the eternal twilight of Great Aunt Kuppai's new residence and was in the front hall, when I heard the loud click of the main gate. This was unusual. The main gate was reserved for Very Important Imperious People and was not to be opened by pygmies. There was a smaller, narrower entrance built into the wall, which is what we used; it allowed only one person in at a time. The main gate was flung open before Mikhale could get there and I realized who the untimely visitors were. It was FishEyes, the mother of Sister-in-law Too and Pigtails, and their father, Dorai Athimbiar.

It was very visibly a peace mission. They came bearing gifts, enormous baskets of mangoes, jackfruit and red bananas, in addition to tins and tins of, presumably, more of the snacks and sweets that Great Aunt Kuppai had, at one time, thrown to the crows in the backyard. FishEyes led the procession, her gold brocade sari end drawn demurely over her shoulders, behind her hobbled Dorai Athimbiar hugging a large stoneware pickle jar, and behind him, the baskets and tins carried in by two sweaty men. I unlatched the front door as FishEyes climbed heavily up the steps to the verandah. At the door, she bent, touched her fingers on the threshold, then to her forehead and her full bosom, turned, took the pickle jar none too gently from Dorai Athimbiar, and stepped into the house. It was a grand entry, much like that of a temple elephant but alas, there was nobody to see it but me.

Within the hour, Komala Nivas was in uproar. Brother One sat in the inner hall, looking as if his afternoon nap had been split asunder by a giant cosmic jackfruit. Every now and then, he shouted, 'What? What did you say? What?' Sister-in-law One clutched a bawling Goblin to her chest and screamed, 'No! I am saying no!'; my mother, at the doorway to Great Aunt Kuppai's new room, and Inga, at the back door, stood frozen, Paru in the side verandah threw back her head and wailed and beat her breast along with three others. Soaring above it all, was FishEyes' shrillness, '. . . so I said better to go and settle quickly. My mother was always telling when you finish deciding you must finish the work also. Quickness is very auspicious. So I called my murukku maami, she is always ready to do anything for me, she made adirasam also on her own. Not just that, we got good mangoes this time so I put them in salt, murukku maami only gave me help. I know Kuppaathai always likes mangoes from our tree so . . .'

My father burst into the room. He was panting, his chest heaved with stacks of ammunition, ready to be set off. Dorai Athimbiar scrambled to his feet, FishEyes merely turned her face to my father and without a break of breath, she went on. 'You have come Anna, that is good. We can discuss although there is not anything to discuss but still, now itself, I can . . .'

'Meenakshi!' my father roared. Everyone fell silent, Brother and Sister-in-law One, Paru and her friends in the verandah, even Goblin stopped her bawl. Two or three party workers whose caste allowed them into the house, entered silently and stood behind my father in a row, arms folded, blocking the doorway. FishEyes gave a tinkly laugh and said, 'O Anna! What a shout! The child will be afraid. Tinkle. Tinkle.' My father lowered his voice, 'Why have you come, Meenu?' he asked. 'You think I will give her to you?'

FishEyes tinkled again. 'Anna!' she said with a horrifying pout, 'you are a one! She is my granddaughter! You have forgotten or what! My dear Raashaati's poor little daughter! My jasmine bud was not destined even to see her.' The pout gave way to a sniff and the fish eyes rolled upwards where, presumably, the jasmine bud now resided.

'Suddenly she is your grandchild is it?' my father said. 'When you sent her off from your house with a whore of a servant girl, she was not your grandchild?'

'O Anna! That girl!' FishEyes clicked her tongue several times. 'You said something very correct. I was so much deceived by that girl! I did not even think that . . .'

My father raised his voice. 'Look Meenakshi,' he said. 'The child will stay here, in Komala Nivas. She is my granddaughter. The child of my son. You take this yours obediently husband and go back in the same way you came. The child will stay here.'

FishEyes screamed. 'Your son? That good-for-nothing, not male, not female son of yours? He did not touch my girl! You think he could do it? He . . .' She realized the enormity of what she had said and stopped. But only for a moment. She heaved herself up and spat out her next words. 'Where is this great son of yours? Where? Is his hand between a woman's legs or a man's buttocks? Tell. Where? Tell.' Sister-in-law One gasped and covered Goblin's ears. My father said nothing.

FishEyes picked up the pickle jar and thrust it into Dorai Athimbiar's belly. 'Hold it,' she commanded and turned towards the door. She motioned imperiously to the party workers to move aside and as she strode past my father, she hissed, 'You think it is over? I will also see! I will get the best lawyer.' The party workers flattened themselves against the wall as she charged out. In the front courtyard, the sweaty men were still standing with their tins, awaiting orders. 'Put it all in the car,' FishEyes said. Then she turned her head towards the house and screamed, 'You corpses! You think even one of you should eat such good things? Made in pure butter?'

The shiny black car sank as she and Dorai Athimbiar clambered in with the pickle jar; a minute later, it jerked into life, groaned a little, shook very much, then spluttered down the road and clattered away.

When I went back inside, I found my father setting off

more ammunition. 'Who opened the door to that raakshasi?' he raged. 'How did anyone dare let her in? Into this temple? Who did it? Who?' I ran to my mother but she was no protection. My father grabbed me. Strangely, it was Great Aunt Kuppai who was my rescuer. 'Leave the girl,' she snapped from the door of her retreat. 'What did she know? Anyway, in better days, that door was never shut.' My father let go. Nevertheless, my ear hurt dreadfully for a long time.

After that, Komala Nivas became a fortress. Every entrance was guarded. Mikhale was posted at the front gate along with two muscular party workers. Paru's cowshed duties were given to her sister Ammini and Paru stationed in the back verandah with as many friends as were available. All other outer doors were either shut and locked or had party workers lurking nearby. Inga was given strict instructions not to talk to anyone between home and school and Brother One declared that except for doing some essential duties, he would not leave Goblin's side for even a minute. Sister-in-law One hung her head and blushed as he said this. I was not given anything to do but was warned against opening any door or any window. Once he was satisfied with the fortification, my father, obviously butted by FishEyes' remarks, began to look for Brother Two in earnest.

⁀

A SHORT HISTORY OF THE AYYARPURI DYNASTY
(Written during the Goblin Fair)

King Kittu was the founder of the Ayyarpuri dynasty. He ascended the throne after slaying his two older brothers and imprisoning their wives in a dungeon. His first task was to ensure the protection of his provinces, to which end he had massive forts built along the borders of the kingdom. Most of these are now in ruins but the fort in his capital city, called Komala Nivas, still stands and is considered a fine example of medieval architecture. The long reign of King Kittu was not prosperous for his subjects, since he was more interested in expanding his rule than in looking after the welfare of his people. He made many enemies and had few allies and left his kingdom in a sorry state.

However the kingdom began to flourish when his only daughter Queen Rapa succeeded to the throne. She was a wise and benevolent ruler. The Chinese traveller Hsing Ku has given a glowing account of the kingdom during her reign. In his words, 'Never have I seen such broad and shady avenues and charming rest houses. The rice is excellently grown and there are many types of vegetables and spices in the market abundantly available. I sought audience with the queen and had the good fortune to be granted it. She is exceedingly beautiful, as fair as a moonbeam in the night. One wished for a thousand eyes to behold her.'

Queen Rapa was a benign monarch. She made allies among neighbouring kings and trade flourished. She had seven ministers who helped her with schemes to protect the poor and needy, to make the kingdom prosperous and to encourage the arts. They were called the seven rays of the sun. There was peace and prosperity in the kingdom and many poets and writers in her court. Queen Rapa herself was an accomplished writer, poet, singer and administrator. Her reign came to an abrupt end when one of her father's sworn enemies invaded the kingdom and . . . (This is rubbish. I should stick to English writers.)

Journal

Brother Two seemed to have disappeared very firmly but my father continued his search. 'Surely she will find her father,' he kept saying, referring of course to Goblin, 'Surely she will pull him back to his home, to Komala Nivas.' Nobody else seemed quite as certain, Great Aunt was openly scornful. 'You are only wasting money,' she told my father flatly one day, when he came into her room. My mother had just brought in Great Aunt Kuppai's mid-morning glass of watery curds which is curiously called buttermilk. 'The boy will come back on his own. Just wait! When she finds one other idiot with good thighs and a full pocket, she will not even remember your son's name!'

'He is no idiot, the poor boy,' my mother spoke up rather astonishingly. 'You yourself used to feel bad for him because he did not have his wife there.'

'That was then,' Great Aunt retorted. Then she turned to my father and snapped, 'See what all is happening in this house. Even your wife answers back. To me. And you are keeping silent?' My father left the room without saying why he had come to see her in the first place. He dived into Goblin Corner and started playing with her, talking baby language, asking her to get her father back thoon. My mother wiped her eyes and joined him; as usual, the inner hall was torn asunder by loud laughter and chortles between the four of them, my father and mother, Brother One and Sister-in-law One. It was sickening.

Later that same day, my father slammed into the house carrying what he and everybody else, with the exception of Great Aunt Kuppai and me, considered alarming news. It had been reported to him that FishEyes was planning to send a young and beautiful woman to kidnap Goblin. 'Or kill the child!' my father roared. 'She has said, it seems, that she will send one Poothanai!' The assembled crowd of Goblin-watchers inside and outside the inner hall was silent. 'I thought I knew that woman, that raakshasi's evil mind, but even I did not think she will go to this length. My poor baby! My jewel!' He picked up Goblin and burst into tears. There was a minute of silence, then came a wave of protestations from all sides, including from Inga, still in her school uniform. 'No! No . . .! We will not let it happen! Never Saar, we will give our lives but this we will not allow to happen . . . Appa! Rest assured. We are here to give her full protection.' The last declaration was Brother One's, in English.

The result of all this tumult was a new rule. No female between the ages of ten and fifty was to be allowed into Komala Nivas. 'They can all see her from the window,' my father declared sternly, and went on, 'she is sending a Poothanai, think of it! Poothanai! But I am not called Kittu alias Krishnan for nothing! I will show her! You, Inga, will not allow anyone even to touch the baby. Do you understand? No one! Not even if they look like Urvashi and talk like . . .'

'But Periappa,' there was a degree of anxiety in Inga's tone, 'Kutti Paapa will not allow anyone to come near. She will cry.' I saw Sister-in-law One lean towards Inga and place her finger on her lips. Inga did not say any more; my father's temper was unpredictable and Sister-in-law One was well aware of that.

A few days later, Prof. Seshu came to Komala Nivas. He sat with my father all day; I did not see him till early evening when I was called to the front courtyard. My father was walking up and down with Goblin over his shoulder and the professor was sitting in a chair looking rather glum. When he saw me, he said, 'Ah! There you are my dear! How have you been?' I said I was fine. 'And what are you reading now my dear?' he asked, rather mechanically I thought. But before I could answer, my father broke into a hoarse song and the professor fell silent. I waited, standing still.

When my father seemed to be repeating a line he had already sung, the professor asked me whether I knew the song. I said I didn't. 'It is a song to be sung to a little child, it is a lullaby,' he told me. 'Am I to believe that you have never heard it?'

'No. Never,' I replied. 'What do the words mean?'

He was quiet for a moment, then he said, 'It is one of the most beautiful songs I have ever heard. But like your father, I too do not remember all of it. In the first lines, the poet says, "Are you the endearing rays of the moon or the softness of the lotus flower? Are you the sweetness of the flower's honey or the light of the full moon?" The song goes on in this way, it is quite lengthy.'

'Does the poet get an answer?' I asked.

'I beg your pardon. An answer to what?'

'To those questions in the song. Are you this? Are you that?'

There was a flicker of impatience in the professor's tone when he replied, impatience and something like pity. 'These questions are not meant to be answered. They are not examination questions, for heaven's sake.' He paused, and when he spoke again, it was like a teacher in a classroom. 'These are not real questions, they are statements in the question form. It is a literary device often used by poets and great orators. In fact, one of the best examples of rhetoric that you will sooner or later come across would be in a poem titled *Tiger* penned by the poet-philosopher William Blake. Perhaps you will then better understand what I mean. In the meantime, I will send you . . .' He broke off suddenly, sat up and stared over my shoulder. 'Who on earth is that?' he murmured softly, almost to himself. I turned.

Inga had come out of the house and was standing close to my father, peering up towards Goblin's head that lolled face down on my father's shoulder.

'Who is that?' the professor said again.

'That is my cousin Inga,' I told him.

'Your cousin?'

'Yes,' I said. I felt a stab of pride in telling the professor something he did not seem to know. 'Her mother and my mother are sisters. So Inga and I are cousins. But she does not know much English,' I added.

All the time, while I was speaking to him, the professor continued to stare intently at Inga. I did not realize till then, that he had not seen her before. He did not seem to have heard of her either. But was I wrong about this? Surely my father would have told him, at some point, that Inga and her mother stayed with us in Komala Nivas. Or were these things not spoken of between men? It was a question that haunted me for a long time as did the memory of that evening.

The courtyard had darkened. My mother ought to have come out by then, with a lit lamp for the evening worship of the thulasi plant in the courtyard, a ritual that I was made to do some months later. Till the worship was done, no electric light could be used. My father must have waited for her with rapidly growing impatience; he would have shouted out to her in towering anger, if it wasn't for Goblin half-asleep on his shoulder. Instead, he switched on the big, steel torch that never left his side even in the daytime. Its beam cast an arc of light across the verandah. It encircled Inga's upturned head, and softly touched the amber of her eyes. The words of the lullaby came to me then, and all of a sudden, I knew what they meant. And I knew why the poet's questions were not actual questions; because the answer to all of them would always be, yes.

Except, I realized, I had never ever felt the softness of a lotus flower, nor tasted the sweetness of its honey. Just as I had never seen a nodding violet or smelt a sweet musk rose, both of which flowers, I supposed, could have been included in the lullaby.

Six or seven days later, Mikhale handed me a brown paper packet; 'From Maasher,' he said, with awe in his voice. I realized he meant the professor. The packet contained the book *The Water Babies* by Charles Kingsley, and two sheets of lined paper, one of which was a letter; the other a poem. The letter said, 'I enclose an English translation of *Omana Thingal Kidaavo Nalla Komala Thaamara Poovo* – a poem written by Irayimman Thampi for his cousin, the infant prince Swati Thirunal who grew up to become a great music composer. Mine should not be regarded as a literal translation of the original Malayalam poem. I have merely penned a few lines which I sincerely hope will convey the sheer beauty and dexterity of the poetic images, and the many similes and metaphors employed by the poet. Alas, the melody of the original lines cannot be expressed in English. The poem itself is much more lengthy; I have picked out a few of my favourite lines. I hope you like it and enjoy reading the book too - Uncle Seshu.'

OMANA THINGAL KIDAAVO NALLA KOMALA THAAMARA POOVO

The tenderness of moon rays,
The full moon's brilliant light,
The softness of the lotus flower,
The honey filled inside –
Is this what you are?
The dance of the swaying peacock,
The chorus of bird song sweet,
The water that quenches all thirst,
The shade that travellers seek –
Is this what you are?

The breeze that comes flower scented,
The lamp that glows in the night,
The fragrance of unfading jasmine,
For me, the most auspicious sight –
Is this what you are?
Are you Lord Krishna Himself
Disguised yet again in play?
Are you the sign on Lakshmi's forehead
That directs good fortune my way?

6

It was the end of Inga's school term and she was free to be with me. It made no difference though. Not a single day did we together creep into the storeroom to gather green mangoes and then into the kitchen for salt. Not a single afternoon did we sit in our secret place, lips stinging with salt and mango acid, and whisper into each other's ears. Inga was always in the inner hall, sitting cross-legged, Goblin on her lap, singing to her, twining the creature's fingers through her own or making funny sounds, while my mother and Sister-in-law One and Brother One watched delightedly, laughing themselves silly. I wished I could pluck that creature off Inga's lap and throw it into the backyard for the crows to eat.

I disliked *The Water Babies*; I wondered even when I was reading it, why the professor had sent it to me. Was it because the book was called a fairy tale? Or because the main character was a chimney sweep, all sooty and black? This boy, from what I remember, turns into a rosy little water baby and has many adventures, good and bad, with underwater creatures. He also meets fairies with horrible names like Doasyouwouldbedoneby and Bedonebyasyoudid.

These beings sounded to me, even then, like Great Aunt Kuppai. It is true that they spoke in a genteel way and in beautifully phrased, very long English sentences, but underneath, it was all the same. Behave! Have adakkam!

I don't know whether other Tamizh Brahmin households were bombarded with this word as often as ours was. Adakkam! It bounced off the walls, it splintered the floors, at night it gnashed its teeth and hissed at me. Adakkam! Like the Biblical 'begat', this one too was blessed with the consonants of a stinging slap. And how often it slapped me and stung me, and tripped me up and hit me across the face. Adakkam.

When I was first attacked with the word, by Great Aunt Kuppai I think, I assumed it meant good behaviour. But gradually I realized that it was a cauldron of virtues, none of which I had. And it was used only against women.

'You! You black-faced raakshasi! You have no adakkam! No adakkam at all! Why is your skirt so up? I can see your both upper legs! . . . You should not open your mouth so much just to smile. Never show teeth to anyone. . . . Better do not smile at all. A Brahmin girl always has adakkam. No! She will never open her mouth and laugh! . . . This jasmine string in your hair I am putting tight. It must not, must not move even one inch when your head shakes. . . . Ayyo! You should not eat so much. You must have adakkam. Food should be kept for men. Poor things. They go out and work so hard! . . . O you stupid donkey! Why you are screaming. If you fall down, it is your blame only. Who asked you to fall? Shut your mouth! You have no adakkam or what? The whole world can hear you.' Such were the custodians of adakkam. Great Aunt Kuppai, my mother of course, all the toothless hags around Komala Nivas, all related to us in various, diverse ways. And Rukku Paati, the cook who could not hear but who could never keep her own mouth shut. Rook the cook!

I still remember the moral at the end of *The Water Babies*. It said, 'Learn your lessons! Always wash. Stick to hard work and cold water.'

But not all the waters of multitudinous seas, cold or hot, can wash away my sootiness, my chimney sweepness. And my . . .

Letter from Inga

Dear Rapa,
What is so bad about having adakkam? It only means having good manners, not talking back to elders, not talking loudly, dressing properly, all that. I believe girls in England are not told such things but we are different no, Rapa? This is not England.
Inga

Journal

I had now been in Komala Nivas for almost two months; the holiday was not one bit the way I had pictured it. It was a ruin of a vacation, a charred heap. And it was all because of Goblin. How I hated it, the ugly misshapen head, the small snake-like eyes, the two strands of sand-coloured hair, the almost constant bawling. Its taking away of Inga so completely, diabolically. Goblin was evil. I was sure of that. Did nobody else see it?

'Pilgrims' continued to throng Komala Nivas. In fact, ever since the fortification, it seemed as if the crowds were larger and their worship more elaborate. Why do people want to go expressly where there are restrictions, to crave to read a book that is banned, to eat the fruit that is forbidden? So it was at Komala Nivas. Those who could come into the house, now brought flowers and incense sticks and coconuts, all of which was returned after Inga touched Goblin's podgy hands to them. (There were strict instructions from my father that no money was to be offered.) For two days before the exams, there were special timings for batches of children to have their books blessed. Of course, those who were kept out in the courtyard could only raise their voices in prayer when they glimpsed Goblin through the upper half of the window. That was all they were allowed to do. But some of those who came into the house, left behind little chits of paper with their wishes written on them; these were read out to Goblin by my mother, when the lamps were lit at dusk and we were all required to gather in the inner hall. The wishes were the usual boring ones; women wanting husbands, babies, sons, men wanting work, plenty of money and r.c. – reinforced concrete – houses. There was, of course, the sick lot too, who wanted to be rid of their own several ailments or those of their children.

Were there any cases of divine intervention, of miracles? I don't know. Paru and her friends would burst out every now and then with the story of a wonderful gift of money come to some Goblin devotee, or of so and so who, having sniffed at the flowers from Komala Nivas, sat up from a death bed, fully recovered. But none of this was confirmed. My father touched his head to Goblin's feet both morning and evening, he was unquestioning, and so of course, was the rest of the family. Except for Great Aunt Kuppai and me.

Letter from Inga

Dear Rapa,

Why are you asking the same thing again and again and again? I tell you I do not know what was true and what was not true. Till you wrote this in your letter, I did not even know that your father was becoming so rich those days, and had such a good name. My mother never told anything to me. If Brother One and Sister-in-law One and other people were thinking that good things happened to them because of Kutti Paapa, it is because of their faith only. Having faith is very very important, according to me.

It will be good for you also to have faith in some one thing.
Inga

Journal

I realized, even at that time, that I did not want to hear anything good about Goblin. Whenever I thought of her, I felt a great surge of something in my throat and mouth, a something that was sickly green, nauseous, stinking. Years later, when I was back in Komala Nivas, grown up, and questioned my mother about those Goblin months, she would inevitably answer with bitter stories about Inga and her mother; or else, she would use her favourite weapon of silence. My father, desperately ill and half blind by then, continued to declare that Mahalakshmi had come to him as a baby and that she had blessed him for all time. When I argued that Goblin was just a malformed child, he shook his head obstinately and quoted the experiences of the devotees who came to see Goblin. 'What wonderful things they told me about what what happened to them. I used to get tears in my eyes when I heard them. Mind you, they were all intelligent, highly educated people,' he would say. He would then abruptly raise his voice. 'They did not know your Shakespeare or your Milton. But is Shakespeare everything? Is English the be all and end all of life?'

And then he would brutally use the one argument that I could not counter, against which I was totally weaponless. 'You know how many boys rejected you? How many houses I went with your horoscope! But one look at your photo and finish! They stopped all talk. Only because of her, that Kutti Mahalakshmi, I got an IAS son-in-law. Remember that.'

But all this was long after that summer when I was fifteen years old. One day, when I went to the outside bathroom used only by the women of the house, I found spots of blood on my underwear. I felt no pain and when I rubbed my hands across my buttocks and peered down my thighs, I found no cuts or bruises. I came out of the dark bathroom, to examine myself in the sunlight. That was when Paru came upon me, standing there, stained underwear in hand, puzzled. She gave a whoop of what seemed to me to be very inappropriate joy and ran towards the house calling out urgently to my mother. The Goblin Fair was still going on; nevertheless, to my great surprise, my mother came running out. She ordered me back into the dark bathroom and made me wash out the underwear, telling me incoherently that I was now a big girl and must have even more adakkam.

In a very short while, I was installed at the far edge of the back verandah, with a thick wad of cloth between my thighs and told to sit there and not move, food would be brought to me. Paru and her friends came to giggle around me, covering their mouths with the towels they wore on their shoulders. They asked me questions which I did not understand, and laughed and nudged each other when I shook my head. After fifteen minutes or so of this idiotic behaviour, they began to leave, at last, and I realized the Fair was getting over for the day. I edged towards the back door hoping I could catch sight of Inga, but I heard my mother's voice coming towards me and I quickly went and sat down as before.

My mother came out and slid an old, chipped enamel plate across to me and began to serve me food, holding the ladles about a foot above the plate, as if the sight of the enamel would curdle the sambar and the vegetable curry, and turn the rice to grain again. I was refused my favourite mango pickles, and instead of the usual curds, she gave me half a ladle of thin, sour buttermilk. My mother's face was puckered with irritability and she stood well away, not letting even her sari end stray towards me. When the unappetizing meal was done, she made me stoop over the low outer wall of the verandah and poured water from a jug held high up. This water was for me to drink, to wash my mouth with, as well as wash the plate I ate off, that hateful, chipped enamel plate. My mother then hurried away, without paying any attention to my request for my books and my school bag; even my plaintive lie about wanting to do my homework she ignored. I sat there alone, the sound of crows all around, the verandah got hotter as the western sun slanted towards the back of the house. I was still hungry. Inside, the chink of steel plates and dishes and the low rumble of conversation had given way to the usual, slumberous quiet of a Komala Nivas afternoon. Goblin was obviously asleep and now Inga alone would be on guard. I crept into the house and tiptoed towards the kitchen. I put my foot across the threshold and all the clamour of several hells broke loose.

I was singularly unlucky. Rukku Paati was not asleep, she was still pottering about in the kitchen and although she could not hear, she could see perfectly well. As soon as she caught sight of me, she let out a shriek so loud and so long, it was as if she had been embraced by her husband, dead several years. Simultaneous with the shriek, she let go the large copper vessel she was wiping dry. This hit the floor with an ear-splitting clang and rolled towards me with loud affection. I stooped to pick it up, which seemed to be a natural thing to do, when there were more, and louder, shrieks from behind me. My mother and Sister-in-law One! 'Don't touch it! Leave it! Leeeeave it!' Rukku Paati moaned and coiled down onto the floor. Goblin woke up and began her howl. I took a step forward, towards Rukku Paati, when my mother screamed again, the copper vessel hit my big toe and rested there heavily. My mother was now at the kitchen door, and yelling at me to move out of the way. I did. Even so, she curved into the kitchen, as far away from me as was possible, as if I was plague infected, tucking in her sari so tight that I wondered how she breathed. But breathing she was, smoke and fire and fume all directed at me, as she tended to Rukku Paati. 'Did you not know you idiot, you are not supposed to enter the house and never, never even look at the kitchen? You brainless fool didn't you know you are not supposed to touch anyone till you have a bath? That you are not supposed to touch anything, a plate or a glass or a towel or anything till. . . .' But I had had a bath as usual in the morning, I protested. My mother's voice, all of a sudden, was stronger than Goblin's. Obviously, indignant virtue gave to itself both high authority and high volume. I saw Inga trying to shush Goblin, her eyes busily cast downwards, not looking at me. Behind her, from the far end of the room, I heard Brother One snigger. I walked out, limping, ostracized, back to my prison.

I remembered suddenly what had happened to me once, at school. I was in Standard I or II at the time, and had had chicken pox. After fifteen days or so, and after several neem water baths, I was sent back to school. Unfortunately, it was old, crotchety Miss Harper who was taking the morning assembly that day, and when she saw me, she started spitting with anger. 'How dare you come to school?' she screamed, spit, spit. 'How dare your parents send you? You still have marks all over your body, you dirty girl!' She pulled me out of the line, first wrapping her fingers in a handkerchief of course, and dragged me to the music room which, apart from the piano, was bare of furniture. There she made me stand, well away from all the walls, right in the centre of the room, till someone came from home to collect me. As I left, I saw her wash the room out with buckets and buckets of what I later realized was strong disinfectant.

Letter from Inga

Dear Rapa,
It is a very bad thing and I used to feel very bad about it. But one day, I asked my mother, and she said that in earlier days, ladies had to do all the work in the kitchen, grinding rice, making sweets and savouries for a big joint family and also they did not get much good food. They also had to be with their

husbands each and every night excepting on the days they were not clean, when they had periods. So these three days was a sort of rest for ladies. I believe some ladies used to make out that they got periods in nineteen twenty days, so they got more rest. Sometimes, two or three ladies used to say they have got it at one and the same time. Then they all would be sitting at the back and talking talking. How angry Great Aunt Kuppai used to get. But who was to know if they were telling lies?
Inga

Journal

I managed to get some of my books to keep me company in my monthly prison, but not my bag. This was apparently because the bag was made of cloth and if I touched it, I would pollute it and then I would have to wash it and since I did not even know how to wash my own underwear, how would I be able to wash a strong school bag? My mother pushed a few books towards me from afar and I found, to my dismay, that they were my arithmetic and algebra textbooks and notebooks, there was nothing to read. Much, much worse, I was not given my 'rough' notebook, which I had specifically asked for, saying that it was where I did all the rough work for my essays and my precis writing. Actually, the notebook contained the first chapters of a novel I had started. On Goblin. I had made her an ugly, evil fairy simply called Miss G, who roasted boys and girls till they were quite charred and under her control, and then she sent them out into the world to turn everyone else black too. I enjoyed writing the book, it was the complete opposite of *The Water Babies*, so I had my revenge on Charles Kingsley too. As I wrote the story, I also made notes of the several evil ends I had planned for Miss G, all immensely nasty and satisfying. Later, when I read the Bond books, I realized I had had much the same ideas as Fleming, except that I had not then, nor afterwards, known enough about firearms. I was more familiar with the torture methods of the medieval period, which caused pain, not just to the body but to the mind as well. And sent the soul to hell.

When I returned to my school bag after three days of imprisonment, my journal was nowhere to be found. I got frantic. I shook out the entire bag, I searched the whole room, the house, I pestered my mother till she slapped me across the face. I tried to find out from Paru whether the cows had been given any paper as feed. She was most indignant when she understood what I was asking her; our cows, she said, were fed the best food in all the land. She made it sound as if they feasted on ghee rice, sambar and vadai every day. She refused to let me search the cowshed and I had to come away. I continued to look for the notebook, much hampered by the Goblin Fair and an assorted lot of people who seemed to be staying in the house. I dived under cots, shook out the folds of mats, and put my nose deep inside kitchen vessels when Rukku Paati was safely asleep. But I kept bumping into waddling old ladies with one or two teeth or none at all, and a slippery young man with hungry eyes and ears. I was asked so many questions, particularly by the slippery sneak, that I was forced to give up the hunt. I never saw my book again.

Later, I learnt from my mother, that Great Aunt Kuppai had been taught to read English by her husband Great Uncle Pichchu. He had been a lawyer, and extremely miserly;

instead of employing a clerk, he expected his wife to keep his notes and papers in good order, especially since she had failed to provide him a son.

Letter from Inga

Dear Rapa,
Great Aunt Kuppai did not conceive at all. One time I heard Paru one day, telling somebody that Great Uncle was not a proper man. That other thing you wrote, that Great Aunt used to read in English, I did not know at all.
Inga

Journal

For those three days and nights when I had my periods, I sat in the far corner of the back verandah, and slept in a windowless room at the back of the house. On the fourth day, I was woken up very early with a harsh shout from my mother, who ordered me into the dark bathroom where Paru waited with oil and soapnut powder. For the first time, I realized how cool the oil was on my head and how welcome the splash of hot water on my limbs. I was also rid of those smelly cloth pads; luckily, I had not bled much, I never really did later either. Paru bathed me gently, singing a song under her breath, of some girl being adorned for her marriage to some god or the other. This seemed to be the famous bath that would allow entry back to the house and to humankind and I was impatient to be done because I wanted to get to my notebook. But once the bath was over, I was wrapped in a wet towel and pushed into an inner room, where there were new clothes laid out for me. A sari!

A slithering silk sari, a blouse (which Inga always called a jacket), and a petticoat.

I still don't know how the sari stayed around me that day, I had not ever worn one before. But stay it did, in spite of the long ceremony I went through, with flowers in my hair and all sorts of chants and songs in my ears. I understood little of what was being done; I was worried about the notebook and the sari. However it did not disgrace me. It stayed on my hips even when I had to kneel and touch my head to various pairs of feet, most of them, I was informed, belonging to my father's side of the family. My mother was at her most daughter-in-law state, humble, submissive, running in and out to get glasses of buttermilk and whatever else, to show how untiringly dutiful she was. The daughter-in-law nonpareil! It made me sick. It did not impress anyone else either because Great Aunt Kuppai was astonishingly affectionate to me, she patted me on the head and slipped a gold chain round my neck. I heard her loudly telling some aunt or the other sitting next to her, toothless, that my mother knew nothing of anything, that a girl's first period was to be celebrated with the lighting of an oil lamp and decorating the girl's hair with flowers, not treating her as an outcaste. 'Poor girl, my nephew's daughter!' Great Aunt said confidentially enough for everyone to hear, 'She is studying in one big English school, what she knows? My brother is seeing her like a princess. Should not a mother sit and tell her all? Only one daughter she has!' The unknown aunt clicked her tongue and began a counter-complaint about her own brother's wife with great relish. Others in the room pressed money into my hand, which my mother took away as soon as she could.

For some reason, my father was at his most jocular and did some loud mock wailing about how he would now have to trudge from house to house with a bundle of horoscopes, looking for a groom for his daughter. 'One IAS only for her,' declared Great Aunt Kuppai, 'with nice height. See her height, even at this age.'

'Good features also she has, Kuppakka,' said the unfamiliar, sans-teeth aunt. 'See her nose and eyes.'

'She is always coming first in her class,' boomed my father. 'So many times she has got double promotion. And her English! Appappa! Even those nuns can't talk like her! Yes! They themselves say!'

'Ayyo! Kitta!' broke in Great Aunt Kuppai, touching the tips of her fingers rapidly from cheek to cheek. 'Don't put eyes on your girl.'

Inga's enormous eyes brushed against mine, it was a fluttery glance empty of meaning; the next moment she was back to the giggling, to the tickling of the Goblin's feet in her lap, looks of pride exchanged with Sister-in-law One as Goblin made inchoate sounds.

I continued going around the room, doing the bend-and-touch-the-feet bit, when Great Aunt Kuppai called imperiously out to my mother, 'Tell Paru to put salt chilli circle for your daughter,' she said. 'Many people have bad eyes. And take her to that sister of yours for blessings.' Then in a loud, grumbly whisper she added, 'I do not want any burning bellies in my house today!'

My mother dragged me furiously to the side verandah where Inga's mother usually sat, cleaning rice, grinding idli batter or simply sitting silently, staring at the hibiscus growing along the compound wall. She was there, my aunt, as usual, but this time, she looked as if she was crying. When she saw me, she wiped her eyes quickly and asked me to go closer to her. My mother stood at the door, not saying a word. I went towards my aunt and wondered how I was to kneel down to touch her feet, there was so little place for me and my sari. But my aunt would not allow me even to bend towards her. She unrolled the waist fold of her sari and put into the palm of my right hand, two worn coins. 'One from me and the second one from your grandmother,' she said loudly as if she was speaking to Rukku Paati. 'Safely keep it.' My mother turned and walked into the house, I followed her in, tripping over the unravelling folds of my sari, wishing I could have Komala Nivas back the way it used to be before Goblin. And Inga by my side.

7

Letter from Inga

Dear Rapa,

*I don't know who did what and why that day. So many years
have passed away and still every day I am thinking about it
and how that all happened. Why that day of all days, your
mother sent off my mother and me to some tailor so far away
to give him cloth to make jackets and long skirts for you? We
never went before like that. If your mother is now saying Great
Aunt Kuppai made her to do it, we were not knowing that.
You know Great Aunt Kuppai never said even one word to
my mother or me when we were living in Komala Nivas. She
never gave her face to us to tell anything. One more thing. I
did not at all want to go to that tailor. Your mother is not
correct in telling that I cried and cried to go out with my
mother. Your mother only made us both to go. Brother One
also was not there, it was Monday, the day he used to go to see
Sankunni Uncle to do accounts. Only Sister-in-law One was
there with Kutti Paapa, Also there was that Great Aunt
Cheetai who was crying so much afterwards. She was related
to Great Aunt Kuppai's in-law's house I believe.*

*By the by, your mother was not in the house that day.
Everything she told from the verandah only. Rukku Paati gave*

*the cloth to us in one bag. The whole time your mother was
also speaking many things from the back door to Sister-in-law
One and also Great Aunt Cheetai. They were inside only. So
when the thing happened at that time, where your mother
was? She did not hear anything or what?*

*Ask that to her. Why she is putting blame us? She only
made us to go somewhere somewhere.*

Inga

Journal

The events after my stupid 'coming out' ceremony remain
hazy for me. Too much happened too quickly. Besides, I was
frantically looking for my notebook and did not pay much
attention to what was going on in Komala Nivas. I realized
there were a lot of people who stayed on after the ceremony,
which included the Aunt Toothless who got very cosy with
Sister-in-law One and my mother. I saw her sitting in the
Goblin Corner quite often, presumably whenever Great
Aunt Kuppai let her. But she was, I realized, a highly
privileged guest; I had never known of anybody else being
allowed to sleep next to Great Aunt Kuppai and to talk to
her most of the night. Slippery Sneak who had also stayed
on, slept in the 'office rooms', separated from the main
house by the front courtyard, rooms I had never been into,
only smelt the cigarette smoke coming from them, and the
more unpleasant smell of what I later discovered was liquor.

The other reason for the haziness of those days, and
which also came in the way of my notebook search, was the
sudden change in my status. I was now a Woman, no longer
a mere girl, and I had to be given Work to do. This meant I

was to get up early, have a bath, then with hair still wet and open, with a small horizontal plait to keep it off my face, I had to water the basil plant that grew on a stone pedestal in the front courtyard. There was also some prayer I had to chant, to get a good husband or some such thing, but I didn't bother to say it; anyway I forgot it soon enough. Then I had to churn the milk for butter which took aeons to form. It might have been easier, less tedious, if I had read Hardy by then; I discovered Tess and her white, dimpled arms two or three years later. But Tess would hardly have been sitting as I did, on a bare, red oxide floor, pulling at the two ends of a complicated system of rope and watching for the white ball of butter to bob up. No rosy cheeks, no clean white smock, no merry Maypole dance on the green. I was not even allowed to be in a short frock anymore, I had to wear a long skirt with a blouse and an irritating length of cloth, a half sari, to cover my non-existent breasts. No fresh-faced milkmaid I.

There were other tasks too, all within the house, all dull, helping a grumpy, unforgiving Rukku Paati carry the food vessels back to the kitchen after everyone had eaten, taking dry clothes off the line in the backyard and folding my mother's clothes, my own and Great Aunt Kuppai's too, into separate piles to put away in the appropriate cupboards, which everyone referred to as almirahs. Folding the saris was like going to war without weapons. My mother's six-yard length of sari was bad enough, but Great Aunt's nine was as never-ending as my father's showy morning worship of all his gods and goddesses. My mother helped me the first time but left me to my own devices after that. I was then surrounded by hostile, billowing waves of sari, all threatening to strangle me, smother me. It was Paru who sneaked out of the cowshed and rescued me surreptitiously when nobody was about. If Paru had been seen touching those wretched lengths of washed cloth, they would probably have been burnt or torn into little pieces. Along with me.

What added to the strangeness of those days was a sudden spurt in my popularity with Great Aunt Kuppai and my father. I found myself high on their praise graphs, which made me quite dizzy. Was it merely because I had begun menstruating? Great Aunt called on everyone to see how easily the butter came up when I churned the milk; she could recall only one other daughter of the house, now dead several years, who had the same ability. 'Pure mind she had, like this one,' declared Great Aunt, 'that is why her butter is so white. Clean mind it needs.'

With my father, it was apparently my appearance at dusk as I carried a lighted lamp from the puja room to place at the foot of the basil. 'Ah ha,' my father said every now and then, 'What grace she shows! What dignity! Like a virgin goddess she is.' Had I replaced Goblin in his religious estimation? For a single, dazzling moment, I thought I had. Of course I was wrong. His praise of me had nothing to do with me. He had merely exposed his unthinking idea of women and of the world, his was the picture book perspective, based entirely on the drawings in cheap Tamizh magazines, where a freshly-bathed woman with turmeric marks on her face was the model of chastity, a courtyard with a lamp lit at the basil plant expressed a serene household within. Fiddlesticks!

O yes. I was just an illustration, a faint imitation of a Raja Ravi Varma painting. My father continued to touch his head to Goblin's feet and to put his lips to them as well. A screeching hobgoblin with kissed feet!

Now when I have so much time to think, I know that our eyes are fools. Fools and imposters at the same time. How is it that we allow our eyes to interfere with our sense of judgement? Our powers of observation are limited, often distorted, and yet what we think we see, overwhelms us. We look at the mask and believe it is the face, we see the face and are convinced it is but painted.

The situation in Komala Nivas changed dramatically one Monday morning. The day began, as most mystery books would put it, like any other day. The sun rose duly in the east and washed the front yard golden as I came out to water the basil, the first of my morning duties. I remember I was a bit late that day and had already got a round of scolding from my mother, sitting in the back verandah. She was more tetchy than usual and said a lot of unkind things but I disregarded her; I had realized she did not like my new-found favour with Great Aunt Kuppai and my father.

Letter from Inga

Dear Rapa.

Thank you for saying you have belief in me. It is only because of that I am now writing a reply to you. Yes, the other question you are asking is also true. My mother told me everything just now. It seems your father's father, Great Aunt Kuppai's brother, was very rich and gave your father even before he died a lot of money. He also gave big dowry for his sisters' marriages. With the money your father got, he built Komala Nivas. Your father was already married. Her name

*was Komalam, she was mother of Brother One and Brother
Two. Great Aunt Kuppai and Great Uncle came for the
grihapravesham, the new house puja, and did not go back at
all. They said Great Uncle was not having good practice.*

*Your father also said that it was all right because when he
was not there, they could look after his wife who was going to
have Brother Two.*

*When your father was in Delhi, Great Uncle wrote your
father's signature on a piece of paper, that he was giving
Komala Nivas to Great Aunt Kuppai. He got registration
and all. By the time your father came to know, Great Uncle
died and Great Aunt said what I can do?*

*Your father also could not do anything. She was in the
place of a mother and she was a childless widow also.*

*Then when you became a big girl, Great Aunt said it seems,
that only you had brains, not like Brother One and Two, so
she was going to give Komala Nivas to you. The lawyer came
when you were still not in the house for those three days and
Great Aunt signed the paper.*

My mother is not saying who told her all this information.
Inga

Journal

As I churned the milk that fateful Monday morning, the
household eddied around me in its usual fashion. Inga and
Sister-in-law One were sitting in the Goblin Corner cooing
at Goblin, my father after having finished his loud worship
of gods who apparently had severe ear afflictions, made his
customary visit to the Goblin shrine, then ate his tiffin and
went out with Brother One. My mother was 'not in the

house', it was the second day of her periods, and she was
giving loud orders to Rukku Paati from the back verandah.
It was a most ordinary day except that I had extra work,
helping Rukku Paati serve coffee and tiffin to everybody,
since my mother could not. I hated this, people either
wanted more or they wanted much less of whatever I offered
them, especially Slippery Sneak who also tried to caress my
hand.

I was relieved, and I am fairly sure that my mother and
Rukku Paati were too, when, on the orders of Great Aunt
Kuppai, the kitchen doors were firmly shut before the
visitors to the Goblin Fair arrived. Great Aunt Kuppai had
insisted on this from the very beginning. So after my morning
duties were done, I escaped with my books to the attic. It
had rained the night before, the ground was still wet and, in
some places, slushy; I could not use the secret place. The
attic was not as secret as I would have liked, my mother and
Rukku Paati came up there far too often, to open sacks and
tins of tamarind and jaggery and coconut to replenish the
kitchen stocks. But the attic was the only place that was safe
and offered some little privacy. I sat down to vent my
irritation on compound fractions and algebraic equations
which I had to finish before I returned to Delhi and to the
raised sarcastic eyebrows of Mrs Jacob, the mathematics
teacher. The house gradually grew quieter, the Fair was
obviously over and I decided I would ignore Rukku Paati
when she called me to lay the plates for the next round of
eating. But there was no call. No clatter of steel on a stone
floor. I did not realize then that Inga and her mother had
already been sent away, that Great Aunt Kuppai was still at

her bath, an unusually long one for a Monday and that, therefore, Rukku Paati had not yet been shaken awake from her mid-morning siesta. There was no sound from the inner hall. I was caught between staying upstairs with my fractions and going down to investigate the strange silence that pervaded the house.

Suddenly there was a loud, long scream and then another. From the inner hall. It was Sister-in-law One. I threw down my fractions and ran down the steps from the attic to the hall. As I entered, I saw my mother at the back door, Rukku Paati clutching at the kitchen door and Great Aunt Kuppai standing still at the doorway leading to the well, her hair wrapped in a towel. Sister-in-law One was at the Goblin Corner, screaming without stop, and next to her, Aunt Toothless wailed, rocking herself to and fro. But the main inhabitant of the Corner was not to be seen, there was no loud, howling mouth, no kicking bundle of urine-soaked cloth. Goblin had disappeared.

As I stood dumbstruck, there was only one thought that hammered in my brain. Inga would be mine again. Then I heard a sudden burst of sound at the front gates, the noisy confusion of an arrival. I turned to look. A car had drawn up, the large gate was flung open by Mikhale, and scores of lackeys were running about, looking important. Bustling up the steps, shouting out to the men to bring all the luggage in quickly, was my father. Behind him were his two sons, Brother One grim, not smiling, and close to him, as if not wanting to show himself, a shade uneasy, a little blanched, the runaway Brother Two.

THE CURIOUS CASE OF THE
MISSING GRANDCHILD

It was a close day in June and the weather had taken a sudden turn to rain, when I called upon my friend Mr Rapa Homes at his rooms in Pater Street. I found him lounging upon the sofa in his dressing gown, a pipe rack within reach, the morning paper unopened beside him, and a sheet of crested notepaper in his hand, evidently newly read.

'Ah! Ingson,' he cried. 'Delighted to see you dear fellow! You have read the morning paper diligently today, have you not?'

'I believe so,' said I ruefully. 'I had nothing else to do. Everybody is out of town or so it would seem.'

'It is fortunate, for you will be able to post me up.'

I cast a glance at the letter he was holding. 'That is a fashionable epistle,' I remarked. 'From a noble client?'

'Decidedly one of the richest in Tamland. If you have followed recent events closely, you would doubtless have read about Sir Kittu Iyer and his grandchild?'

'O yes, with the deepest interest.'

'The letter is from him. 'And as I have observed frequently, a letter is always instructive. This is what it says:

"Dear Mr Rapa Homes,

A good friend of mine whose name I do not wish to disclose, tells me that I can place the utmost reliance on your judgement and discretion. I am therefore determined to call upon you at four o'clock this afternoon. Should you have any other engagement at that time, I trust you will postpone it. The matter I wish to discuss is of the greatest delicacy.

Yours faithfully etc."'

'He says four o' clock,' said I. 'He will be here in a quarter of an hour.'

'Then I have time, with your assistance, to be apprised of the delicate matter he mentions. It involves a child, I gather.'

'His grandchild,' said I. 'The paper is full of it. Here it is: Parliament has risen but in the home of Mr Kittu Iyer, the eminent Parliamentarian, there is dismay and consternation. Mr Iyer's granddaughter, not yet a year old, has reportedly disappeared. What has added to the mystery is that the child has been under heavy guard over the past months, ever since she was proclaimed the incarnation of the Goddess of Good Fortune.'

'Proclaimed a what?' asked Homes with a start.

'The residence of Mr Iyer,' said I, 'has, for many months now, been considered a place of pilgrimage by the devout. The child is believed to have had divine powers and many swear that their lives have been miraculously transformed after they have seen her. However, it was not easy to see her. Visitors had to undergo detailed questioning before being let into the house, visiting hours were strictly regulated. And apart from family members, there were young men from Mr Iyer's political party whom he had appointed to guard the child as one would guard the Royal Jewels.'

'Men loyal to him?'

'Indisputably.'

There was a ring at the bell and the sound of a heavy step ascending the stair.

'That, if I mistake not, is our client, Ingson,' murmured Homes.

The door was thrown open and a gentleman entered, with a scowling face, strong-nosed and dark, almost a

INGA | 101

mahogany, with a stretch of skin from chin to throat, which gave him the appearance of something, perhaps, of the bovine. He had a steady eye and the air of a man whose lot it had ever been to command and be obeyed.

'Good day, Mr Iyer,' said Homes, rising from the sofa. 'Pray take a seat. This is my friend Dr Ingson before whom you can speak as you speak to me.'

'This is an extremely painful matter,' said Mr Iyer. 'Every passing minute is a minute lost. Pray tell me Mr Homes how you will restore my grandchild to me.'

'I know only that which is in the public prints. I take it that the account in the morning paper of the disappearance of your grandchild is correct?'

Mr Iyer glanced over it. 'It is correct.'

'Who was in the house at the time?'

'My widowed aunt, a female relative who is visiting, my wife, our daughter-in-law and the cook.'

'I believe you have a daughter?'

'O yes! But she was at her books.'

'Pray, tell me in your own words what happened at your residence that day. Be precise as to details.'

'It was Monday morning,' said our visitor. 'I had reason to believe that my younger son, whose whereabouts were not known for some months, had taken the eleven-fifty passenger from Madras and was on his way home. I determined to meet him and as the station is some considerable distance from my house, I set off with my older son at about half past nine.'

'Did anyone in the household know of your mission?'

'I mentioned it to my aunt and begged her not to divulge it till my son was safely under my roof. Who could predict that a tragedy of this measure was to occur on the very day . . .?'

'Quite. Pray continue your narrative.'

'Unusually enough, the train arrived on time, and my sons and I returned home much earlier than I had thought possible. As we entered, I heard my daughter-in-law scream. I ran into the inner chamber and found the child gone.'

'Snatched from your daughter-in-law's arms?'

'No. She had left the child in the care of the female relative and gone in to fetch a clean towel. The child had been strangely quiet and sleepy all morning and my daughter-in-law felt that a brisk rub down would help revive her.'

'Where were the other members of your household?'

'My aunt was in her bath, the cook who is extremely hard of hearing was asleep, my daughter was at her books, probably up in the attic and my wife . . .' here Mr Iyer gave a discreet cough, 'was not in the house.' He paused for a moment, then continued. 'There is something else baffling. My wife's niece, her sister's daughter, to whom my grandchild was particularly attached, was away on an errand with her mother that very morning.'

'Was that an unusual occurrence?'

'To the best of my knowledge, it has never occurred earlier!'

'What is her explanation?'

'She says my wife sent her.'

'And your wife?'

'Denies it. It is true, my wife was requested by my aunt to send her sister to the tailor with an urgent commission which, I understand, could not have been undertaken by a servant. My wife says that her niece insisted on accompanying her mother.'

'To return to your account of the events of that morning, did you notice anyone on the road to your house as you came in?'

'There was nobody, I would have noticed if there had been. It is an unfrequented road with houses standing well away. Since it had rained the night before, the ground was slushy and the carriage slow. I am certain there was not a soul about. My sons confirm that.'

'Who benefits from the child's removal from your guardianship?'

'Her grandmother. A cruel, unnatural woman, Mr Homes. I refused to entrust my grandchild to her when she applied to me after the mother died in childbirth. The child belongs to my family.'

There was a long silence, during which Homes leaned back and stared into the fire. 'This is a perfectly trivial business,' he said at last. 'My services are redundant in the matter. You will find soon enough, Mr Iyer, that the child has been safely deposited with her grandmother. I bid you good day.'

'Ah! You put me off, do you?' screamed our visitor, rising from his chair. 'If, as you say, the child is with that woman, how was she taken there? How did the villain get in? The house was guarded as closely as the Treasury. And tell me Mr Rapa Homes, how did he smuggle her out without being seen? There was nobody on the road, the alarm had been raised, yet nobody was seen coming out of the house with the child.'

'The child was still in the house when you entered it.'

'What!'

'Consider, Mr Iyer, you returned unexpectedly early, your

men would certainly have left their posts to receive you and your sons – there would have been a great deal of confusion at the gates. It would be easy for a clever man to wait, perhaps in an inner verandah, and slip out when the coast was clear.'

'That is all very well. But how did he get possession of the child?'

'It was a well-laid plot, planned and executed to near perfection. The female relative had been invited on purpose and there would certainly have been a young man in the picture.'

'Heavens! My nephew once removed is also visiting. He stayed in that morning, saying he had a fever. How did he have the impudence to . . .?'

'He was lured, perhaps with the promise of money, and given very precise instructions.'

'By whom?'

Homes drew out a slip of paper from the desk, wrote something on it and passed it to our visitor. Mr Iyer glanced at it and sank back into his chair. 'My aunt?' he gasped.

'A clever and devious lady, Mr Iyer. She would be a formidable foe.'

Our unfortunate visitor was in a state of pitiable agitation. 'What shall I do, Mr Homes?' he cried. 'For the credit of the family, it is essential to avoid scandal.'

'I recommend that you call off the search for your grandchild, and make peace with her grandmother,' said Homes. 'As you go out, Mr Iyer, do remember to close the door behind you, for there is a decided draught.'

'You know my methods, Ingson,' said Homes after our visitor had gone, a broken man. 'I saw from the first, that it was a conspiracy from within the household. You recall the curious incident of the road?'

'There was nobody on the road.'

'That was the curious incident.'

8

Journal

There was no news about Goblin for more than a week, only rumours. Somebody had seen a shiny black car in a shady lane behind the cinema, and somebody else had heard a baby cry in the same shady lane that day or maybe the previous day, she was not sure. When Aunt Toothless was questioned, all she could say was that she had put a sleeping Goblin down on the mat and gone into the kitchen for a drink of water. 'When I came out, your grandchild was gonay gone,' she wailed. 'Gonay gone!' That is all she would say; she said it many times and she wailed each time she said it. 'Gonay gone! Gonay gone!'

Who else was there to question? My mother was apparently talking to Paru near the outer bathroom, two alibis that could not be shaken. Rukku Paati was safely asleep, Sister-in-law One had dragged herself to the room where the towels were kept, and Great Aunt was of course in her bath, which gave her the immunity for not being questioned at all. Inga and her mother returned, just as I was carrying the evening lamp towards the basil. They were pounced on by Brother One and Mikhale and pounded with questions. I could see Inga's face in the half dark, looking more and more lost as she turned from one urgent questioner to the other; she did not even know what had transpired in the house. When she finally understood, she broke away and ran in. And then, there was a wail from the inner hall that cracked open the sky and tumbled the trees and upturned the birds flying home, mid-air. Then silence, complete, total. When I rushed in, Inga was sitting still in the Goblin Corner, with Sister-in-law One weeping beside her. Inga would not speak even to me, she would not eat, she was like stone. When the night deepened and the kitchen closed, she was carried by her mother to their back room, as if she was a piece of irritating furniture.

After the day's cross-questioning and cross-webbed recrimination, the only clear fact that emerged was that Slippery Sneak had disappeared; he, his dirty cloth bags with his clothes, and an old wristwatch belonging to my father, had all gone with him. Aunt Toothless wailed higher when she heard that he had gone, a thief. Apparently, it was he who had escorted her to Komala Nivas, her brother's son, a god-fearing, obedient boy, filled with respect for his elders. When her wailing rose the next day, my father gave her some money and packed her off with one of the now unemployed guards, to be deposited at her house. He did not speak to Great Aunt about it, nor, strangely, did she raise any objection though it was unceremoniously done.

I did not see Inga the next morning after a stretched night. I was told by Paru that she had a high fever, my mother told me fiercely that I should keep away from her, 'It might be I don't know what kind of fever, and we have enough trouble in the house as it is.' Paru told me quietly when my mother returned to the kitchen that Mikhale had got medicines from the 'dagtar' and I was not to worry about my small sister. I was too dispirited to argue with her about always referring to Inga as my small sister.

The days felt endless and vacant. I was furious with Inga for having fallen ill. Because Goblin had gone? I do not know what I might have done had it not been for Brother Two. He had brought with him two trunks full of books, and had promised to let me read the best mystery stories ever written. As the rains came down, and the speculations, the arguments, the reproaches, the quarrels continued to coil and uncoil downstairs, I sat in the attic as much as I could, meeting the residents of No. 221 B, Baker Street.

A week or so later, a small, much-folded note was thrust into the hand of one of the lackeys at the gate by a thin, rainwet boy who did not stay for an answer.

'Letter! Come! See!' shouted Brother One through the house. All of us, even I, dropped whatever we were doing and ran from wherever we were to the Goblin Corner, and gathered round the note. It was short, and written in English, the letters scratched by a shaky hand. Brother One read it aloud. 'Said child safe with Meenakshi. Stop search.' There was no signature to the note.

'It is from Dorai Athimbiar,' Brother One said triumphantly. 'I know it surely. It is only his handwriting.' He pushed the note to his father and brother so that they would confirm his assertion. Neither did. My father had sunk into moroseness since Goblin's departure, from which he made no attempt to rouse himself. Brother Two was indifferent.

Brother Two's girlfriend, 'that low-caste slut' as Great Aunt Kuppai called her, had found herself a much wealthier lover. So, when not reading one of his many books, Brother

Two played the much maligned man, beautifully blending the cynicism of the rejected eloper with the droop of the dejected widower. He did this to great effect; my mother quickly recovered from Goblin's absence, and as expected, gushed over him. But so did Paru who now acquired a dreamy look in her eyes, and a swing to her hips, and threw herself in his path whenever she could get away from the cows. She had a daunting rival in Rukku Paati, who suddenly began remembering old and secret family recipes which involved much pounding and grinding; she therefore kept us all hungry till she was done.

Brother Two's looks gave him an enormous public advantage. He was fair-complexioned with large speaking eyes, sported a delicate moustache, and thereby resembled, ever so slightly, a popular film hero of the time, whose hairstyle he copied. Why should a disappearance, a mystery, matter to him?

But even with Goblin gone, Komala Nivas did not return to being the place it used to be. I was strictly forbidden to go anywhere near Inga. I had to scour for news of her from Paru when she was not looking out for Brother Two, or from Mikhale whenever I managed to stop him in the midst of his scurrying about. Inga was ill for a long time, they said she was infectious, but I was never convinced of that.

Sweet coz! My pretty coz! Prithee be merry. Let us sit and mock that good housewife, the blind Fortune, from her wheel that her gifts may be bestowed equally. For she doth most mistake in her gifts to women; those she makes fair, she scarce makes honest. Sweet my coz, pray be merry.

Within a day of Goblin's disappearance, Great Aunt Kuppai had got her swing-seat back into the inner hall and she sat on it fanning herself, as of old. But her brief days of amiability were gone; her grim, closed look was back and reinforced. Sister-in-law One would not stop crying and Brother One went about like a man struck down by disillusion. He must have thought, after the note was received, that his father would march to FishEyes' village and with the help of the army, lay siege to her house and return triumphantly with Goblin. But my father did not move. Apart from his oil bath and a few desultory meetings with his party workers, which he held at Komala Nivas, he did nothing. He ate little, spoke hardly ever; he was like a large, humped lump of granite. Later, when I read Shelley's despairing sonnet *Ozymandias*, it reminded me of my father, particularly the way he was in those Goblin-gone days.

The only person who conversed with me was Brother Two, and he liked so much to talk, that it was not really a conversation. He liked being secretive too; every now and then, he would signal to me with his eyes and eyebrows to meet him behind the office rooms, where there was a narrow, hidden verandah. Brother Two smoked, and this was the only spot, or so he thought, where he would not be seen; I did not ever tell him of our secret place, Inga's and mine. Brother Two also considered himself a Poet, a misunderstood, unappreciated genius, far ahead of his times. He wrote in Malayalam of the seductive embrace of alcohol, of full-breasted women with black-lined eyes, who sported endlessly in jasmine-packed moonlight. I did not understand much of the craft of his writing, what I supposed were the metaphors and similes sounded quite awful to me. There was also a lot of repetition; how much can one do with rounded, female limbs and scented black hair? His muse-women also seemed to be the kind who only acquiesced and never spoke, and of course, they never went into the kitchen and diced vegetables or churned milk. Brother Two maintained that every man – every man – was a poet until he got married; I wasn't sure where he placed himself. Wreathed he certainly was, but whether as a poet bachelor once again, or a poetry-exhausted widower, I did not know. Actually, he moved randomly between these two positions, sometimes; like Donne, he chided the unruly sun, at other times, he was Keats' knight, alone and palely loitering. Strangely, but perhaps it was not so strange, he hardly mentioned Sister-in-law Too, his official wife. His monologue was about the low-caste girl whose name I discovered was Lata. He called her his Mohini, the eternal seductress whose breath was nectar and whose eyes were ambrosial or sandal or something, I never did understand how.

Why did she leave you, I asked him. Brother Two pulled at his cigarette and rested his back against the wall, tucking his mundu between his thighs; I realized it was going to be a long reason. But when he spoke, it was of her in past perfect tense, as if it was she who had died, and not his wife. Anyway, it was not in answer to my question at all. Instead, he told me in great detail of their first meeting at her house, the instant electric current between them, their ache for each other. All this he had to tell me in instalments because I was constantly being recalled to duty and much of his story, where he described her divineness, was excruciatingly boring. I realized later that Brother Two had been excessively inspired by Spenser, the long-ago English poet falsely placed on a high pedestal, when all he did was to translate Dante's

Italian into his own native tongue. I noticed also that Brother Two had a curious trick of repeating certain words and phrases, which made his story sound like the recitation of an Indian poetic composition.

Finally, one damp afternoon, while Komala Nivas snoozed, I extracted the whole story from him; by then I had perfected my skill in pulling him back to the main road each time he strayed into a smelly, romantic alley.

'I longed for her, for my Mohini,' he said. 'I longed for her day and night. I could not concentrate on my studies, I could not eat, I could not sleep, I could not think, I could not . . .' After he had given me an exhaustive list of all that he could not do, he went on with the story.

'I was not allowed to go to her house anymore, all because of that old man Venki, that old impotent Venki. He was angry because my green parrot would not entertain him. Can you imagine he wanted her? He actually wanted a divine nymph only as old as his daughter?' Brother Two took a couple of jerky puffs at his cigarette to show his great remembered rage. 'Anyway, late one stolen evening, sitting on the sands of the beach in the dark, I caught hold of her lotus-like hands,' he said, catching hold of mine, after placing his cigarette down on the ledge. 'I caught hold of her hands like this and pleaded with her. I said that I was going to die if she did not come away with me, she had to come away with me. She laughed like a pretty waterfall and wanted to know where we could go, oh she looked so enchanting when she asked me that totally irrelevant question. What did it matter where we were, as long as we were together? But my softest dove, my sweetest doll, she was such a practical little moonbeam. We need food, she reminded me, and a bed, she added mischievously.' He chuckled and I wrenched my hands away from his. He picked up his cigarette, took a long puff, then continued with his memoirs.

'I had to agree with her, of course. We would need food, definitely we would need food, and a bed or at least a soft mat and a safe roof over our heads. So I promised to get some money together and to meet her outside a certain cinema house near the beach. She used to go there with her cousins for a first day first show.' A lost-at-sea look crept into his eyes.

I hastily asked him what happened after that. 'Well, I begged and borrowed as much as I could. I must admit that Prof. Seshu was generous, quite generous, especially when I said I needed money for books and stationery. I told him I was writing a novel, in my spare time of course, in the style of Jane Austen.' He giggled as he remembered his lie. 'I knew very well that Jane Austen is his favourite author, his most favourite author, next to Charles Dickens.

'Anyway, when I thought I had got enough of that dirty but essential thing called money, I put down a deposit for a set of rooms in a non-Brahmin colony, some distance from the city. Then I sent word to my champaka bud that I was ready, quite ready. I wrote a note telling my light of the new moon that I would be waiting for her at our cinema house that evening after sunset. She never got my note.'

'What?' I asked. This sounded promising.

'The servant girl to whom I had given a lot of money and saris and all that, was caught just as she was entering the house. The work of that old rogue of course, that old rascal.'

'Then?'

'Then? Then what? I was at the appointed place an hour

ahead of time. And there I saw not her, no sign of her, I saw her mother and that scoundrel Venki with a couple of hefty men holding brooms.'

'Brooms?' I asked.

He clicked his tongue impatiently. 'Brooms to hit me of course!'

'What did you do?'

'What could I do? I ran! I ran to the rooms I had rented and hid there for three days. The landlady thought I was sick so she gave me food and looked after me. I used to cough a lot in her hearing. In the meanwhile, the lamp of my eyes was told that I had returned to my house, to my wife.' He paused, threw away his spent cigarette and lit another.

'And she believed it?'

'What else?' He spat out the words. 'That rogue is very clever in telling lies, very very clever. He makes it sound exactly like the truth. But luckily for me, after three days of staying inside and coughing less and less, I went back to the cinema house. It was a Friday and I knew that my sugar candy would not miss the first day first show. She was there with her cousins, laughing at something one of them said. She had to pretend she was all right, though I knew she was crying in her sweet, soft heart. She caught sight of me but made no sign, the sly rosebud. But during the interval, she crept out, half crying and half laughing and we met under the staircase. I quickly gave her the address of the rooms I had rented and she promised she would be there. She kept her promise, though all night I lay awake wondering what new plot that old man would come up with. But, she was there the next morning, in my eagerly waiting arms, with all her clothes and some small pieces of jewellery.'

Brother Two stopped. I waited. He was silent still.

'Then?' I asked finally.

'I just wanted a quiet life,' he murmured. 'Just a quiet life with my beloved, my Mohini. I wanted to gaze at her all day, at her neck so like a swan, her ears like seashells, her butterfly-like lips, her thighs like . . . anyway, I wanted to do nothing but look deep, deep into her eyes, and write immortal lines of poetry. Better than Kalidasa, much better than Keats. I would have left Tennyson far behind, I would have been called India's Shakespeare. But life is not fair, not fair at all.' He stopped.

'How come?' I asked, though I had guessed why.

'My Mohini,' he said in a voice that is sometimes described as strangled, 'the Mohini I loved with a passion so rare that it was not understood, not even recognized, that Mohini died before my eyes. A stranger took her place, a woman demanding money and clothes and jewellery all the time, a woman jealous and quarrelsome, a woman who did not even like that sweet landlady who was so good to me. I tried so hard to bring back my ray of moonlight, my jasmine bud, but she was gone, she was lost to me forever. It only remained for the landlady's nephew to promise her great riches and then I was finally rid of her. She had spent all that I had, she took away even the rent money, so I had to sneak out like a common thief one night and go back to my old room. The next day, I borrowed some money from Prof. Seshu, sent a wire home; then I caught some train, sat in an unreserved compartment and came here.'

He got up as if disgusted, threw his cigarette into the hibiscus bush, hitched up his mundu and loped off. He had not mentioned his daughter Goblin even once.

Letter from Inga

Dear Rapa,
I really do not know what what medicines Sister-in-law One
was having. Why should anybody tell me about such things? I
just used to sit there near to Sister-in-law One and Brother
One because of Kutti Paapa. Afterwards, I never sat there, I
never even went to that side.
Inga

Journal

By the time Inga became well enough to come out of that
wretched back room, the rains had started in right earnest.
Komala Nivas was curtained off by thick swathes of monsoon
water sheets; it was as if we lived on an ocean bed, secret,
hidden. All around was the drumming, dancing, dappling
sound of water. It drowned out every other voice, it allowed
no intrusion of any element foreign to it. And it made my
heart grow monstrously heavy.

I was getting tired of Brother Two's tales of a dead-alive
woman, I suspected that her apparently mesmerizing beauty
was his imagining. But since he allowed me his books, I had
to tolerate him till such time as Inga was able to be with me
again. Then I had to tell him that I could no longer be his
audience, that I had to go on with my homework. Brother
Two sulked, he had a rather beautiful sulk; he complained
that I was the only other literary one in the family and that
he was 'suffocating due to the fumes of unrecognition'. But
soon afterwards, I heard him giggling near the cowshed;
obviously Paru was providing him sweet enough ventilation.

When Inga finally emerged, it seemed as if she had shrunk,

she was smaller and looked much younger than her age, but with none of the laughter, or the quickness of the younger pre-Goblin Inga. She was almost transparently pale, a baby leaf completely listless. It was as if no rough winds, not even a storm, could rouse her; there was a streak of obstinacy about her that I had not noticed earlier. She refused to come up to the attic, she hardly spoke to me. All she did was to sit in the front verandah, looking at the rain endlessly, motionless, as she did in our grandmother's house. She also returned to her old infuriating way of allowing everyone to coddle her. Anyone, everyone could seat her on his lap and give her loud, wet kisses, caress her, run their hands over her, she even allowed the postman to paw her with his dark hairy hands.

I tried to stop this, to pull her away; I guarded her, I sat next to her doing my wretched fractions. But the moment I was called away for more of those hateful household duties, some counterfeit uncle would show up and pull her onto his lap and smother her with kisses and call her his precious pudding doll. I remonstrated with her often, I explained to her that the attic was a safer place, but she said she wanted to sit only in the front verandah, she wanted to see the rain from there. There was nothing I could do, but one day when I saw her in the arms of one of my father's lackeys, my patience broke. I was sharp with him and he got up hurriedly, half laughing. I dragged Inga through the house to the back verandah, where I knew her mother would be. The back verandah was damp and smelt heavily of wet lentils and rice, of spinach, curry leaves and curds, of cow.

Even now, the smells from a south Indian kitchen bring the scene back distinctly. In the far corner, well away from

Rukku Paati, stood Paru, mixing what must have been cow feed, in a huge cauldron. Rukku Paati herself was sitting in the middle of high piles of green stalks, muttering to herself and pinching off their leaves. Inga's mother was at the other corner, grinding an enormous quantity of rice and lentils. She sat with her legs on either side of the huge black grinding stone, her faded green sari pulled up to her knees. I remember how white, hairless, her legs were, like blue-veined marble. In contrast, her arms looked rough, almost brown, her hands were puckered and the skin of her palms a kind of dirty yellow. As she turned and turned the monstrous pestle, stone grating against stone, the lentils heaved and frothed up with a plopping sound. The rain was drumming all around us. I went up to my aunt, and called out loudly to her, still holding Inga tight. The hands stopped their circular motion, my aunt turned to look at me. Her face, bare of the vermillion mark, was, even so, like that of a goddess, painted in tints of saffron and milk cream white, glowing, her eyebrows like the arched back of a swan. But her eyes! Did I imagine it or did her eyes actually blaze as harshly as diamonds do when they catch the light? Diamonds are anger-filled stones, even the small nose and ear studs my aunt wore, looked as if they had declared war. I told her, stammering a little, that Inga was allowing everybody to pick her up and touch her, touch her everywhere and that this had to be stopped. My aunt sat very still, looking at me, listening, not even wiping off the small beads of sweat forming on her forehead. When I had finished, she turned to look at Inga, who, by then, was sitting limp on the top step, her wrist thin in my clasp. Then, still looking at her daughter, my aunt said, 'You speak very big. Like forty years woman, not like fifteen-year-old girl. I suppose your city school teaches you such things no? That is good. But Inga is just a village fool. Like her unlucky mother.' Then she turned away, bent forward, pulled at the black pestle with a grunt, deftly pushed the dough that had surged up back into the hollow, and returned to her grinding. It was a dismissal.

As I helped Inga up to take her back into the house and to the front verandah, I saw my mother. She was standing at the doorway; her face, so like my aunt's, and yet so unlike, was shuttered and said nothing.

Why did I do what I did? What did I expect would happen? That Inga would return to her sweet ways? That we would go back to the time of stolen green mangoes burning and puckering our lips, Inga's heart-melting laughter ringing out and, so often, quickly shushed? Such stuff that fantasies are made of, just airy nothings?

Little coz, my pretty coz, shall we seek our fortune in the Forest of Arden? Alas, what danger will it be to us, maids as we are, beauty provoketh thieves sooner than gold. So I shall with a kind of umber smirch my face, the like do you. And were it not better because I am more than common tall, that I did suit me all points like a man? Lie there what hidden woman's fears there will, we'll have a swashing and martial outside, as many other mannish cowards have, that do outface it with their semblances.

9

Journal

Nothing happened, nothing changed, and on a weepy, rain-smeared morning, my father, mother and I found ourselves on the train back to Delhi. It was as grim and silent a journey as I had expected it to be, the rain that washed the train windows clean stopped abruptly as we crept northwards and, by the time we reached Delhi after three days, it was as if the sun had never left off burning the earth. And again, as it happened before, just as we arrived at the station, one of my father's Delhi lackeys ran up, panting, and thrust a telegram into his hands. This time, it was an express telegram from Brother One to say that his wife, Sister-in-law One, was 'suddenly being able to walk'.

After that first, transfixed, disbelieving moment, I wondered how it would have been at Komala Nivas. Would Great Aunt Kuppai have cried and laughed hysterically as my mother did at the station? Would Brother One have shouted incoherently as my father did at passers-by in three or four languages, his eyes streaming? Would sacred bells have been rung joyfully in front of my father's gods and would crowds have gathered? Would flowers have rained down from the skies? Would there have been such scenes in Komala Nivas as there may have been at Lourdes?

Letter from Inga

Dear Rapa,

I am telling you I did not at all know whether she was having any medicine. I never saw her with a medicine bottle or anything. She used to put some oil on her legs which was quite smelly. But I think that also was only on Friday. She had the same food, like us only. Your mother used to tell her to have more green things but she never used to listen.

Inga

Journal

The journey from the station to the house was chaotic. My mother, still crying and laughing alternately, did what she had not done even once in my life – she hugged and kissed me, and called me by Sister-in-law One's name. My father's one-sided conversation with her, conducted at the top of his voice, lurched drunkenly between bafflement, some lingering disbelief and a total conviction in the powers of Goblin. 'She has not abandoned me,' my father cried again and again. 'She is still with me! Devi! Bhagavati! How could I have imagined that you were gone?' In the middle of all this, he managed to convey to us that he had decided to return to Komala Nivas immediately, as soon as arrangements were finalized; he might even leave the next day. 'By flight,' he announced, recklessly. This was emergency behaviour. My father was closefisted, even though he might have charged the air ticket to Party Work. But, in addition, he was frightened of letting go the known, the brown earth, the stinking but familiar train bathroom, the crowded and noisy railway stations. Did he feel his power would diminish if his feet were not firm on the ground, that he would become a small man if he were suspended mid-air? I had never heard him wanting to be nearer the skies, to soar.

As soon as she heard of his plan to go to Komala Nivas, my mother turned away from me abruptly, mid-embrace and asked, 'And me?'

My father rotated his head and looked through the window. 'We are almost reaching the house,' he said. Then throwing a glance at me, he went on, 'You have to be with her no? She has become a big girl. I will come back soon.'

My mother said nothing, but she hurled a dagger look at me, a look that cursed me for being female, for having started menstruating and therefore not to be left unattended. Her tears began again, but now for a different reason. When we reached the house, my father jumped out of the car before it had stopped and ran in calling for the telephone. My mother followed him, not as quickly since she had to exhibit her bitter disappointment, but hurriedly enough. The lackeys were in a car behind us, so I left them to bring the luggage into the house and went in with my own bag of books. I had decided during the train journey that I must shed my Enid Blytons now that I had started menstruating. So I read them all one last time, as a farewell, and found that even the boarding school ones were wanting, they lacked disorder, the dilemmas were too easily resolved, mysteries too quickly explained away. I had to grow out of such childishness and come to woman's estate. I did not know what this was exactly, I'm not sure of it even now, but I intended to find out through the books I had stolen from Brother Two's collection. *Jane Eyre*, *Wuthering Heights*, *Pride and Prejudice*, *Emma* – I had purloined them all and they must be my guides. Brother Two never missed them, not even later; I recall now that many of the books he boasted about – I remember Tolstoy and Marx among them – had many uncut pages.

As I went into the house, I heard my father shouting into the phone. He seemed to be talking to his party office, to somebody who was either naturally slow-witted or who had become so because of my father's manner. My father was demanding that the man drag Brother One to the office, in order that he, my father, could speak to him, his son, immediately. In between barking out these orders, and obviously much to the consternation of the slow-witted man, my father raged at Great Aunt Kuppai for refusing to have a modern 'yantram' in Komala Nivas. 'It is for such times no?' he roared. 'If there was one phone in my house, why I should waste time talking to fools like you? Tell me that. But she says, no yantram should be there. What yantram? This is good instrument, it will not cause injury, she should know that. I am yantram mantram doing man or what? You! Why you are still on phone? Go ask that son of mine to phone me. Now itself. Not next year! Now! Urgent.' I knew that my father had been quite happy to allow Great Aunt Kuppai her way about the telephone, it allowed him to keep his secrets.

Brother One phoned a couple of hours later. My father and mother had not moved, not eaten, not even had a bath to wash off those train smells. They sat by the phone, stinking, keeping vigil. Naturally, the first words Brother One heard from his father, were those of anger for keeping everyone waiting. 'What you were doing?' my father raged. 'We are sitting here for so many hours! What? I am not hearing. O! Your in-laws have come? Many people? All right, all right. So what happened?'

I stood by the door, having bathed and eaten, and listened. From what I could piece together, from my father's grunts and ejaculations and frequent shouts at the operator, Komala Nivas was still afire with confusion. What had happened was this. The day after we left, Sister-in-law One had felt some strange sensation in her legs. She apparently said that it was as if hundreds of ants were biting her 'from inside'. This was at night. The next morning, very early, when she woke, something made her hold on to the wall and stand up. She did. She was alone of course, Brother One was sleeping in the office room as usual, and Great Aunt Kuppai was washing her face outside, near the well. Sister-in-law One then made her way to the inner hall very slowly, still clutching the wall, and holding on to the door to cross the threshold step.

The first person to see her upright was Rukku Paati who was standing by the kitchen door, with a glass of coffee. This redoubtable lady saw Sister-in-law One, dropped her jaw and the coffee and began to scream. The hot liquid must have scalded her quite badly. Anyway, Great Aunt then came in and, quite calmly, helped Sister-in-law One to the puja room and made her kneel and thank all the gods there. The brothers were hurriedly woken up. Brother One turned mad, Brother Two rubbed his eyes, muttered 'aascharyam' twice and tottered back to sleep. But the amazement, the wonderment obviously set ablaze those less slothful, and grew a thousand-fold. Within an hour, Komala Nivas was choking with visitors. I gathered that those who came to scoff remained to gaze and as they gazed, so the wonder grew.

'What about that aunt of yours?' shouted my father. 'Your Meenakshi Athai! Anyone has told her?' Brother One did not seem to have understood the question. So in English for emphasis and clarity, my father shrieked again, 'Meenakshi! Has she been informed?' There was no answer. The line clicked dead.

I ran back to my room. How could I have ever expected some mention of Inga?

Letter from Inga

Dear Rapa,

That day was really a funny day. I was still sleeping. Mother was taking bath. Then I heard Rukku Paati shouting something. Mother also heard in the outside bathroom. By the time she tied her sari and came, I also washed my face and cleaned my teeth. We both went inside the hall and we saw Brother One dancing and singing and clapping his hands and we saw Sister-in-law One standing up. She was looking very tall. When she saw me, she said, 'Come Inga come. You only must take me to every place.' So the whole day I stayed with her. I even took her to the bathroom because she was still a little little afraid that she will fall down. But she did not at all fall.

Later on, her father mother and two sisters and all came, first time to Komala Nivas. The house was so filled with people. It was like a marriage. Brother One even called a man cook for helping Rukku Paati. I am telling you, it was really like a marriage.

Inga

Journal

Much as he tried, my father was unable to speak to his office again that day, the trunk line remained obstinately dead. But he stayed on the phone, calling the Party Office in Delhi and all the south Indian clubs and associations in the capital, telling them of the Great Event in his life. With each conversation, the story was exaggerated just a bit more, so that by the end of the evening, when the house was full of visitors, Sister-in-law One had been transformed into a living goddess. Goblin was, of course, the divine baby, and, in addition, according to my father, heavenly choirs sang regularly at his native home, while a host of gods showered down fragrant flowers and gold coins on the said house.

The first visitors to the Delhi house, once the news began to spread, were a sceptic lot. Many of these were north Indians who brought with them sad, summer-scorched bouquets and boxes of sweets with greasy undersides. I watched from the far corner of the front porch, hidden behind a pillar. I saw their faces unconvinced, I could see them telling themselves that this was some clever kind of Madrassi hoax, but that it would be best to exclaim and be reverent because one never knew how the political wind in Delhi might turn. I saw them come and go, shaking their heads as they muttered the word 'chamatkaar', a term that to me sounded manipulative, conniving, far removed from things wondrous. The south Indians came too in clusters, empty-handed but ready to seek the divine anywhere, breathing the air my father breathed, standing close to him, but especially tasting godhead in cups of coffee, plates of upma and in glasses of buttermilk. As the evening closed in, they began to see themselves as gods, helped by large gulps of my father's secret store of liquor. My mother, who had supervised the vegetarian part of the evening, retired when the conversation and the cuisine – brought from outside – became unbearable.

My father left early next morning even before I had got ready for school. My mother who, it seemed, had made up her mind the previous day to adopt the Quit Smiling movement, obviously had not bargained for his leaving so soon. When I returned from school, I got the brunt of her sulks, leftover food from the night before which I refused to eat, and bitter looks all evening. When she finally spoke, it was because she was compelled to, I could see that. I had once overheard Great Aunt Kuppai telling my mother of some woman who was mistreated by her son and daughter-in-law. She kept it to herself, so ashamed was she to complain about her own son. But one day, when the torture became unbearable, she left the house and went into the fields where she found an old abandoned shed. There she stood and there she vented all the anger and hurt she had kept unexpressed for so many years. Apparently, when she let out her pent-up grievances, the walls of the shed crumbled and crashed to the ground.

So when my mother finally opened her mouth, I had to let go *Jane Eyre*, which I had just opened, and listen to her. 'So many things I have not told you,' she began. 'But now you are big, you should have some idea about all these things. Family things. You know that your father, Kuppaathai, even me, we were all cheated?'

'Cheated?' I had to ask. 'Who by?'

She sat on my bed and made herself comfortable. 'By your

older sister-in-law's father mother. Saroja's family. Such cheats they are. And now, they all are staying in Komala Nivas is it? After the marriage when did they come? Did they come once even? For my second boy's marriage they came or what? Some some excuse they gave. How they could come? They had no face.'

'Why?'

'How they could come, tell me. They cheated us no? They tied one cripple girl on our head. The whole world was knowing that the girl was not all right. But we were not knowing. Girl's horoscope was matching so your father said it is very good family, three girls only, they have big village house, lot of land and coconuts, they will spend very much on girl. So your father and Kuppaathai went to see. Very far away village it was, no road, nothing. In the last part they went by walk, even the cow cart could not go. The girl's people gave much honour to your father and Kuppaathai, that all was very good. But when Kuppaathai went inside to see the girl, you know what they did? The cheaters? They showed the younger sister. They both look same same, only one year difference, same nice colour, nice face, everything. That girl brought coffee, that girl stood and sat, her hair she opened to show it was her hair only. So Kuppaathai agreed for alliance, and marriage date was also agreed. Your father even got good road for them before marriage. Just think. Then that Meenakshikka started saying why Kuppaathai went to see girl, it was not correct.'

'Why shouldn't she have gone?'

'She is widow.' My mother spat out the word. 'But your father will not believe in all this. He is big Gandhi no? So Kuppaathai said she will not go for marriage, and we only went. Very good arranging they did, everything was nice. But even on marriage day, we could not make out. The girl was brought by her uncle, her elder maama on his shoulder to the mandapam. That is part of our ceremony, you know. Only after the thaali was tied, we found out. The girl was not able to walk. The eldest daughter-in-law of Kittu Iyer's house was one cripple.'

'Then?' I asked.

'Then? Then nothing. What was there? Garlands were already exchanged, thaali was tied. Girl belonged to this house now. Your father started shouting in front of every people. Seshu Anna also. We came out without eating even one mouthful. Her father ran and fell on the ground in front of us. He was hugging and hugging your father's legs so tightly. He cried and cried and said he has two more daughters what will he do now? Then your brother only said it is all right, let us take her to our house.'

My mother paused. When she spoke again, her tone had changed. She was now not the narrator, but the scornful wife of an imperfect husband. 'Your father makes big show saying he is like Gandhi no?' she asked. 'You are big girl now, you tell, what Gandhi he is? Gandhi, he is calling himself? He should see his son. His son took that cripple girl to his house, our house, he kept her, gave her food, gave her one place to sleep. How many boys will do that?'

Haven't other men done things similar? Behind closed doors and closed faces, who knows what goes on? My mother's long monologues were only partially true. I realized later, that she had kept so much away from me, she had hidden the most crucial of all truths. Did she not cheat too? What is hidden is secret, what is secret is often sinister.

Letter from Inga

Dear Rapa,

Yes, I remember. You acted the part of a boy in that drama. It was about a boy and his sister who saw Mother Mary. I do not remember the name of the place but it became a place where many miracles used to happen. Blind people could see, lame people walked and people with leprosy got cured. This is all because of faith. If you go to see, even everything and every minute is a miracle. You take one leaf from a tree and you look how it is made, it is a miracle. Who made that leaf made you and me also.

Inga

Journal

It was nearly a fortnight after he had left so hurriedly, that we heard from my father. I remember that it was about eight-thirty on a Sunday evening, the Delhi sun had finally set, albeit reluctantly, its heat still shimmering all around us. My mother had finished her evening bath and was telling the cook to bring the food to the table, when the phone rang. It was an explosion of sound in a house that was, with my father away, as silent as a cleared desk. My mother dropped the glass she was holding, its contents splashed across my feet, buttermilk, sticky and cold. From the innards of the kitchen, one of the lackeys yelled, 'Phone! Eda! Phone!' But my mother was quicker than the lazybones who had been called; she ran into the office chamber and picked up the phone with hands that trembled. It was my father, as I thought; he had obviously overruled Great Aunt Kuppai and had had a phone installed in Komala Nivas. As the MP of the place, he had got it done in less than two weeks. I heard my mother shoot a fusillade of questions without waiting for an answer. 'How is she? How is she? She is holding and walking or not holding? She is going to kitchen or no? What is doctor saying? Steps she is going up and down?' Then abruptly, she stopped, she said nothing, only listened in a silence that grew ominous. I heard the phone click and I rushed out to wash my feet clean, I did not want to get the first fiery blast of her displeasure.

I need not have worried; my mother did not eat at all that night. She apparently told the lackeys while I was still in the bathroom, that she had a headache and was going to sleep. So I ate alone, with *Jane Eyre* for company and wanted for nothing. But I needed to know what it was my father had said to her. I was certain it was not an upbraiding; if that, he would have raised his voice high enough for the whole household to have heard him. Besides, what had my mother done in the last two weeks to anger him, so far away? No, it was something else, some bit of news. Surely she would tell me once she had cooled down. So after an hour or so, I knocked at her door. She did not answer, she had latched the door fast and all I heard were muttered invectives and a storm of sobs.

My mother did not seek me out the next morning, she did not even sit at breakfast with me as was her custom. Nor did she wait to have lunch with me when I got home from school. I went to look for her, and found she had locked herself in again and would not speak. She did not emerge from her room in the evening either. I suppose Brother One or Brother Two would have been able to coax her out of her sulks and persuade her to talk to them but I lacked that talent and after some trying, I gave up.

My mother's strange behaviour continued for a whole week. What she expected me to do or whether she expected anything at all from me, I did not know. Even later, she refused to talk about this time, especially in front of my father. Sometimes I brought it up deliberately, in my father's hearing, but she always steered the conversation away adroitly. How did going without food help anything? When Gandhi fasted or took a vow of silence, the government of the day, an entire nation, was alarmed. But when my mother did not seem to be eating, I did not really worry. I knew she ate because I saw two plates being washed as also the special steel glass she used for her coffee. Her wet clothes hung on the line, a fresh set every day. Whom was she fooling? And why? I will never know.

And I did not care. Neither then nor later. The Sunday after my mother went into self exile, the phone rang. I was sure it was my father, it was just like him to call us when the trunk line rates were lower than during the week. I picked up the phone and spoke our number as we had been taught at school.

'Where is your mother?' my father barked.

'Not well,' I replied.

'All right, all right,' he said in English. 'Tell her my programme stands. I will be coming to Delhi next Sunday. Monday itself, I have to request your Mother Superior for a seat for Inga.'

'Inga?'

'Your mother did not tell you? I am bringing Inga and her mother with me.'

He cut off the call without another word.

I was still holding the phone, stupefied, when I heard a

sound behind me. It was my mother, red-eyed, wild-haired, not trusting her voice. Before I could say anything, she turned and jaggedly, half-stumbling, ran back to her room, slammed the door shut and shot the bolt across. It was as if she had stoppered up all lips and tongues that talked.

She is coming, she is coming, my dove, my sweet; she is coming, she is coming, I hear my heart beat. The mogra says she is near, she is near; the jasmine cries she is here. Come my beloved, let us go forth into the garden, let us watch the fountains play. Come my beloved, that art in the cleft of the rocks, in the secret places of the stairs, let me see thy countenance, let me hear thy voice, for sweet is thy voice and thy countenance comely. A garden enclosed is my beloved, a spring shut up, a fountain sealed. The night queen insists she is late, she is late, the gulmohar whispers I wait.

Letter From Inga

Dear Rapa,

No, my mother did not say even one word. You have seen her talking to your father any time, tell me? Your father only said we have to go to Delhi. It was like a order. Mikhale came and told. He also brought one black trunk to put our clothes. Before that, we did not have anything. Even in the train, my mother did not open her mouth. What can people in jail say anyway?

Inga

10

Journal

It was the slowest week that ever was. It dragged by with dreadful, painful sluggishness as if its feet were bound in irons. Yes, time acts in diverse paces with diverse people. But surely, no happy bride could have awaited her wedding day with as much anticipation as I did Inga's coming; no anxious mother with a sick child watched for the first light of recovery with as much impatience. In the meanwhile, I decided to make preparations. I wanted that Inga sleep in my room and asked the lackeys to put in another cot. They nodded but did not do it, despite all my reminders.

Mid-week, my mother began appearing feebly at meal times, still red-eyed and wild-haired, but refused to speak about what arrangements were to be made. When I asked her about it, she looked at me as if it was I who had gone mad. However, there seemed to have been some sort of orders from my father to the lackeys, because all of a sudden, on the Thursday of that week, they opened up an unused room near the kitchen, cleared it of its cobwebs, cleaned the windows, swept the dusty floor, then washed it down with water that turned brown, and finally carried in two cots, one full sized, the other small. When I returned from school on

Friday, the two cots held a mattress and pillow each, and violently coloured bedspreads. The windows were uncurtained. When I mentioned this to them, the lackeys nodded vigorously in agreement, but did nothing about it.

The train was late. I had gathered from the conversation between the lackeys that it was to arrive in the middle of the morning on Sunday. I had, with great effort, finished all my homework on Saturday. As Sunday morning turned into Sunday afternoon, and the sun waxed in the high blue sky, I could not stay still. No chair held me for more than a minute, nor no book either. I hardly had any tiffin in the morning and lunch I could not face. They were supposed to have been home by then. When I finally heard the sound of a car, it was almost three in the afternoon. I flew to the front porch, my bare feet burnt on the cement steps, the sun blazed on the roof of the car as it drew in and stopped. My father clambered out first, from the far side; I could see my aunt struggling with a limp, half-fainting Inga. Before I could reach them, one of the lackeys rushed forward. But Inga clung to her mother, moaning, and had to be half carried, half dragged into the house by my aunt. It was not the arrival I had waited for, that I had embellished with laughing joy, a lingering hug, a tight clasp of hands. How often expectation cheats us.

My mother did not come out at all. She remained in her room as I knew she would, and, as was his wont, my father bustled in, calling out to her imperiously. But this time, she chose to keep away, to be unresponsive. My father frowned, spoke her name sharply, then strode towards her room and kicked open the door. It took a week for the latch to be replaced. In the meanwhile, Inga and her mother and the black trunk were escorted to the curtainless room and then, that door was closed to me as well.

Nobody ate lunch that day, except my father.

The afternoon lay heavily upon me. My room felt airless, the fan creaked and rotated but to no great effect; it was as if I had to breathe and move in a sea of oil. At about four-thirty or so, I heard my father's voice telling one of the lackeys to send word to the driver. 'I have to go out,' I heard him say. 'In five minutes.' I crept out. My father was standing at the half-open door of his room, buttoning up his shirt, and speaking to my mother. 'You want what?' he asked in Tamizh. He did not yell as he usually did in Komala Nivas, but his tone was savage enough. 'If I do that, it is wrong, if I do this it is also wrong. That time, you cried like a new baby, wanting to go back, you even were prepared to leave the girl here alone. Now what has happened?' Then in English, he said, 'I have decided. I will go and talk to Vembu now.' He turned and went towards the front porch. A moment later, I heard the door of the room slam shut.

It was only much later, when the sky began to darken and I heard the crows cawing their way home, that the door of the other room opened and Inga came out, timidly, almost as if she were afraid. I had gone by the room several times, knocked at the door twice, but to no avail. Now when I saw her at last, it struck me that she was not as pale as she had been, and had grown a little taller. She had been scrubbed clean of the soot marks that the journey had deposited on her arms and her hair, her eyes were enormous in her thin face. She was dressed in a rather rough cotton frock that ill fitted her and wore no footwear. She smiled when she saw me and asked in Tamizh, 'Will it always be so hot like this all the time?' My heart bumped; it was the first time she had spoken to me like that, before Goblin separated us.

I laughed. In winter, I promised, it will be as cold as it is hot now. Then I held her by the hand and took her to my room where there was a spare pair of rubber slippers. The slippers were two sizes too large for Inga, but she put them on obediently, the heavy blue straps made her feet look like porcelain, delicately fashioned, fragile. I took her by the hand again and we went around the house and the garden. There was nobody about, my mother was still behind a firmly shut door, the lackeys were in the kitchen and my aunt was presumably unpacking or something. The world held only Inga and me.

I took her from room to room and I saw everything as if for the first time, the heavy dark furniture, the huge sofa set in the drawing room where my father sat with his Party Big Ones, the office chamber, the dining room still smelling of the lunch not eaten. Then we went into the garden. Night had descended but was there ever such a night as that? The sky was a dark velvet, sprinkled with thousands of glittering star sequins. The night queen flooded the front lawn with her scent, and, as we turned the corner to the side lawn, the mogra and the jasmine clamoured for attention. I plucked a fat mogra flower and tucked it behind Inga's ear. 'You put also,' she said. I did. Tomorrow, I told her, we would string the flowers as Sister-in-law Too used to do in Komala Nivas, and wear them in our hair. Inga laughed. Then we raced each other across the watered grass on bare feet, my feet drew dark lines where I ran, Inga's hardly bent the grass heads. Then we heard a car drawing up at the gate. Inga stopped abruptly; by the light in the front porch, I saw that she had pulled a shutter down her face, she plucked the flower from behind her ear, thrust it into my palm and ran into the house. I picked up both pairs of slippers and followed her, calling her name. But she ran unerringly to her mother and shut the door. My father was in the house by then.

We were a silent company at dinner that night. Inga sat next to her mother and the two ate only curds and rice, not allowing the slightest sound to escape them, not even the faint scraping of the steel ladle against the sides of the rice vessel. My mother ate nothing at all, she sat with hunched shoulders, staring at her empty plate. My father and I alone had a hearty meal, I was ravenously hungry, my father rarely missed a meal. He slurped up his rice and rasam as if he had not seen such food for days, he belched over the curd rice and mango pickles and then, as he pushed back his chair to get up, he announced to nobody in particular, 'Tomorrow, Rapa's mother will go to Komala Nivas. I have found a good escort.' He then got up, belched again, and strode heavily to the washbasin.

Letter From Inga

Dear Rapa,
So many wrong things your mother is saying. Again and again she is doing this. My mother never knew about what your father was going to do. How will she have been able to know?
  Inga

Yes this is true that my mother knew that Sister-in-law One was going to have baby.
  Inga

Journal

After dinner, when I was in my room, packing my school bag, my father shouted to me from his office chamber that I should, 'find some nice clothes for that girl Inga. I have to take her to your school tomorrow.' I ran to my cupboard and pulled out the old suitcase from the bottom shelf. Here were clothes I had grown out of and which I kept hidden from my mother so that I could take them to Komala Nivas for Inga. I chose two or three sets of skirts and blouses, these were my school summer uniform, and a few frocks. As I ran to give them to Inga, my father called out again. 'They have to be ironed first,' he said. 'Give them to this fellow and go and do your homework.' One of the lackeys took the clothes from me and I was forced to go back to my room.

Of course, I did not do my homework, I had already done it, hadn't I? So I rebelled; I stayed up and finished reading *Jane Eyre*.

That night, a strange thing happened, I had a visitor.

⌒

UNTITLED
(I resisted using a title like 'RAPA EYRE' or 'JANE IYER'; I was sorely tempted though.)

A FRAGMENT

'. . . And this dream weighs heavily on your spirits now, Rapa, when I am close to you? Forget visionary woes. That was merely the creature of an over-stimulated brain; nerves like yours were not made for rough handling. What is there more? But I will not believe it to be anything important. I warn you of incredulity.' Her disquietude, the apprehensive impatience of her manner surprised me.

'Depend upon it, my nerves were not at fault. The thing was real, the transaction actually took place.'

'It may have been one of the servants.'

'It seemed a woman, tall and large with thick, dark hair hanging down her back. I know not what she wore, it was white, but whether sari, sheet or shroud I cannot tell.'

'Did you see the face?'

'Fearful and ghastly, I never saw anything like it. It was a discoloured face, a savage face. I wish I could forget those bloodshot eyes and that fearful, blackened visage.'

'Ghosts are usually pale, Rapa. What did this one do?'

'It stopped at my bedside and thrust up the torch it held, close to my face, and extinguished it under my eyes. I became insensible . . .'

Journal

It was long after I had gone to sleep, that the visitor came to my room. I was wakened by the creaking of the door which I always left unlatched, in keeping with my father's orders, and through sleep-heavy eyes, I saw the dim beam of a torch at the half-open door. The bearer of the torch entered the room and closed the door softly. In the wavering light, I saw the outline of a tall shape that seemed to be a woman's. I shut my eyes tight as the beam hit my face. Then I heard my mother's voice, ask, 'You are sleeping?'

I grunted. What was I supposed to say anyway?

The torch light was moved away, and then extinguished. I felt my mother sit at the foot of my bed. The room fell back into darkness and silence. After a few minutes, she spoke again.

'You will be all right?'

I grunted again. She fell silent. Again. Then she said, 'You will be careful no?'

'Of what?' I asked.

'Of everything. Your studies and also . . .'

'Also?'

'Also . . . also Inga.'

I sat up. 'Inga? What do you mean Inga?'

'That girl not straight come and straight go.'

'You mean she is not straightforward?'

'Yes. Yes. That is very good English word. Yes she is that.'

I thumped my head down on the pillow. 'I am going back to sleep,' I said. 'I have school tomorrow.'

She went on as if I had not spoken. 'Her mother also, very like lizard she is. Yes, yes, I know you are saying, but she is your own sister, born in the same mother's belly, how you can say this thing, that like snake, like lizard she is? But all fingers in one hand are not same no?'

I did not answer. She was silent too. Then she started sobbing, small sobs that might have been false. I took no notice; instead, I breathed long, deep breaths to show that I was fast asleep. After a while, she clicked on the light of the weak, wavering torch, and went out of the room, closing the door behind her.

The household woke up very early the next morning. Even before I was ready for school, Vembu Maama, who was to escort my mother, had arrived; obviously, he had been invited to have morning tiffin with my father. My mother moved like a shadow between the kitchen and the dining room, she would not meet my eyes. There was no sign of Inga and her mother of course, their door was shut tight. My father was in his loud, public mood, he introduced me as the 'genie-ass' of the family and spoke eloquently of how I had impressed Prof. Seshu. 'He fell down from the chair almost,' my father lied. 'When she just opened her mouth. "Ah, ah ha, what English," he said. "What perfect accent." He said, "Kitta, she is sure candidate for IAS, even ICS she could have done."' Vembu Maama said something I did not hear, to which my father replied with a huge guffaw, 'Tamizh? Malayalam? All poojyam only. Zero. Even her mother has to learn Shakespeare to talk to her.' Then he switched to English and said, confidentially, 'In today's world, Vembu, English will have the upper hand. Only those who are good in English, will come up. Even in office, I have noticed, work is better when it is done in English. And what good work these Christian nuns and paadris are doing? What discipline! How much effort! We can't touch it.'

I left for school soon after, my mother came to the porch to see me off, she did not say anything particular, and even before I moved off, my father yelled out to her from the dining room, 'Yediye! Have you put battery in your torch? Or that also you have forgotten?'

It was some years later that my mother spoke to me about that journey, of how she had been sent off so unceremoniously from Delhi.

'But you wanted to go,' I reminded her. 'You wanted so much to see Sister-in-law One after she started walking.'

'Why you are not calling her, her correct name? Just say, Saroja Manni. Or Periya Manni. This English is having no respect for elders.'

'Sister-in-law One is a perfectly respectful title,' I retorted. 'I don't even pronounce her name. But that is not the point. You did not want to go to Komala Nivas then, is that it? Why did you cry so much then?'

'I was not wanting to leave a big girl like you in that house with so many servants.'

'That is why my father brought Chitti to look after me.'

My mother did not speak for a moment. Then she said, 'You know what name that Vembu has? All people were saying, how your husband made you come with that Vembu? He has one one wife in one one town.' My mother filled her eyes with tears. 'We were in coupe, just think. Only two berths. You know what he told ticket checker? That we both are husband and wife.'

'So did he do anything to you?'

'So so afraid I was. After we ate food, he locked door and started removing shirt. I put my face next to window. My sari I pulled tight and sat. He said, you are not going to sleep? So I said I never get sleep in train.'

'So you stayed up all night? And the next night too?'

My mother wiped her eyes. 'You are having no pity for your mother,' she said.

I remembered something else. 'Why did you come with this same Vembu Maama in his car, when you returned to Delhi alone?' I asked. 'That was all right is it?'

'That was ten minutes only,' she said sharply. 'Is it same like two nights alone in that train?'

'What happened in the train anyway?'

'He sat on my berth and he said you are just like my sister only. I will not do anything. Now you sleep.'

'That means he was a good man, in spite of all that people say about him.'

'No, no, he is like that really. Everybody is knowing, your father also. You did not see him? He wears ring on all fingers. Who will say he is one Brahmin? Still your father made me to go with him. If I was having a brother, he will have given your father nicely.'

'You do have a brother,' I said.

My mother looked at me as if she could not believe her ears. Then she burst into tears and ran out of the room. I must confess, I felt a small spurt of vindication.

Letter from Inga

Dear Rapa,

Sometimes feeling hate for somebody is not the reason for war. Hate may be there but elders say that, many times, the quickest reason for going to war is because of insult. In Ramayana, *the sister of Ravana was insulted by Sri Rama and Lakshmana. They cut off her nose and breasts and then made fun. She went to her brother crying, and that was how the fight started between Rama and Ravana. In* Mahabharata *also, Draupadi laughed and laughed at the oldest Kaurava brother Duryodhana because he lifted his dress when he thought there was water in the tank. It was only a illusion. This laughter or making fun, we call as parihaasam – I have put two 'a's but it is looking funny – I don't know what you say for it in English.*

Inga

Journal

Parihaasam, derision. I still remember how my father had jeered at me once when I brought home my report card from school. I remember every word Mother Superior had written. 'An intelligent and diligent child with a reserved disposition. However, she shows a marked inclination towards intemperate behaviour on occasion and is too easily provoked.' My father had laughed. He continued to laugh and to loudly repeat the words of the judgement. He explained the lines to my mother, who joined him in mocking me. He never let me forget it, always leaving out the first part of the observation, through my school and college days and even later. It became a family heirloom, a conversational nugget, to amuse and to insult.

The day my mother left for Komala Nivas, I went to school feeling a little anxious. My father was to bring Inga to meet Mother Superior. What would Mother Superior say? How would Inga behave? Would she be frightened? Would Mother Superior call me when they came?

I was not called. Neither was I able to find out when Inga and my father came to the school, how long they stayed and when they left. All that morning, every time I could, I looked out of the window of my first floor classroom; I had been given the desk near the window because I was rarely distracted by what went on outside. But that day was different. I was so restless that even my English teacher had to call my attention back to the lesson. 'Are you looking for daffodils in the school garden?' she asked and the class rolled about laughing, much more and very much longer than necessary. It was only when I returned home in the afternoon, that I learnt of the morning's events. I was not told anything directly of course, but as I entered the house, I heard my father speaking in English over the phone, and I stopped to listen. '. . . Yes, yes, they all behaved very well but you see they had to give the girl a small test as per their rules. What? . . . Yes, yes, there and then, they went through the answers also. It seems she did very well in mathematics, but her English was no good. What to do? So I thought that since you know the principal of that other school, what is the name . . . Ah? What? . . . Yes. Yes. I will be thankful. . . She is about eleven or twelve years. Yes. Very good of you. What? No, no, not like that . . . I am just a small man, helping in my small way. The father? No idea. He disappeared just like that. Frankly, I don't ask about these things. As I said, just try to help and support . . .Yes. Very good of you. Very good of you.'

I flew to the curtainless room near the kitchen. My mother had obviously left, and the lackeys were chattering around. They stopped when they saw me and rushed around fussily to put my lunch on the table. I knocked at the shut door. It did not open, nor was there an answer. Had they gone? Had Inga been sent away because she had failed the English test? I remember how my stomach went stone cold, as I stood outside that silent door. Then one of the lackeys shouted to me from the kitchen. 'They both are sleeping,' he said in Malayalam. 'Such a long journey they had no?' Then, for some reason, all of them laughed.

I had my lunch alone, my father was still on the phone, and the dining room was like a witch's tureen. My room, with the curtains drawn and only the table lamp switched on, was infinitely cooler and I decided to finish my homework quickly, so I could go out of my room without being ordered back. The afternoon grew steadily hotter and still. About an hour or so later, it suddenly became dark. The wind began to howl around the house like a wild dog, doors and windows slammed shut, I heard my father shout, there were running footsteps, then the lights went off. This was the north Indian 'loo', the yellow dust storm, more fierce than any Mongol looters, invading the eyes and the nose, the dust penetrating through every chink, the smell of grit everywhere, the dreadful reminder that the desert is never too far away. *Ozymandias.*

I hated it, hated that madness of yellow dust swirling like a dervish gone berserk, hated the complaining, moaning wind. I sat with my eyes and ears closed in the afternoon dark, and tried to remember the prettiest English poetry I knew, bits of Shakespeare, Keats, Tennyson, all that was civilized, as ordered as a walled sunlit garden in Sussex. Then in a small and sudden interval of silence, I heard a little peal of laughter. Inga! Inga? I crept to my door, the wind picked up again, I opened the door with some effort and went out, pressing myself against the wall. And there in the inner verandah, looking up at the dervish wind, was Inga, holding her arms out to the dust and sand, laughing, laughing, as if she were at the seashore and the sea spray was running up to her, greeting her with delight.

I watched her, not knowing what to say or what to think. Then I heard the first raindrops fall, they were large, sand-dirty drops, but they quenched the wind and the air cooled. I saw Inga run out and pick up something from the ground.

She looked at it with wonderment as it melted in her palm. It was a hailstone, more of them pelted down and she danced about trying to catch them, till the hail stopped as suddenly as it had started.

When I remember that day, the day of the storm, after all that has passed since then, I wonder whether I ever knew Inga. Every time I thought I had come closer to her, that I was important to her, the joy I felt was quenched, suddenly, inexplicably, and I felt myself pushed away again, out through the door, beyond the paling, onto the bare, lonesome heath.

But these were not my thoughts as I watched Inga that day, delighting in her as she danced her delight. At that time, nothing mattered except that Inga was with me in the same house, I could see her, touch her, talk to her. We were together again and we did not need green mangoes or a secret place. However, it is true that when Inga arrived in Delhi, I had fervently hoped that she would join my school, I would then have eaten tiffin with her at recess, I would have taken her through the school and the grounds, talked to her about the teachers, showed her off. But when she joined the other school, I found myself strangely relieved. I realized that I did not want to introduce her to the north Indian snobs in my class. They were, each one of them, unfriendly, hostile, both because I was dark-skinned and because I was far superior to them as a student. I was constantly held up as an Example by Mother Superior and I could see how angry that made them. But there was something else too. Inga had a rather stubborn attitude towards English that puzzled me. I felt that she would excel in the language if she but tried. She wouldn't. Sometimes I even felt that she deliberately used wrong grammar or paltry words like 'nice' just to provoke me. When I asked her about it once, she laughed and crinkled her noise in that Inga way, and I felt my question squirm with embarrassment. It was only much later that another question struck me. Did Inga believe that using the English language, and allowing it to pattern her thinking, was a kind of betrayal?

But then, who betrayed what, Inga?

Letter from Inga

Dear Rapa,

I felt very sad that I did not pass that English test in your school, but I am not so good in English like you. I know that. I also became very afraid of your Mother Superior, so white she was, and even that room where I did my test had strange smells. It was better I went to another school. It was a nice school, fees was not much and everybody, the teachers also and the principal, were very nice. I was not afraid even once over there.

Inga

11

Inga was given admission to her 'nice' school without an admission test. She began to attend classes immediately, and, by the end of the week, was dressed in a not very smart uniform – a blue and white salwar kameez set that hung on her like a tent, and which made us both giggle very much as we got ready together every morning.

About a week or so after Inga started school, I had another surprise; my father appointed a music master for us. 'He is brother of cook in my maternal uncle's house,' my aunt said with pride in her voice. 'My uncle only gave money for his fees in music college. Now he is here doing music classes. Very good he is.'

'If he was in your uncle's house, my mother would have known him too, isn't it?' I asked.

My aunt nodded. Then, after a small pause, she said, 'But your mother does not have much interest in Carnatic music like me.' Clever, clever aunt!

The music master came to the house on his bicycle, wearing a spotless white mundu and a 'bush' shirt – a half-sleeved shirt. In winter, this changed to a full-sleeved shirt, over which he wore a sweater, but the mundu remained, a thin piece of bordered cloth that flapped open when he moved and which he swiftly, deftly pulled together. On very cold days, he wore socks as if it was a great concession to the weather gods. He had a strong voice and a harsh temper and insisted that we practise every lesson he taught us for at least an hour after he left. My aunt was as insistent that after the music practice, we attend to our school work equally assiduously; between the music master and my aunt, Inga and I were like worker bees in a hive. But on Saturday afternoons and on Sundays, we were allowed a game of caroms in my room, then in the evening, to play hopscotch or hide-and-seek in the garden and to play silly paper games, laughing very much, before we were sent off for a wash, dinner and bed. We rarely went out of the house. My father remained amiable and in Delhi; he seemed too happily occupied to find time to go to Komala Nivas. Every now and then he spoke to Brother One over the phone but never, I think, to my mother, whom he seemed to miss even less than I did.

It was a time perfect in its ripeness, a time of indescribable sweetness, more honeyed than the inside of a lotus flower, more fragrant than any heaven-hosted feast, a time of dancing, yellow daffodils, a pearly time, as perfect as a dewdrop. And as briefly lived. It lasted only six months and four days.

When I think of that time, I remember being constantly surprised by my aunt as much as I was by Inga. My aunt did not seem to be the same woman who sat in the back verandah at Komala Nivas, grinding enormous amounts of rice, like an undertrial breaking stones in a prison yard. In

Delhi, she was different, and in a way difficult to explain. She appeared like a trick of the moonlight, sometimes seen, sometimes hidden in the shadows, oftentimes half visible in the milky light of the night, and then again, not. It was like that joke about a black cat walking on a zebra crossing – now you see her, now you don't. Yet, I felt my aunt's presence everywhere, in the quiet way the furniture was rearranged, the carpet in the dining room removed so that it was less like an overstuffed oven. It must have been because of her that there was a newfound politeness in the attitude of the lackeys, and certainly, she made them cook better food. My father displayed a certain gentleness of manner which I had seen only in the Goblin days, and then, only towards the child. Now, he was universally affectionate, and, to my amazement, as we practised our music, I distinctly heard him hum along; he seemed to know all the ragas, he was not very tune true though.

Letter from Inga

Dear Rapa,

What you are saying about my mother is quite strange. Your mother has said some more things or what? My mother is very ordinary. Only thing is when she is happy, she is nice. When she is not happy, she is not at all nice, she acts very badly. But we are all like that no?

One more thing is my mother can say a lot without opening her mouth. She is very quiet that way but just by her look, she can speak quite loudly. My mother also has suffered very very much.

Inga

Journal

Whither shall we go coz, my pretty coz? Shall we seek happiness in the Garden of Arden? We shall fleet the time carelessly there as they did in the golden world, find tongues in trees and good in everything. Come into the garden, coz. Come. My beloved is unto me as a cluster of camphire in the vineyard of my garden, the beams of our house are of cedar, the rafters of fir.

We learnt music, Inga and I, classical south Indian music, Carnatic music. It was nothing like the hymns I had heard the nuns sing in the school chapel, great soaring notes that seemed to fingertip touch the rafters of heaven. Carnatic music was also quite unlike the English tunes I used to listen to secretly on the radio – when my father was not around – request programmes where listeners asked for their favourite songs to be played. Jim Reeves. Elvis Presley. Cliff Richards. And The Beatles. I understood those songs, they were in English, they used rhyme and they told stories. Of strangers falling in love in an instant, of subsequent betrayal and heartbreak, of the phone not ringing, the letter not written. This was the stuff that went on between boys and girls, frothy and inconsequential. Much later, when I grew to know what love could be, I dared not use the word at all. It was far too powerful; like the eyes of someone who could look into me and see what lay there.

And then when I did say the word out loud just that once . . .

The music we learnt from the master was very different. In Komala Nivas nobody was 'musical'. I had never heard my mother or Great Aunt Kuppai sing, not even to their gods. Brother Two would croon syrupy Malayalam film songs that were mostly about women draped in moonlight. But that was all. I was travelling into what was, for me, unfamiliar territory when I began learning Carnatic music. After a few lessons, I discovered something almost Brahminical in its rigidity. There were structures of authority everywhere, unyielding; everything had its place and function, there were no sudden alleyways that met a hidden, tree-darkened pool. It was a landscape as unlike the English countryside as steel to sand; its ordering was mathematical, absolute. No whirl of whimsy had any place here.

Did I like being there? I don't know. I could have rebelled against its authoritative temper, so like my father. But strangely I didn't. Why didn't I? When Inga was with me, I did not ask myself that question. When she wasn't, nothing else mattered.

The Carnatic music system seemed to me to be based on taalam, the beat, not so much on melody. Inga and I were taught to keep the beat by slapping the five fingers and palm of the right hand on our right knee as we sat cross-legged in front of the master who taught us a prodigious number of combinations of beats and half beats. We were also told, by my aunt and the music master, of a great many ragas – combinations of musical notes – and lyrics in languages I did not understand at all. Inga took to the music like a sapling enjoying the first rain, and because of her, I stuck to the lessons too, although the music master's attitude annoyed me often. Whenever he met my father, he would tell him that I ought to be removed from that 'stupid English school' and admitted into a music school. 'Your daughter,' he told my father in a mixture of Tamizh and Malayalam, 'she has very good grasp of taalam. Very good. She is using her mind to learn, not just doing copy. Ten, fifteen year after learning, she can even go to stage. Why she should learn this Shakkes Paiyer and all? Your niece has got sweet voice, light music like that she can do. But your daughter! Appappah! Like her I have not seen for many years. Hear me saar what I am saying.'

What names the ragas had! They were even better than the names in Dostoevsky's and Tolstoy's books. Hindolam, Karaharapriya, Surutti, Aarabhi, Shankarabharanam – they sounded like names from a register of royals, all purple and gold. My favourite was Hamsadhwani – the song of the swan – not a swansong at all. It was a raga that emerged like a whisper from the sea bed, pirouetted on the surface of the water, then swirled into the arms of the winds, tossed itself like a ball up high, very high, where the horizon met the heavens, then came down again like a sleepy child, back to its bed in the sea. My description of Hamsadhwani made Inga laugh, she said she also liked the raga very much but that was because her favourite song, which was about Ganesha, was composed in Hamsadhwani.

Delhi quickened into the Garden of Arden. As the weeks went by, Inga grew taller and began to fill out a little, the wan look was now gone. Although my aunt was very strict about our doing our school and music lessons well, she enforced the rule gently and with humour, unlike my mother. Whatever it was, I found myself at the top of the class in the humanities section all through Standard XI, my last year in school; I did not slip to second place as I had done, much to my mortification, in Standard X.

How strange! As I write this, I suddenly see the face of one of the busybody lecturers in college. She took the history subsidiary classes, and often, in the middle of the Battle of Plassey, she would break off, and tell us that when we prayed to the Almighty, what we should ask for always, was for work and the capacity to do it. 'Don't pray for money and a good husband and all that,' she would say. 'All that is nonsense. Ask for work.' Maybe she had a point there, maybe if I had insisted that I be allowed to finish my graduation, to work later, things may have been different. And yet I know not. I wanted to write, that is what I most wanted to do. A thatched cottage with a pretty garden sloping down to the river, a typewriter and Inga by my side – that is all I wished for. I could have been one of the Brontë sisters, or a Jane Austen, or a Dickens. Why was I born here, in this country? Here, where the colours are always violent, the languages taste tart like tamarind, acidic, unsubtle. This is a country made intemperate by the heat and glare of the sun.

No woman in India would like to be compared to a summer's day.

But Delhi, at least, had a winter. When the cold fingers of November first touched our cheeks, I was worried for Inga. How would she take it? Would she have to stay inside all day, shivering in front of a spluttering room heater? But she drew in her breath on the first cold morning as we were getting ready for school, and said her face felt as if it had been rubbed with green mangoes cut and dipped in salt.

Winter became her. Wrapped in warm, bright coloured woollens, Inga looked like a little English girl, her cheeks rosy, her light brown eyes shining in the pale winter sun.

Was it a particularly cold winter that year? I don't remember. What I do remember is that my father arranged for us to watch the Republic Day parade from the second floor windows of an office building on Curzon Road, it was a cultural centre of some sort. Why he did not take us to Rajpath, I don't know. Was it because he could not explain my aunt away, especially in the absence of his wife? For a man deft at manufacturing stories at a moment's notice, this should not have been difficult. Whatever the reason, we were not taken to Rajpath for an unbound view, sitting within touching distance of the parade. The weather conspired with my father I remember; the sky was leaden and threatened rain. So, protected from the elements, my aunt, Inga and I, along with some others belonging to the centre, watched the soldiers march by, the guns and armoured tanks, the caparisoned camels and elephants. Inga clapped loudly and long for the columns of school children who, she said, must have practised their marching for many years, they were so perfectly in line.

At one point, when Inga and I were alone at the window, I asked her the question that had vexed me for months, 'Do you still miss Goblin?' She stilled, then she turned towards me. She examined my face for a long moment, her eyes filled with tears, then she turned away. She said nothing.

After that, while she was with me, I never asked her about Goblin again.

It struck me only later, that in all that time, Inga and I never talked of the dramatic events in Komala Nivas. It was not just Goblin; we did not discuss Sister-in-law Too, or the 'miracle' of Sister-in-law One walking, or of Inga's own illness. Perhaps it was because anything I might have wanted to know was related to Goblin, directly or otherwise. Everything, somehow, returned to that wretched infant, she was always at the centre of all happenings, she seemed to have the inevitability of the law of gravity.

Letter from Inga

> Dear Rapa,
> Please do not ask me about that part so many times. I am telling you, I do not know what happened. My mother and I we were sent off to that tailor. How many times I must tell you this. Yes. Every day I feel sad about Kutti Laxmi. She loved me and I loved her.
> Inga

Journal

Four days after Republic Day, my mother arrived in Delhi unexpectedly and with Vembu Uncle. Much, much later, when I was hardly in the mood for it, she told me that Brother Two had brought her to Madras and put her into a ladies compartment of the Grand Trunk Express to Delhi. She had told him not to inform my father. When she reached Delhi station, however, she did not know how to get home. She knew little Hindi and did not know the streets at all. It was then that Vembu Uncle spotted her and brought her home. 'Very lucky!' he boomed at the gate. 'That coolie was just going to start one fight with her. Another train had come you see, he wanted to snatch money and go. And I just came to see off one friend. Really lucky. Where is your father, Blackie?'

My mother had chosen a bad day for her arrival. My father was already at Rajghat singing hymns, Inga and I were playing hopscotch in the driveway, my aunt was in the kitchen. It was all very proper. My mother took leave of her benefactor at the door, ordered one of the lackeys to bring her trunk and bags into the house, stalked into the room where she had always slept, and slammed the door shut. She did not have a word for any one of us.

My father returned about an hour later, quite self-satisfied and singing the Ram Dhun. He waved Nehru-like, to Inga and me sitting on the lawn nervously doing our homework. Then one of the lackeys murmured the news to him and he flew into a rage, the like of which I had not seen for six months. 'What nonsense is she doing?' he screamed at the lackey in Malayalam. 'Her head is off or what? She came with that man? She does not know what sort of name he has?'

My mother suddenly appeared at the door of her room, and began to explain that 'Vembu Anna' had only given her a lift from the station.

'Oh! So now he is your brother, your anna, is it?' My father roared. 'Yedeeye! You know what people will say? You climbed into his car, alone? You, wife of one MP? Whole world saw.'

'Yes,' my mother yelled back. 'Same whole world saw that you sent me off with same man. In one coupe compartment I was with this man. Up to Komala Nivas. Whole world laughed.'

My father suddenly switched to English. 'I asked him to

escort you,' he bellowed. 'You had your husband's protection then. You understand that? My protection! Not like this, getting into his car without my prior knowledge.'

My mother broke into sobs and went back into the darkness of the room; my father followed her in and slammed shut the door.

With that the gates to the Garden of Arden slammed shut too; gardens enclose but they also exclude. The world outside was lawless. Was it the same world that my father and mother always used as a moral thermometer? I have never understood this. Which is this world and how does it matter what it says? What great ones do, the less will prattle of anyway; are we to pay attention to prattle? When my mother returned so ill-advisedly to Delhi, it was my own world that closed to me, my own precious garden sphere, all blue and green, that spun away. In its place were thousands of quick-cutting slivers, lacerating my feet, my palms, and most of all, my ears, they bled.

The regime changed overnight, Inga and I did not dress together for school as we used to, I did not see her at all in the morning because she took to leaving by the side gate for her bus; she and I came together only for our music lessons. For a time, I thought these too would be banned but they continued. My mother had to exhibit her own vast store of musical knowledge and dexterity, which, according to her, she had pushed away because of her 'big household duties, looking after so many people with different different demands'.

But the classes were no longer the way they used to be. The music master stopped telling us stories about his early days in Delhi, which he would as he slowly sipped the coffee my aunt used to bring for him in the middle of the lesson. I realize that she brought the coffee then so we could rest a little too. But the music master seemed not to enjoy my mother's coffee as much, and anyway, she brought it after the lesson was over. It did not seem to be steaming hot either, the way he liked it. So instead of mellowing with tales of his own glory, unrecognized by Delhi's barbarism, he made us sing the scales over and over again, forwards and backwards and in all three beats, till our throats and fingers were sore. Inga and I were not allowed to practise on our own either; my mother said very loudly that I should remember I had very important examinations at the end of the year, not like other people. So she locked away the harmonium once the music master left so that there was no 'noise' to disturb me.

As winter gave way to a hard summer, everything began to wither and sour. Inga and her mother stayed away completely, they ate separately, I did not even see their clothes on the washing line. The house lost its honeyed quality, my father found his bad temper, the lackeys remained subdued, the cooking was devoid of charm. Then, on the last day of term before the summer holidays began, I came home to meet a terrible, echoing emptiness. Inga and her mother were gone.

It was one of the lackeys who whispered the news to me as I stepped out of the car. 'They gone,' he said in Malayalam; he did not have to tell me whom he meant. I flew into the house and to the room near the kitchen. The doors were wide open, the room was completely empty. The beds and the table had been removed, the pretty curtains my aunt had hung at the windows had been pulled down and lay in a cruel heap by the door. The floor had been washed down, it was still damp which meant it had just been done, the smell of antiseptic was strong. There was no sign of my mother, her door was shut. Even later, in the evening, my mother said nothing about their departure, my father even less. Was theirs a flight or a removal? How did they go? Where did they go? I tried to ask the lackeys but they only shook their heads and scuttled back into the kitchen, including the one who had given me the devastating news.

What kept me going? I don't know. Maybe, the mechanics of the everyday took over, as it often does in times like these, the routine of having to study all day, even during the holidays that year, of having to bathe several times just to stay sane, of having to chew and somehow swallow some food at heavily silent meal times. But there was also a black anger that grew in me, monstrous. It blinded me, it stoppered my ears, I refused to take any more music lessons; my mother was forced to trot out the same examination excuse to the music master, he disappeared into Delhi's unknowns and I never saw him again. The house fell into a long, unbroken silence, the sedge had withered from the lake and no birds sang.

Some two weeks later, Pandit Nehru died. My father broke into loud sobs when he was told the news, claiming that it was the Chinese who were the cause, they had betrayed his friendship, broken Panditji's heart much earlier, with their aggression in 1962. I remember wondering why I didn't die too, for much the same reason – betrayal. But I was already dead at the time; the news of Panditji's passing came to me like a distant gunshot. Nevertheless, I went with my mother, escorted by the lackeys, to see the funeral procession that came down the avenue a few yards from the house. The streets bulged with people, most of them wearing white, many weeping openly. The body was carried in an open vehicle, high above all the moving heads so I saw his face clearly, eyes closed, his nose sharply etched, Panditji, still handsome in this, his last sleep. Yet I could not cry. Wherefore could I not cry?

As our own procession made its way back home, I heard a wave of laughter. Two good-looking young men were trying to hoist a young girl on their shoulders, presumably to give her a better view of the cortege as it moved away. She was a rosy-cheeked girl, as fair as Inga, laughing. And for that moment, she laughed Inga's laugh.

12

School reopened, the exam drill went full throttle, and strangely enough, I continued to stay ahead of the rest of the class; it was as though I was some kind of machine, I clicked open in the morning, functioned as I was expected to, and clunked shut when I was alone. Outside my room, summer gave way to colder days, the wind grew chill, and I forlorn. Sometime around then, definitely before my final exams, two bits of news arrived at the house. Goblin had died, and Sister-in-law One had delivered a 'healthy' boy. My father left for Komala Nivas immediately.

Letter from Inga

Dear Rapa,

Mother and I heard about Kutti Paapa, sorry Laxmi many days afterwards. I will not tell you how we got that news. It was very, very sad news. She was lesser than three years. But I think she was one great atma who came to this world to finish some work from past birth.

That person also said that Brother One has got son.

Inga

Journal

As far as I remember, the two bits of news did not come together, but within the same week, certainly. My mother later swore that we heard of both on the same day, a few hours apart. 'One news came in letter, first post,' she claimed. 'Good news your brother phoned from his in-law's house. Even in those days,' she went on with complete irrelevance, 'they used to have phone in their house itself. Immediately he heard the child first crying, the poor boy phoned.' The letter about Goblin, a postcard actually, was from Dorai Athimbiar; I found it, faded but readable, some years later in a file, along with what seemed to be a wedding invitation in Malayalam, and some horoscopes. The postcard read, 'Regret to inform the death of my granddaughter Laxmi, at my house on 20th inst., after prolonged illness.'

Even at the time, I realized dimly that there was great significance in the yoking of the two events – Goblin's death and the birth of Brother One's son. 'My Laxmi has come back!' my father exulted on the phone to Brother One, predictably in English. 'I knew she will not leave me just like that. Now you see how your son will bring wealth and fame to our house. You just wait and see.' Then in Tamizh, he asked, 'You have given correct time to astrologer no?' For horoscope?'

I could neither verify nor disprove for myself this alleged transmigration of souls till much later. I had to wait till my exams were done with; my mother and I left the next day, I did not need to return to Delhi till the summer, when college admissions would begin. I could now, at last, look for Inga, find her wherever she was.

Did I really think Inga would be in Komala Nivas? Or somewhere in the neighbourhood? As soon as we arrived, even before the mandatory wash, I ran wildly to all our favourite places inside and outside the house, calling out to her, whispering her name. I dashed up to the attic, ran to the storeroom, now empty of green mangoes, to the back room and the back verandah, sped to our secret place near the cowshed. What a fool I was! It was the stupidest thing I could have done; I had exposed my eagerness, allowed my mind to be known and therefore made myself vulnerable to the severest of criticism. The lackeys sniggered openly at me, Rukku Paati glared, Paru gave me a pitying, scandalized look. But that was nothing compared to what my mother did. She was lying in wait for me, watching as I made my despairing way past the cowshed. That is where she caught me, twisted my arm viciously, and slapped me across the face. 'What you are doing, you prostitute?' she snarled as low as she could. 'Madness has caught you or what? Go. Bathe.' What is it I had done? I had not evoked Lucifer, or Paru's chathan, I had merely looked for my cousin, my friend, my . . . But behind my mother's fierce anger, I could see another flame of rage and suddenly, unbidden, I remembered what Inga had said once, a long time ago. She had been telling me about Rama's stepmother Kaikeyi, who was instrumental in sending him into exile, just as he was getting ready for his coronation. 'Because of that,' Inga said, 'because she was so bad, so jealous, nobody will call their daughter Kaikeyi. That name is like poison.' It seemed to me then that in Komala Nivas, there was a new Kaikeyi.

. . . But if there is any name that is not to be perpetuated, it would surely be mine, isn't it?

I could not find Inga, nor get any news of her or her mother from anyone, not from Paru, not from Mikhale; as for the lackeys, the party workers, I was not allowed to speak to them nor did I wish to. Who else could I ask? Brother and Sister-in-law One were still away at her parents' house, Brother Two had stayed on in Madras, and there was no joy to be had from Great Aunt Kuppai. Her face had that familiar, closed look, like a door that had warped and stayed stuck.

I tried other devices to find them. Since I was not allowed anywhere on my own, I flattered my mother into taking me with her when she went out one day. She visited the general store on the main road to replenish Komala Nivas' stock of umbrellas and torch batteries, to the cloth shop to get blouse pieces for Great Aunt Kuppai and then, finally, to the tailor's. I looked for Inga everywhere, standing on the narrow road while my mother haggled with the shopkeeper over half a rupee. I searched for that face, those little hands, everywhere. There were several chattering groups of women and children walking down the road, some disappearing into shops, there were men with devout expressions coming away from the temple, eyeing the women as if gauging their flavour; their glances did not rest on me. Neither did mine on their ash-streaked, unholy foreheads; what I was looking for was not among them. But my greatest expectations were from the tailor's establishment. I was certain I would find Inga there or get news of her; surely this was where Inga and her mother had been sent the day Goblin disappeared.

What an idiot I was! What a blundering fool! Would my mother have allowed me to go with her if Inga could have been seen? The tailor we went to was the wrong one; it was a woman tailor, quite close to Komala Nivas, who had apparently lost her husband and returned to her mother's house only two months ago. She may have been a poor relative; my mother was very much the lady-of-the-manor with her. I was in complete despair.

It then struck me that I ought to make a round of the temples around Komala Nivas. I decided to turn religious and asked to be taken to every temple within walking distance. I told all the shocked faces in the house that I wanted to make sure my exam results would be brilliant, and so I was seeking divine help. 'This before exam you are supposed to do,' my mother said sharply.

'Then, I prayed in my heart,' I lied. 'Not just that, I did not even know whether there are any temples in Delhi.'

My mother was silenced, she could not quarrel with me. Great Aunt Kuppai stayed ominously quiet, her eyes watchful. I had made a splendid move because my request for a temple visit could not be refused, however suspect. Not taking me to temples! God's wrath would descend on them! So, with much low muttering, my mother took me first to the Devi temple near the house; this was a small cove-like shrine, I sensed that it was a regular meeting place for my mother and her cronies, and I knew Inga would not be there. The following day, she took me to the huge Shiva temple near the bazaar, and then to the massive Bharata temple, which Inga had told me was the most important one in the area. 'One time when the king went there,' Inga had said, 'the diamond from his crown flew off and went inside the diamond on the God's forehead.' But neither my mother nor I could see this diamond-fond deity because Brahmin women in the 'reproductive age group' were not allowed to enter the inner shrine. 'He is in tapasya and we should not disturb him,' my mother told me curtly as we went round the temple courtyard in a curtailed version of worship. I detected a certain pride in her tone; she drew her sari tightly around her breasts, she walked delicately, her eyes cast demurely on the stone paving. The temple's rule gave her status, it told the world that she was still young, desirable and could easily tempt a god out of his celibate meditation. But above all, it proclaimed that she was Brahmin. She spoke again after a pause, just as a group of priests walked past us. 'Poor boy!' she sighed. 'It is only temple in India for Bharata, he was Rama's brother you know? What sort of sad life he had. His mother was that Kaikeyi, that raakshasi.'

No part of any temple anywhere, held Inga.

A month or so later, my father arrived at Komala Nivas; he had returned to Delhi only the evening before we left, for the all-important month of January. Now de-Gandhied and de-martyred, he wanted to go immediately to see his grandson again, the new fortune-giver, the new family deity. Or should I say the old one in a new bottle? Of course, I was wild to go, Inga could be somewhere there. If not, I was sure to get news of her from Brother One or Sister-in-law One. As it happened, neither of them had any time for me, they were so taken with their loud, greedy son. Never have I seen a baby who so clearly showed the markings of the tyrant he would grow to be. He had taken and embellished the qualities of both his grandfather and his father, the arrogance, selfishness and an opaque uncaring of all concerns other than his own – the father, the son and the holy terror.

No, he was not like Goblin. He kicked when my father tried to kiss him in reverence, he spat milk on my mother and he screamed all the time while we were there. My father indulgently said, 'We must remember he is not one year old only.' My mother was less certain I could see, but would not admit it of course. In her book of reference, everyone other than Inga's mother, Inga and Rapa, were basically good, sometimes misunderstood, always to be forgiven. She spoke against her husband only to me; to the rest of the world, she was the model wife and daughter-in-law of the house, a shining example of chastity and that celebrated adakkam which I did not possess, the virtue of female submission.

Even in my misery, I noticed that nobody mentioned the 'miracle' of Sister-in-law One suddenly being able to walk. This was the first time I was seeing her after it happened and I felt a curious tremor of shock when I saw her standing upright and walking about, albeit a little ungracefully. Had she so completely forgotten her earlier existence? Had the extraordinary become the everyday so quickly? But then, what had I expected? That she would be constantly singing halleluiah or its Brahmin equivalent? That she would be thanking Goblin every half an hour? She did not mention her even once; her ability to walk had become as commonplace as the betel leaves she offered my parents after they had eaten.

Much later, I thought of Sister-in-law One when I came across the parables of Oscar Wilde. There was one where Wilde narrates how Jesus returned to Nazareth and met three men he had miraculously cured. None of them were grateful, none at peace with themselves. The leper he cured was now a drunk, the blind man ran after a prostitute and the man whom Jesus had raised from the dead, wept ceaselessly. When he asked them why they were like this, each of them said, 'What should I do otherwise?'

Letters from Inga

Dear Rapa,

Why should you be angry with Sister-in-law One? She is thinking of so many other things no? I am very sure that inside, she is saying thank you to God every time. We should also be saying thank you no? God is giving us life, prana. That is itself a miracle.

Inga

Dear Rapa,

After so much time, you are thinking of Sister-in-law One because of this story? This story you have told about Jesus Christ is so sad. But we people are like this only, our minds are small. How we can see what God really is? Sometimes when I think about this, I feel that my mind is like a balloon and it will burst.

So it is good I think, to have small minds that are only thinking about small, daily things.

Inga

Journal

On our way to and back from Sister-in-law One's house, I tried to get a sliver of information about where Inga might be. But my father's talk was all about his decision to go to FishEyes' house, too late to see the body but not late enough to miss FishEyes' lamentations. 'So angry she was, that woman,' he said, 'because people did not come like in Komala Nivas. First few days, yes it seems, some people were there, but the sick did not become better and the lame did not walk. You remember what all great things happened in Komala Nivas and how much people said how many good things happened even months after they saw her?' He wiped his eyes and murmured in English, 'Remarkable! Very remarkable!'

After a few minutes, my mother asked how Goblin had died. 'I don't know,' my father answered. 'According to that woman, she got high fever for two days, then her eyes went up, she vomited. Somebody called a doctor at that time but what was the use?'

'What was that Athimbiar doing?' my mother asked angrily.

'Sitting with two fingers inside his nose, and the other hand between his legs,' my father snarled. 'What else he does? That woman did not take care of our child, she just threw her in one servant's lap. Anyway, Bhagavati has sent Bhagavaan Maha Vishnu himself to our house, just see!'

The journey to see the holy terror had taken the whole day and part of the night. When we finally arrived at Komala Nivas, it was past midnight. Paru opened the gate, holding aloft a spluttering hurricane lantern. As I crossed her, she squeezed something into my hand with a warning look. I glanced down quickly and realized it was an inland letter addressed to me in Inga's hand. A letter from Inga! From Inga! Little tendrils of life sprang up in me. I hid the letter in the folds of my skirt, ran to the bathroom and turned on the tap. There, with the water splashing all across my feet and legs, I read the letter over and over again, till I knew it by heart. I now had a post bag number.

Dear Rapa,
I am writing this letter to Komala Nivas because you are there
now. Do not ask how I am knowing this . . .

I bumped into my mother as I came out of the bathroom, she was at the door. She looked at me suspiciously; the letter was safe, deep inside my blouse. 'What?' she asked, 'Already started?' She did not realize how I relished her question, she had flung me a rescue line. 'I thought it started,' I said in her lingo. 'So I ran inside to look. But there was nothing. Anyway, time is not yet come.'

'Yes. Three days more there is,' she agreed. 'But sometimes this type long journeying can make it come early.'

In the morning, I went back to writing. It was difficult at first; I had been numb for so long. Then I remembered the stories Inga used to tell me and the stories I was told in school during the moral science periods, some of which I recollected, but a little imperfectly. That did not matter, it was a piece of fiction, my creation or re-creation, and I could turn it to my purpose. As I could the tales Inga told me, in her way.

So I wrote. To Inga. To myself.

TWO STORIES
(written at sixteen)

Rapa once told this story to Inga:

Long ago, in another land, there was a rich man who had three loyal servants. One day, the man decided to go on a long tour. Before he left, he called his three servants and told them that he would return only after a year and they should look after his affairs well. He gave the first servant five talents or gold coins and asked him to use the money well. He gave the second servant two talents and asked him also to use them well. To the third servant, he gave one talent and said the same thing. Then he left.

The first servant looked for some rich land along the river, and when he found it, he bought it with the five talents his master had given him. The land was so fertile that within a year, he had three harvests and was able to multiply the five talents to fifteen.

The second servant bought a big house with the two talents that he had been given. He rented out the house to some rich people and, by the end of the year, he too had multiplied the money he had been given, from two to four talents. The third servant was not sure what he should do with the one talent the master had given him. Finally, he buried it under a bush, and slept most of the time.

When the master returned after a year, the three servants stood before him. The first servant proudly showed him all the money he had made during the year; the second servant did the same. The master was very happy with both of them and rewarded them. But when it was the turn of the third servant, the master flew into a rage. The third servant merely handed over a mud-stained coin to his master and said, 'I looked after this for you.' Needless to say, he was thrown out of the house, to a place where was much weeping and gnashing of teeth.

The moral of the story is 'When you are given a talent, use it.'

In answer, Inga narrated this story:

One day, Paramasivan and Parvathy were looking at this earth. They saw a beggar. He was going to eat some food that he had begged from somebody. But before he started, he closed his eyes and folded his two hands and said thank you to Paramasivan for that food. Then only, he started to eat.

Parvathy saw this and felt very angry with Paramasivan. She said, see this poor, hungry man, this beggar, is thinking of you so many times, even before he eats his food, why you are not helping him? Why he is still one hungry man who begs every day? So Paramasivan gave a smile and said, all right, you only help, let me see.

So Parvathy took one gold coin and threw it down, near to where the beggar will walk after he finished eating his food. She said, now he will see the coin and take it and he will become one rich man. But after he finished his food, what did the beggar do? He said, now I am a beggar only, but I have eyes, I can see. Supposing I am blind, then how I will be? So he got up, closing his both eyes and walked on that road where the coin was. But he did not see it, why? Because his both eyes were shut. Some minutes after that beggar went off, another man who came on that road, saw the gold coin and he took it.

When Inga stopped, Rapa asked, 'So what is the moral of the story?'

Inga said, 'I don't know.'

Then she asked, 'Should there be?'

Journal

I wrote a reply to Inga and gave the letter to Paru secretly. She tucked it in the waist fold of her mundu and whispered her promise to post it as soon as she could. She and I made excellent conspirators, we were never seen together and nobody knew that I had learnt enough Malayalam to converse with her. It was much later that my mother suspected that Inga and I had been corresponding regularly, perhaps she got a whiff of it from Paru. By then it did not matter anyway.

There was something about the clandestine letter exchange that excited me, the furtive locating of Paru, the seemingly casual inspection of the backyard and the cowshed, the sauntering up towards Paru, her apparent indifference, and then the quick sleight of hand, either receiving a letter or handing one over. In the thrill of it all and the joy of talking to Inga, I did not stop to think of how Paru knew which letter from the bundle that came to Komala Nivas was meant for me; she could read only the Malayalam alphabet. This was what Brother Two had once told me, when he, apparently, was giving her lessons in poetry appreciation. So who picked out the right letter for Paru to give me? Was there a third conspirator?

Then there was the other question of who was giving Inga news of us. There was somebody who knew of the goings-on in Komala Nivas, who was alert to the implications of certain visits and conversations and who reported it all to Inga, and therefore to her mother too. If I had bent my brains to it at the time, I would have also realized that there was more than one informer. But I was too happy, much too full, too rich, to think of anything other than that I had regular news of Inga. And that I would be able to continue writing to her even after returning to Delhi.

I seemed to be the only one in Komala Nivas who was happy. Everyone else moved in an orbit of gloom, it was as if their Ali Baba's cave had been looted. My mother complained bitterly about Brother and Sister-in-law One staying on at his in-laws' house. Rukku Paati mourned over Brother Two having gone to Madras and then ordered by my father to finish his law course. Paru too was affected. My father expressed his prayers and his grievances loudly and with equal ferocity, while Great Aunt Kuppai kept her grim, silent, vigil over the house, sitting on her swing in the inner hall, fanning herself.

13

Three or four weeks after that momentous day when I finally got a letter from Inga, Komala Nivas received visitors. FishEyes and Dorai Athimbiar arrived in their shiny black car. They were not alone, there were two strangers with them, two men. How they all fitted into a single car, was a puzzle for Houdini – three men, the driver and the buxom FishEyes, her various pillows, water jugs, tins of fried snacks, towels and all other paraphernalia that must travel next to her. In fact, the younger of the two men was quite tall and when he came out of the car, it seemed to me that he had to unfold himself like an accordion.

FishEyes was in sack cloth and ashes, metaphorically so. There were fewer necklaces noosed around her podgy neck and only half a dozen bangles down her arms. She began a high-pitched wailing at the front gate itself, and as soon as she tottered into the house, still wailing, she stumbled towards Great Aunt Kuppai sitting on the swing, and flung herself down at the grand lady's unwelcoming feet. 'Forgive me, forgive me,' FishEyes cried. 'Whatever punishment you want, give! Give!' This dramatic declaration was blunted by the swing suddenly, smartly moving forward and hitting her bent head.

My mother rushed up to help but FishEyes waved her away. 'It is nothing, nothing,' she sobbed, not even rubbing the sore spot. 'I deserve more. More. A sinner like me. A maha paavi like me.' With that, she banged her forehead down on the floor a few times, then moved to the mat my mother had spread out and poured herself upon it. Dorai Athimbiar who had most likely waited for the scene to be over, then came in with the two other men, and presented their credentials to Great Aunt Kuppai. As usual, there were no names spoken, only relationships were drawn; the older man was a cousin 'twice removed' to Dorai Athimbiar and the younger man, the accordion, was the cousin's son.

Great Aunt Kuppai smiled, suddenly, entirely unexpectedly. 'For your poonool, your thread ceremony, I have come,' she said when the younger man touched his head to her feet. 'Your father has named you Padmanabhan. Maha Vishnu's name. See I remember! So tall you have become. What you are doing now?'

The young man was not allowed to answer. FishEyes announced, 'He has given IAS exams. Big Collector he will be,' she added triumphantly. 'Speak no Paddu. You tell.'

My father, who had entered with the men and stood with his back to FishEyes, burst out with, 'Very good, very very good! You are one big blessing to your family.' He then switched abruptly to Tamizh. 'You women speak your gossip, we will go that side. Bring some hot coffee and some eatables.' He led the men out to the front hall, shouting for chairs to be brought from the office rooms. A few minutes later, he called out to my mother in the mildest tone I had ever heard him use. 'When the coffee is ready,' he said surprisingly, 'tell Rapa to bring it.'

FishEyes swept a swift upward glance at me when she heard my father's command, but said nothing. My mother pursed her lips and sniffed her disapproval as she handed me the plate with the glasses of coffee and the fried snacks. My father seemed to have transgressed some code of privilege. I served the coffee and snacks to Dorai Athimbiar and to the two guests, while my father boomed my praise. 'English only she knows,' he said. 'Shelley, Keats, etc.' Then he began to declaim, flinging his arms about. 'To be or not to be that is the question, whether it is nobler in the mind to suffer, or whether, there is the rub . . .' The younger man, the accordion, spluttered over his coffee. I sliced through my father's literary bumbling.

'That is from Shakespeare, mixed up,' I said. '*Hamlet.* It's not either Shelley or Keats.'

My father burst into a loud, insincere, guffaw.

'See! See!' he bellowed. 'How her old father she corrects!' He continued his false good humour even after I left the hall. I wondered why. Two years later, I understood.

It was quiet in the inner room. FishEyes was feeding my mother's ears with something that sounded distinctly undelicious. Great Aunt Kuppai did not seem to have opened her grim mouth at all. I thought I would escape through the kitchen door but FishEyes stopped me halfway.

'Child, come here,' she said imperiously, and gestured that I should sit next to her. She smelt strongly of the talcum powder that was Sister-in-law Too's favourite, and of stale sweat. 'So what you are doing now?' she asked and without waiting for an answer, she went on, 'My second daughter is in Ernakulam, doing BA fust year. In hostel she is, what to do? Our village has no college no? She is not so lucky like you, with MP father and Delhi school.' Then without a pause or a change in tone, she turned to my mother and said, 'You must try goat milk for her. Goat milk mixed nicely with green gram powder and put on whole body. In one week she will become white. I use that only, my daughter also. See me.' She thrust out her round bejewelled arm and laid it next to mine, the colour contrast could not have been greater.

'Why she came?' Great Aunt Kuppai asked my father as I served them and my mother their evening meal. The visitors had left as dusk fell, 'Because,' FishEyes had whispered loudly, 'driver he is having eye trouble in night.'

'Why she came?' asked Great Aunt Kuppai again.

My father grunted. 'For his second daughter Dorai is looking for groom. IAS groom it seems,' he said.

'So now whole world must know she has big big relations from mother's side? So she came? Or to show off her son-in-law to come? All that drama that is why?'

My mother answered. 'First time she is coming no, to our house,' she said, 'after that poor child went.'

Great Aunt Kuppai snorted in disdain.

My father did a final, comprehensive lick of his hand and began to get up. 'This Kittan if she thinks she can fool,' he growled, 'she knows nothing. I did not get born yesterday. Big mistake she made, bringing that boy here.' He exchanged a swift look with Great Aunt Kuppai and left the room to wash his hands. I sat down to eat and the rest of the meal passed in silence.

A few days later, I was surprised to find a harmonium being brought into the house. 'This is for you, it seems,' my mother said, 'for practice. Your father is also finding a teacher.' She sniffed to show her complete disapproval. The teacher turned out to be a scared-looking woman. 'What all I know I will teach,' she said to my mother in a self-deprecating way. 'After that, you yourself see.'

Astonishingly, when she began to sing, she became a different person. Her voice was strong and clear, it had resonance and it had softnesses too. That was not all. What she was able to do was to maintain the mathematics of the system and to go beyond to a melodiousness I had not thought possible. She sang Hamsadhwani. The music began to speak like Inga, here was the soft murmuring when she talked to herself, here the green mango giggle, the gasp at the first rainshower, and then the transforming laughter that washed into my hollow and upturned me as if I were a piece of driftwood in a vast sea.

So as the music grew inside me and Inga's letters reached me regularly, my mind blossomed with words. I had not kept a diary since I lost the notebook in which I had vented my anger against Goblin, but now I began to make jottings, which would be incomprehensible to anyone else, of events and feelings that were important to me. I recorded what I remembered of things past and went back to a practice I had given up, of closely studying the style of other writers to decide who was to be my model. How stupid I was! How little had I read till then.

Those jottings are my memory bank now, my store of reference. One remembers, one forgets, one remembers again, but while the snob boasts of being absentminded, I know now that not remembering is foolish in the extreme. And forgetting is never innocent.

It was a time of great contentment. Komala Nivas, its crevices and corners, its sun motes and shadows, filled with music; there was now a translucent quality about the house, as there used to be before Goblin. I have read somewhere that one should not ever become attached to a house, to brick and mortar. But Komala Nivas was not just a structure of stone or of reinforced concrete, that favourite of Kerala builders.

Komala Nivas was my growing up, it was my epic, it meant Inga.

I realize now that it was Komala Nivas that bound us together, Great Aunt Kuppai and me. In that brief time before my exam results arrived, I often found her looking at me with a kind of iron regard, curiously enough as if she were fearful for me and wished me to seek protection. She said nothing though. Should she have? Watched over me more closely perhaps? But she used silence just as stupidly as I did, thinking it was the most efficient way to hide the truth, the unmentionable, the terrifying.

We both used silence; like a shroud that attempts to cover what is so unmistakably the naked face of death.

The exam results came by post with a personal letter of congratulations to me from Mother Superior. Her letter said everything right and ended with, 'We are proud of you my child'. I had stood first in school, scoring 1 in all the five subjects that were considered for the final tally, the best grades possible. I was one among three across India with those grades. My father exploded with pride. Although he said nothing to give me happiness, he phoned his party office in Delhi, asked them to spread the word, called Prof. Seshu and then everyone else who had a phone and shouted his exultation. However, as always when he spoke of me, he let his imagination go wild. I could see that the marking system puzzled him; I had tried to explain it but he did not pay much attention. He told Prof. Seshu that I had come first in all of India and my marks totalled twenty or twenty-five. When Prof. Seshu obviously did not accept this, my father changed that to two or three.

The results did not signify much to anybody else. Paru said it was not a surprise, Mikhale nodded his head excitedly and gave me a broad smile, the party workers looked at me sideways and murmured that it was solely to my father's credit that I had done well. Great Aunt Kuppai grunted. My mother sniffed.

All of a sudden, it was time to return to Delhi for my college admission. A few days before we left, Prof. Seshu came to Komala Nivas with a set of books for me, 'for doing us proud,' he said. 'I have asked your father,' he went on, 'to seek admission for you to the Honours course in English. There is an excellent women's college where the sister of a friend of mine is Principal and also Head of the Department of English. A brilliant girl and, most important, from our part of the country. She will look after you. Enough of that. Let me hear you sing now, your father has been telling me about your music classes.'

I brought out the harmonium and sang a small geetam, one I remembered well. 'Good! Shabaash,' he murmured as he hummed the lyric as I sang. When I finished, he said, 'That is one of my favourite raagams, Mohanam. Thank you my dear.'

We were alone in the front hall at the time. As I got up and bent to take away the harmonium, he stopped me. 'You are a lucky girl, but do you know how lucky you are?' I shook my head. He was about to say something more when we both heard my father's heavy footstep approaching the room. The professor turned and spoke to him as he entered. 'Kittu, I was just telling your very talented daughter, that she is very lucky. Do you know why? She has two great civilizations to drink from. The Western and our own. Drink deep, my dear, drink deep.'

My father said something coarse about drinking deep, and they left the room laughing. I put away the harmonium and went back to my journal, still wondering what it was that the professor had wanted to say to me.

The decision about what I was to do next, what course of study, was taken even before I boarded the train to Delhi. I was not asked for my opinion; I was not supposed to have any. During the long journey, I read the books the professor had given me, authors I had not heard of till then – Wilkie Collins, Thomas Hardy and, surprisingly, P.G. Wodehouse. When I read *The Moonstone* by Wilkie Collins for the first time, I understood how the same events could be told by more than one narrator, from his or her particular perspective, and in their own style. I wondered what it would be like if the Cinderella story was told by her wicked stepmother if she was interviewed by a newspaper reporter. The stepmother calls Cinderella 'kari', coal in Tamizh.

KARI

Yes, yes, you think she is so sweet and all that. Just see her no. Such a black face and black hands. What is so very sweet about her, uh? What you said? She is black because she is in that kitchen full day? But she can bathe no? There is lots of water in our well. Best well we have in this town. Such very cold water it is. Myself and my two daughters have to bathe in hot water. Otherwise we get pain in our body. Kari is there no? She fills that big boiler and brings hot water to our bathroom itself. She brings six or seven buckets because we need much water. We are clean people, not like her. How she is called Brahmin girl itself I do not know. So dirty she is. Actually, about her mother, I have doubt. I used to ask my husband so many times, but he never told anything. Even on that last day, he wanted only her face to see, this girl's black face. Once also, he did not call my sweet girls, like pearls they are. But he did not call their names at all. That is type of man he was. What to do? Woman in my place has to go through many, many problems. I am here for my two girls only. I just want to get good husbands for them who will be from old, rich families, then I can close my eyes.

What? Yes, Kari. So anyway, I am looking after her no? All these days, I was giving her food and place to sleep. Even after her father died, I still kept her. If you go to see, why I should keep her? She is not my relation. What? This house? Yes. Yes. You are right. Her father wrote it in her name only. So much I did for him and still.

So anyway, that day when they came with that one slipper, I was sure one of my two gems' foot will fit. They went for that puja also, to the palace. Yes. Yes. They were there. My second one's swan foot almost fitted also. Then Prince said,

'No, no. It is not this one. There is no more girl in this
house? I was going to say no, but that palace servant said yes,
there is one kitchen girl. Before he closed his mouth, Kari
came out with all dirt on her face, her clothes. Then Prince
jumped and stood up and he said, it is her, it is her, this is
same girl. Then the slipper fitted her and Kari took out
another slipper just like that one, and Prince took her off
and now they have fixed marriage date also.

You are from newspaper, there is some cheating business
going on. You only tell me how that girl went to palace?
Who gave her new clothes? How she went there? You are
believing all lies like this. Some enemy only has given Kari
all this kind of help. There should be government enquiry.

⇌

THE STORY OF KARIGUMANI

Oh it is all very very exciting. I am thrilled, thrilled to bits.
Do you know he has promised me a huge huge diamond
set? Even a diamond belt? Imagine that! A diamond belt!
What? How did it all happen? It was so funny, you know. I
was just sitting in the kitchen and thinking if I should have
mango pickle or lemon pickle with the curd rice and then
this next door aunty came. She only made me wear all those
nice nice things which were all her daughter-in-law's. Anyway,
then she made me go to the palace in a cart. It was so funny
because she herself was driving the cart with a big turban on
her head.

Yes. Yes. He saw me immediately because you know, this
aunty pinched me suddenly just when I entered the big hall.
She pinched me so hard that I screamed very loudly. So of
course, everybody turned to look at me. He also. I was so

afraid when I saw him coming near me and asking for my name. I ran and ran and my slipper fell off.

The aunty brought me back and made me to change into my old clothes. I was angry about that because the new dress was so nice. Anyway, she said I can keep that one slipper but she told that I should show it only to the prince. After that, he came to my house and I showed him the other slipper and it was all just like in a story. So funny!

⁓

LOVE IS BLIND

The rags-to-riches true life story that has grabbed all the headlines in the kingdom since it broke yesterday, is truly a spectacular one. The story of how the heir to the throne found his beautiful bride reads like a fairy tale. His beloved, whose name we understand is Karigumani, is an orphan and had been relegated to the position of a kitchen girl in her father's house, allegedly by her stepmother and two stepsisters. It was a kindly neighbour who appeared as a fairy godmother and reportedly helped the young girl to attend the coronation ceremony at the palace where she caught the royal eye. However, as the prince tried to approach her, the young girl seemed to have got alarmed and left hurriedly. There seems to be no truth to the rumour that the auspicious time for the coronation had been missed because the prince abandoned his royal duties to pursue the young lady. Palace sources told this reporter that the coronation had already taken place secretly the night before – an ancient tradition observed by generations of this royal dynasty in order to confound their enemies.

To return to last evening's events, it is alleged that in her hurry to return to her house, the young maid left behind a single jewelled slipper, reportedly belonging to her right foot, which was found by His Royal Highness as he followed her. However, he was unable to see which direction she had taken. Consequently, the next day, the prince and his attendants embarked on a house-to-house search to find the girl. It was in the last house in town that she was discovered. The future queen of the kingdom was found dressed in rags and sweeping the kitchen floor!

In an interview to this newspaper, the stepmother of the bride-to-be confessed that she had no idea that her stepdaughter could be so enterprising and conveyed her best wishes to the young maid in her new career as consort to the future king.

The young bride, who was interviewed in a private chamber of the palace, where she was selecting footwear, expressed her great happiness at the turn of events and hoped her stepsisters would find good husbands soon.

Journal

When I think of it now, I realize that my father was pleased that he did not have to puff and pant and take me hither and thither for admission to an Honours course in literature. Any college would have been happy to have me as its student; I was, after all, a trophy of sorts. I applied for admission only to the college Prof. Seshu had recommended and did not have to go through an interview. I did meet the

Principal in her office, a stout, sharp-tongued woman, who, in another time and place, might have been caricatured by Wodehouse. But her imperiousness could not undo the five points. 'How she can refuse?' my father told my mother later. 'Who I am? She knew that fully. And of course, the girl's marks.'

In July of that year, I was an English Honours student in a south Delhi college and about to discover Bacon's essays. I was seventeen.

Letter from Inga

Dear Rapa,

Yes I remember Cinderella. What you sent was quite funny. Was that stepmother supposed to be somewhat like Great Aunt Kuppai?

Actually what you are saying about different different ways of seeing one thing is very very true. In our own case, see in how many ways, we all saw Kutti I mean Laxmi. I was seeing her as a sweet baby, Sister-in-law saw her as her child, other people were believing that she was Bhagavati, goddess. Who knows what she was, poor thing.

God is also somewhat like that, I feel. He is the centre. From our side we see something and we call him that. From another side, they see something else and call him that. But he is still the centre which we cannot see fully.

Inga

Journal

I was lucky in that I found a fellow conspirator in the Delhi house too. I had been a little worried about how I was to receive and send letters without my mother or my father getting a whiff of it. I was ready to be brazen about it, if needed. But fate helped, in the shape of the lackey who had first given me news of Inga's departure from the house. He understood what I was trying to say in my stammering Malayalam and he kept his word. I had managed to hide away some of the money I got at my 'coming out' ceremony where I was blessed with currency notes and coins by those whose feet I touched, and had been able to give Paru enough for postage stamps. Then, in Delhi, my father decided, much against my mother's wishes, that I should be given pocket money. 'She is college-going girl,' he told her. 'Small, small things she will need.'

What did he think or perhaps hope I would buy? Clothes? Face creams and lipstick? I now think my father felt a trifle uneasy about my indifference to things feminine. From his pedestal, his daughter could be allowed intelligence, even academic brilliance, and he could accept praise for this. But she was never to forget that her true function was to captivate a man as well placed as possible, and entice him into wedlock. To this end, she had to make men's eyes turn towards her and rest there long enough for it to be interpreted as approval. When I thought deeper about this, I realized that all those who are born with the female apparatus have to parade themselves and use the arts of a prostitute no matter to which household they belonged. What is the difference between a woman who traps a man into marriage and another who uses the same wiles to entertain him for a night?

Such thoughts would never trouble my father, of course, nor my mother neither. Never. She was virtue incarnate, wasn't she? As for him, after handing me the money in a careless kind of way, sometimes with his left hand, and often in front of his party workers, he would say, 'More sari buying aa?' and look around and bellow a laugh. Saris? What did that stupid man know? I wore my mother's discarded saris, of which she had a great many, and spent the money I was so kindly granted on books, letter paper, and, of course, on postage.

I was one of the very few girls who went to college in a sari. It was a tiresome garment, most complicated in its wearing and the cause of great anxiety since it had a humiliating tendency to slip off at the waist, all in a heap. I had to watch the way I walked, bent down, carried my books; it was like being in a very strict prison. Once, at home, while wrestling with a particularly perverse sari, my mother, watching me, jeered, 'When there are no hips, how it will stay? Hips you need no, like one proper woman.'

I shouted back saying that if I could wear a salwar kameez, I would not have to worry about hips and the like. Unfortunately, my father was at home and he heard me. 'That north Indian costume?' he thundered. 'You call it a dress? Will any girl from a decent family wear it? It shows everything, everything that a woman must hide. Have you seen the bottom thing spread out for drying? So vulgar it looks, like a woman with legs spread out. Karmam. Karmam. I have to close my eyes when I see it hanging in that Punjabi's courtyard. Do you understand this, you idiot girl?'

I never did wear a salwar kameez, but I remember the scandal caused by one of the senior girls in college. She decided one fine summer morning to discard her dupatta, calling it a veil of hypocrisy. She came to class without the

customary piece of cloth across her bosom. The college was
bullet shocked, the crows screamed, she was labelled 'fast'
and sent to the Principal's office. Everyone thought she
would be expelled; our Principal, unmarried and ugly,
apparently played tennis in 'Collumbia' University wearing
a sari. My father spoke highly of her. 'From our land and see
how far she has made it! I know her family very well. Old,
respectable family of Kerala.'

But the girl was not expelled. She continued to come to
college in a salwar kameez sans the dupatta, bare-breasted as
it were. In a very little while, she had a huge fan following
and was dubbed a 'fashion leader'.

Letter from Inga

Dear Rapa,

*That was a very funny story. Society has such funny ideas no,
about what kind of dress girls should be wearing? Here also it
is like that but there is nobody who is so brave as your friend.
You must be liking her a lot and talking very much to her. It is
always good to have one good friend.*

Inga

Journal

How had Inga known? I had told her nothing more than
the story of the rejected dupatta. I had said nothing about K
herself. But Inga was right, K was the only friend I made and
I'm not even sure whether 'friend' is the term I should use.
There is no other word I can think of, however.

K was two years older, a third year student of political
science. She might have been a student of literature, for all

the reading she did. We met on a rainy August afternoon as I was wading up the stairs to the staff room to hand in my essay on Bacon. I had a clutch of books to hold on to, while trying to free my legs from the wretchedly clinging embrace of a wet sari. I had tripped and almost fallen, face down, twice. The rain had kept most people away, and I thought that there was nobody to see me. So I hitched up my sari as high as I could, tucked my pyramid of books firmly against my non-existent hips and continued my journey. Somebody, however, was standing on the upstairs landing, leaning over the low balustrade watching me, and she laughed.

Strange that I was not offended. I remember looking up to a square, spectacled face framed by straight-falling black hair. I laughed too. I do not think I even pulled down my sari then. What K remembered of that first meeting was looking at my legs after she had finished laughing – 'The legs of a dancer, delicate yet strong, tapering to deliciously trim ankles'. She told me this much later, after many weeks of sitting in the canteen or some deserted bit of corridor, talking of Plato and Marx and Eliot. She introduced me to Ayn Rand and Simone de Beauvoir. We discussed our favourite books and I discovered that she had not read Graham Greene's *End of the Affair* or Charles Morgan's *The Fountain*; I bought a copy of Green's book to give her. I could have got her *The Fountain* and shown her the part where Morgan so deftly evokes the power of a woman's presence. But I didn't.

The choice of Graham Greene's book turned out to be significant in a way I had not foreseen. I had bought it for K's birthday and thought I would give it to her when we met in college. But to my surprise, she wanted me to go to her house for 'a small birthday party' that evening. It was a Saturday, just before Deepavali, and my tutorial classes were tepid and short. I hurried home, wondering for the first time in my life what clothes I should wear. What sari. It did not occur to me that I might not be allowed to go to K's house. My mother was at her scolding best. 'What you know of this girl? Who is her family?' she asked angrily. 'Your father's car you want to keep outside some slum house? You know who is your father?' Fortunately, my father came home early enough for me to rush to him and ask for permission before my mother could get a word in.

'Birthday party?' my father barked. 'What nonsense and stuff.' I remember my eyes prickling, his party workers were all around him. 'What party? We go to temple on birthday, you want to go for party? All right, all right. What is this girl's name?'

I told him. And K's address too. My father's air changed dramatically. 'Aa! That is the girl's father? Very high Government Official, he is. Secretary to Government. Yes. Yes. Very good friend she is to have. Go. Go. Wear one nice sari.' Then as I turned to go to my room, not hiding my glee from my mother, he said grandly in English, 'Take a cake. Take a birthday cake. They always have a cake in a birthday party. You have bought a book, is it? All right. What can I say? You young girls have your own ideas.'

K's house was not far from mine. The car went past the spread-eagled lawns of India Gate, already darkening with the long shadows of a winter afternoon sun, and turned into a quiet road lined with handsome two-storey houses. K came running out to greet me at the gate; her 'small birthday party' was actually tiny, it turned out that I was the only guest. I did not see anyone else in the house either. K took me upstairs to her snowy white room and flung my book down, unopened, on the bed.

'Let's finish all the food business,' she said. 'Then we can sit and talk or whatever. Come. Eat. Help yourself. It's all vegetarian. You see I remembered.' A small table in a corner of the room was stacked with plates full of fried snacks, sandwiches, sweets and a pretty birthday cake with a single candle.

'I hate all this candle-blowing and cake-cutting stuff,' K went on. Her eyes were glittering strangely and she chattered in a way I had never seen her do. 'But I thought one candle was fine. And you can blow the candle out and make a wish for me.'

'A wish?' I remember asking.

She laughed. 'Don't you know you have to make a wish when you blow out the candle?' I didn't know; I felt sick.

'That is a very nice window,' I stammered. 'It really makes this an E.M. Forster room. With a view.'

'I thought we had sworn never to use that word,' she answered, laughing again. 'The empty "nice". But you are right. It is a lovely window, a window with a view. Come and see.'

I stood beside her at the window, and looked out to see what seemed to delight her so much. It had grown quite dark and I saw that one of the downstairs windows in the next house was lighted. There was a figure standing there, arms on hips, head turned upwards.

'Why is that person staring at us?' I asked. 'Shall I draw the curtains?'

'Leave them be,' she said. 'He is always doing that. Watches me undress.'

I didn't know what to say. I was still at the window, uncertain, unsophisticated. Gauche. K clicked on the lights, murmured something I did not catch, then without warning, she scooped me up into her arms, her lips warm and wet, prising mine open.

I do not clearly remember how I managed to scramble out of her arms, out of the room, down the stairs, out of the house, through the evening gloom and into the car. I do recall having composed myself enough to face the many questions my parents asked when I reached home. I also remember that the lies I told were artistic and very believable.

When I reached my room at last, I saw that a letter from Inga had been pushed under my door.

As I bent to pick up the blue inland letter, it struck me that I had never mentioned Inga to K. I still don't know why I didn't; perhaps something that is sacred is also something secret.

I did not speak of K to Inga again. Whether Inga wondered about it I do not know. Even without my saying it, she always seemed to know my feelings; it was as if we fitted together like word and reaction, memory and recollection. That is how I thought it was. Then.

14

Letter from Inga

Dear Rapa,
I hope you are all safe over there. I am getting afraid about the
war we are having with Pakistan. Please you don't go to
college every day if classes are not there. Please also switch off
all the house lights in the night. This is the advice they are
saying here. Please write daily. Thank you.
Inga

Journal

I remember kissing the letter again and again, even though
it was full of ink smudges. Had Inga cried as she wrote? Or
had there been rain somewhere during that long journey
that the letter had undertaken before it reached me? I
preferred to think that Inga had wept. For me. That I may
be safe.

The birthday present I gave to K took on greater
significance. Graham Greene's book was set against the
backdrop of the bombing of London in the Second World
War. As I read my own copy of the book, I could hear
sirens wailing too and my mother screaming at me to put off

the light and get under the bed. India was at war with
Pakistan.

Delhi became a military fortification. There were trenches
everywhere and sand bags, the home guards patrolled the
streets all night, shouting out to householders to douse the
lights, to blacken windows. The radio broadcast only patriotic
songs, women sitting on string cots busily knitted warm
scarves and socks, and sewed together small squares of
leftover wool to make blankets. 'For our brave boys fighting
those dogs in the snow and ice.'

In college, the girls who stayed in the hostel boasted of
how they were ever ready to sacrifice themselves for the
country.

'We wear our prettiest night dresses,' one of them said,
giggling. 'And put on makeup and all.'

'In case one of the Pakistani planes crash-lands in the
college compound,' another explained.

'A whole plane? In the college compound?' someone in
the class wondered.

A third hosteler clicked her tongue. 'O god! Don't be so
pious yaar,' she said. 'A Pakistani pilot can bail out isn't it
when his plane is hit? And land in our compound?'

'We hear Pakistani pilots are very handsome,' her friend
added. 'So we do lots of exercising also.'

The three of them stood in a line, swinging their elbows
in and out, chanting, 'We must, we must, increase our bust,
That's what the boys expect from us.'

Sadly for them no handsome pilot parachuted down to
the college grounds. A peace treaty was signed very soon,
much to their disappointment, and while I lived through

the London blitz with Graham Greene, the trenches in our garden were refilled with soil and saplings planted.

We did not go to Komala Nivas that summer, and so I had the time and the freedom to do what I wanted. I read. When I was admitted into the English Honours course, my father had, with loud announcement, become a member of the library run by the British Council. 'For the sake of my daughter,' he boomed to everybody. 'Where is there time I have for reading? But she . . . appappa . . . she reads like some drunkard.'

It was the only thing he had ever done for me, and for which I was grateful. I went there every Saturday and as often as I could during the holidays. It was not very far from home, and in the cool season, when I first began using the library, I walked there. My father did not much care about what I did as long as I did not cut classes, but my mother displayed great horror that I should walk on Delhi roads for such a distance, and on my own. 'You do not know these men. Like animals they are,' she said. 'Why you must always go to read books? We have so many books in the house! Why you will not read them?'

I did not care to tell her how safe I was; Delhi's male animals did not walk close to dark-skinned girls, or even look at them.

The walk to the library gave me a feeling of being independent of my parents and allowed me time to spend in the reading room, looking through British newspapers and journals that smelt of English printing ink. I could pretend I was in England, that Inga was in our tiny cottage near the vicarage, getting ready for the day, while a crowd of daffodils nodded their heads in our small, well-tended garden. I remember the sense of calm I felt as I sat there reading a week-old British newspaper. It was as if all that was jumbled and chaotic in the world had been brought under control by the English language, had been teased apart, then rearranged. Every piece of writing was as ordered as a walled garden that changed gently with the seasons, unemotionally, noiselessly and always with the Shelleyian hope of springtime.

However, as the summer heat steadied, it was not possible to continue the walks. I had to ask my father for the car, which did not much please him, even though he hardly used it himself, especially in the afternoon.

When I was grudgingly allowed the car, I could not spend time reading, I could only change my books quickly. Sometimes, in my hurry, I brought home books that were unreadable after the first few chapters. But I also discovered treasures – all of Rilke, Hardy, Dickens, the Brontë sisters, George Eliot, Austen, Camus, Richardson, Kafka, Gaskell, Butler, Lawrence Durrell, Gerald Durrell, D.H. Lawrence and of course Dostoevsky and Tolstoy. I read the Bible and quite a lot of poetry, I remember reading Samuel Pepys but there are writers I don't recall, the list is comprehensive but not complete. About this time I think, I persuaded my father to subscribe to a book club that sent home, every month, two books by Indian writers. And breathlessly read Raja Rao's *Serpent and the Rope* in one sitting.

I look at the authors and books I have listed and find it a rather motley collection. Yet, isn't that the way people read anyway? Looking, discarding, selecting, and adopting. How am I different? Except that I am an Indian and read only English. And think and write in that language. So? What's wrong with that? It's an accident of history that I was born dark-skinned, my mind English pale.

Letter from Inga

Dear Rapa,

What language you use for reading and writing is not any big problem. People must have understanding about what you are saying, that is only thing to see. For example, my English is not good but I know Tamil and Malayalam quite well. You did English medium, I went to Malayalam medium and my mother made me to learn Tamil. But we are still both Indian. Because you are using English words, it means you are not loving India? What rubbish that is.

We are safe. Hope the same with you.

Inga

Journal

I slid into the second year of college almost imperceptibly. College re-opened in July and I attended classes with the assurance of a senior. K had graduated and left the college; I was splendidly free once more. Freshers looked at me with awe as I strode towards the classroom or sat in the library. I sometimes heard them whisper to each other. 'She carries so many books . . . why is she always alone . . . sssh . . . she's brilliant they say . . . a sure first.' And once I heard one of the seniors say, 'She is good enough for Oxford.'

Oxford! Was I meant for Oxford? For Oxford?

Letter from Inga

Dear Rapa,

What is supposed to happen, that only will happen. People like astrologers will tell us many things but they also are not fully correct. God's plan is like that. What fun is there if we know what all is going to happen?

Hope you are safe. We are all right. I am now learning accounts for my school final exam.

Inga

I am sorry that there are so many blots in my letters. This fountain pen is leaking a lot.

Journal

Were those weeks the happiest in my life? Perhaps they were, I don't rightly know. There were regular letters from Inga, I was far ahead of my classmates in college, and my first term exam results were excellent. My tutor gave me a special reading list that included Freud, Jung, Marx (Karl not Groucho), Nietzsche, Kierkegaard, which introduced me to literary theory as well. Suddenly I realized that literature was structure, the architecture of words and sentences, a contrivance of language. One cannot judge any piece of writing, in terms of its fidelity to life, just as one cannot compare a Van Gogh sunflower with the actual.

My classmates, though they too were in the second year, continued to look at literature as if it were a prescription for life, the characters in a novel were to be either loved or hated depending on whether they were 'good' or 'bad' people. They were ecstatic about Austen because her books were 'just like' the cheap, paperback romances that they devoured. They read her only to make sure there was a marriage at the end, they sighed over her heroes, especially those that were brooding and rich, and would not tell of their 'heart's desire'. Worse, they began to model themselves on the heroines who 'got their men'; they were vivacious, they stopped giggling (which was a blessing), but they also indulged in arch looks, some tried to shape their hair into ringlets, others took to tossing their disobediently straight locks to show disdain. Those who considered themselves born exquisite beauties, decided to put on a sullen, silent aspect and to produce great sighs during the weekly tests, as if they had been forbidden by the state to bury any dead brothers they might have.

None of them saw literature the way I did, as something created, a construct, a synthesis of word, meaning and form. When I read the great books of English, nay, of Western literature, I felt myself back in the land of Carnatic classical music – here were the same stately mansions, the castles, the small, neat habitations, the well-planned roads and lanes, nothing out of place, nothing, not a brick laid wrong. But as I wandered through this map, this land of books, I discovered gardens too, and orchards, glens, shrubbery, walks, clearings, woods and streams. I had not found these in music territory.

As I read on, through those days, the heat of Delhi summer turned to winter chill. It was now December. The air stung my face and hands as I went, all bundled up, to college; I may well have been in England. In Oxford. All English writing opened up to me as I felt the wind sharp, as I saw people's breaths curl out from their spouts, and watched the darkness gather, twittering, outside my window at four in the afternoon. Everything I read, both in prose and poetry, became real and vivid in winter. I knew why Austen's heroines looked despairingly at leaden skies, I sought the warmth of a fire (a two-bar electric heater in my case), I felt Dickens' silent, smeary fog in my nostrils. How fortunate they were to have weather that spoke so much to them. That burnished the leaves of autumn and made steaming tea and soup desirable, that snow-feathered the redbreast and heralded the spring crocuses with such joy. When the heat blazed during our summer, which seemed to last most of the year, my imagination had to work very hard to transport me to cooler climes, to England, to France, Germany, Russia where people wore shoes because the ground, as Keats found, was always hard. And cold.

It was December and I was studying for my second-year mid-term exams. I had read a great deal, but unlike my classmates, I had not looked very much at literary criticism. I felt I ought to assess and analyze literature on my own; I needed only the creative work, with no interference of a critic. After all, literature is meant to be read by the reader, every reader, directly, not just by those with heightened sensibilities or through the keyhole of literary criticism.

I had realized that every piece of writing is a construction with its own geometry and geography and has to be judged accordingly. It also has its place, its context, in literary, social and political history. But I had found something else. All great writers, across historical periods and genres, wrote what they did, because they were haunted by the thought of death. Death was, to them, a consciousness that throbbed like a pulse, it could not be turned off or denied. It could not be diverted, it was 'the eternal footman'.

I could not tell whether they wrote because it was a temporary way of escape, or because they hoped their work would give them immortality. What use is immortality to someone already dead?

Letter from Inga

Dear Rapa,
All you are telling about, is in our country also. In our own languages. You should see the sahityam in Tamil and Malayalam. Sanskrit also. There is a saying that what all there is in the world, it is there in Mahabharatam *and what is not in* Mahabharatam *is not there in the world also. Why you are not seeing our greatness? Why only English English English? Why you do not read some translation at least?*
Inga

Journal

Translations! O Inga! Didn't she remember the Sanskrit textbooks I had to study in school? How we laughed over them! Rama is a good boy. Sita is a good girl. Rama plays. Sita cooks. Rama eats one mango. I eat one mango. You eat two mangoes. They eat many mangoes. Where is the mango of Sita? Verily, verily where is the mango of Sita?

. . . Mangoes, stolen green mangoes. Salt stinging our lips. Inga screwing up her face, crinkles gathering around her little nose. The sun flush on her face. My coz. My pretty coz. Shall we be ever sundered? Shall we part, sweet girl?

I don't recall when it was, but I do remember telling Prof. Seshu about my Sanskrit textbooks and how utterly boring they were. I remember asking why we could not have had a mystery story in Sanskrit, it would be very much more fun. He wasn't amused. Instead, he lectured me about Sanskrit being the language of the gods and how it ought to be treated with respect, with reverence. 'And not with levity,' I remember him saying. I had never before or since, seen him this stern, he looked different, he sounded like my father. My ready argument, half in jest, died away.

I had learnt, over the years, not to argue with my father. But I did try, once more, a complete debacle; from then on, I sent him to Coventry.

Letter from Inga

Dear Rapa,

You are giving me new way of seeing sahityam, our literature. It may be you are correct. But what about funny stories or songs? Also you are always forgetting about religion. Belief in God is very good for taking away feeling afraid of death. Actually what is full of sadness is that God never comes even after calling him so many times. Does that mean he comes only when a person is going to die?

Inga

Journal

Inga's letter, with its contents so irrelevant by then, was squeezed into my palm as I was getting into the car to leave Delhi. Forever. Yes, what Pakistan could not do to Delhi, my father did to me. I was blitzed. Reduced to rubble. To nothingness. I was to be 'married off'.

15

Journal

Did I say I had learnt never to argue with my father? Some lessons are not totally learnt, many remain forever unlearnt. So with my father, who begat me and therefore thought he had the right to treat me as a piece of dark, ugly worthlessness.

Did he not consider that my dark was his, that it came from him, my worthy begetter? I had not asked to be born of him. To be born at all. Yet it was so; my father, the semen spreader, the master manipulator, twisted my fate into a knot so complicated, that its ends could not be discerned, a Gordian knot that Alexander himself, with all his Greatness, could not have sliced. What use then, were my arguments, my tears, my fury? I fought bitterly, but, ultimately, I lost the war.

Letter from Inga

Dear Rapa,

I am very very sad to hear about what happened to you. I know how big a wish you had to go for higher studies. Now you are so angry. I am really feeling very bad for you.

Inga

P.S. There is no use being angry like this.

P.S. again. Please remember this is life.

Journal

It was at the end of December that I was transported to
Komala Nivas with the kitchen utensils, the grinding stones,
the clothes and the trunks. I came home after my second
day's paper to be commandeered by my father into packing
my books and getting into the car again. My cupboard had
been stripped of my clothes. Furtively, surreptitiously.

The return to Komala Nivas was bitter. I was told of the
impending disaster only when the train was on its way. I
yelled and screamed, and then cried through the journey,
even in the presence of the ticket checker. It made no
difference. A day after our arrival, I sat in the back verandah
with my books, and began my fast for freedom. My father
sneered, 'Let her starve, she will know.' I fainted after three
days. My mother slapped me across the face, she held my
mouth open, while Rukku Paati poured gruel into my
throat, and Great Aunt Kuppai watched. I was helpless and
I was hungry. I gulped it all down. After that, it seemed
utterly stupid to refuse food; obviously I was no Gandhi. I
went back to my books and to silence, I spoke to nobody but
Paru, and to her only a few words as I collected Inga's letters
or handed her one of mine with a generous dose of money.

But not Jane Austen or Thomas Hardy, not even Dickens,
could hold my attention. My thoughts whirled as I tried to
think of who might help me. Brother One? No. He would
never raise his voice against my father. As for Brother Two,
I had no idea where he was and even if I did, what surety did
I have that he would bestir himself for me? His inclinations
changed as rapidly as the skies over Bath. What about

Prof. Seshu? Yes. He would help me, he would be on my side. It was not too late, I could join the hostel and finish my Honours course and then . . . Then I would apply to Oxford . . . But wait . . . how was I to get his address in Madras or his telephone number? I hated myself for not asking for it earlier, during happier times. I could have been writing to him all these years . . .

I heard voices in the front hall; my father's, subdued for once, and another's. It couldn't be. It was. I flew down the stairs from the attic and almost pitchforked into him at the doorway. Prof. Seshu himself.

'Oh Professor, I was thinking of you because . . .' I gabbled, totally ignoring my father.

He cut me short. 'Rapa my dear,' he said. His voice was strained, as if it did not belong to him. 'My dear girl, I have brought something special for you.'

He held out an envelope and I took it from him in my ignorance. 'It is a rough translation of the meaning of the most important ritual in the Hindu marriage ceremony,' he said. 'This is the Saptapadi, the seven steps taken around the sacred fire by the bride and groom. You will like it, it is much like the lines from the Christian marriage ceremony, though to my mind, it is more particular, more legal in its phraseology. . . . Wait. Wait my dear,' he said, almost pleading, when he saw what I was about to do. 'Don't tear it up please. It is my own translation. For you.'

I looked at him full in the face. He dropped his eyes. I turned and left them both without a word. I heard the professor call out my name. I heard him say, 'Your comments on literature are truly remarkable.' But I did not turn around. I went back to the attic, doomed once again, and put the sheet of paper he had given me between the pages of my journal. In my heart I had contracted myself to someone already, and I wanted to find out whether the Hindu marriage lines, in any way, resembled my feelings.

It was a long, long time later that I suddenly remembered what the professor had said about my comments on literature. And then it was that I wondered how he knew of them. The only person to whom I had communicated those thoughts, was Inga.

Fool! Fool that I was not to see!

The professor's betrayal blotted me out completely. I realized I had nowhere to escape, nobody to rescue me. Sometimes, I considered killing myself, but I wasn't certain of how to set about it. Moreover, I thought of how it would affect Inga, and I gave up the idea. I decided instead, to submit to everything for the present, everything that my father and my mother and Great Aunt Kuppai, the professor and all my other enemies had planned. I would submit to it all, and then, then when I sniffed a mouse route, I would disappear. I would find Inga. We would be together. I would sell whatever they put around my neck and arms – what earthly use were these to me – and we would buy our passage out. To England. To our cottage in the Lake District. . . .

So I dreamed, and plotted, so I kept my mouth clamped as they began a series of tortures, the likes of which only the condemned know. My limbs were pulled and twisted and lathered with evil-smelling milks and pastes in an attempt to bleach my skin. (I wonder they did not plunge me into a jar of acid). My hair was oiled with demonic vigour, then beaten and claw-cleansed and smoke-dried as if it had to be exorcised. As if I had to be exorcised. I was the one possessed, wasn't it? The cackling, wicked-witch spirit lodged in me had to whipped out, slashed out. For all these honourable tasks, a far-flung cousin of Paru's had been summoned, a dour woman with the arms of a hairy wrestler, who seemed to delight in inflicting pain and took umbrage at my refusal to cry out.

Letter to Charles Dickens

Dear Mr Charles Dickens,

Would you have written a book about me if we had met? I am not an interesting orphan like David Copperfield or Pip, certainly cannot draw tears the way little Nell can, nor do I possess Estella's proud and cruel beauty, not at all. However, my present situation is similar to that of Madeline Bray. Her father was compelling her to marry an old greedy money-lending villain. You must surely remember that, Mr Dickens. But with your characteristic love of suspense, you allowed her to be rescued, at the very last moment, by that besotted young man, Nicholas Nickleby, and made sure her father dropped dead as well. In my case, I am not certain whom my father has chosen as the bridegroom. What is without doubt is that there is no headstrong, desperate lover risking life and reputation to save me. It is also true that in India, marriages are arranged by the parents and accepted, almost without exception.

Is that enough of a plot for you? Perhaps I can tempt you with the vast range of characters that surround me, characters who would delight you, I am sure. Here is your midwife-nurse-torturer supreme Mrs Gamp who exerts herself violently to blanch my skin white. Here too are many pretty Dora-like dolls, all chatter and no talk. There is a sort of Mr Barkis, though we call him Mikhale. There are several hearty, Pickwick-like men, though not nearly as benevolent. There are plenty of schemers and devisers, especially in my own family. You must know that the scale of villainy is astounding. The younger of my two step-brothers, Brother Two, mixes the traits of the seducer Steerforth with the pathetic features of the rejected youngest gentleman in Mrs Todgers' boarding house. Brother One is the slimy scoundrel Uriah Heep and some more Steerforth. My mother has all the coyness you could wish for in a heart composed of the treachery and malignancy of Charity Pecksniff. My father! My father combines the evil of all your villains, of Madeline's father, of Squeers, Gradgrind, Ralph Nickleby . . .

Thank you Mr Dickens for your books. I owe much to you. Rapa.

P.S. I almost forgot Prof. Seshu. He is the one who introduced me to literature. He is a little like Mr Dick, but unlike your eccentric, dream-filled friend, Prof Seshu works for his living, and is much more worldly-wise. Very much more.

P.P.S. My cousin and I are called Inga and Rapa for short. Inga is a sort of diminutive of her very proper, official name – Ranganayaki. My name has been formed with the first syllables of Rajalaksmi Parvathy. Goddesses! What a pompous set of names these are. I hate them.

Letter from Inga

Dear Rapa,

I know how angry you are feeling. But why are you showing your anger on Indian names etc.? If you go to see, our names are very very good in putting all the people in their right place *in society. Name of person's birth place, house name, family name is all there. And the other common names are also good. You can make out whether so and so aunty or uncle is from your father's side or mother's side. So you can talk to them in the right way.*

But I am not agreeing with one thing in this. It is all from the man's side. Why a woman should only have father's or husband's name connected with her name? She should have mother's name no? If you think, you will agree we all have come from the stomach of a mother. The father may be any man.

Inga

Journal

On a hot, March morning, I was smeared with turmeric, bloodied with vermillion powder, handcuffed with scores of bangles, and noosed with a million necklaces. On a hot, sneering March morning, sieved savagely by bullet holes and knife wounds and razor slashes, I, Rajalakshmi Parvathy Krishna Iyer, was transferred as a burnt offering to the family of Padmanabhan Harihara Aiyer IAS.

I heard hate words spitting out all around me, as I was made to walk in and out of the inner room, made to change my sari, forced to keep my head lowered as I was inspected, assessed, judged.

'She is so black. How she got IAS boy?'

'Ssh. She can hear.'

'So what? I am only telling truth no? Anyway, she does not know our language. Only English she knows.'

'You saw bridegroom? Like Manmathan he is. Like God of love. What colour! Like lotus flower only.'

'Girl is tall also no?'

'Yes, yes! Like one coconut tree.'

'The boy's mother did not even see this girl till today, you know that? The boy said yes. So it became fixed.'

'He even did not see her?'

'No, not like that. He once saw her in this house.'

'What he saw in her?'

'His mother is very angry. You saw her face? Like a balloon it is. She is not even coming inside.'

'Good this happened to her, that Ailandam. She was showing off so much.'

'Such headweight she had when her son got IAS.'

'The girl's mother is wearing so many big big diamonds you saw?'

'Now she is wearing. We will see after some months.'

'Why you are saying that?'

'You are not knowing about father of girl? He has lost that parliament seat. So Kittu Anna is now ordinary man. Poor man.'

'Poor man?'

'His money is going no? That older son is wanting his share. The other boy took all the money and went off.'

'What about this house?'

'It is in that Kuppai's name, eldest sister of Kittu's father. But I am hearing that she has written it for this girl. That Kuppai only rules this whole house.'

'Oho! So Kittu Anna gave big dowry must be.'

'No, no. The boy is big follower of Gandhi. He said no to dowry.'

'But Ailandam will squeeze it out. I know her.'

'Yes. Yes. She has done that. And Kittu Anna also has to show he has money no?'

There was a pause. Then another bejewelled woman joined the group. She started off a new round of malice.

'You know that Meenakshi?'

'Kittu's second son married her first daughter only.'

'She had one eye on this boy. For her second daughter.'

'Yes. Yes. Almost fixed it was. Very pretty girl that one is.'

'Then what happened?'

'Meenakshi came to this house with the boy and his father two years earlier. Boy just finished writing IAS exam. Meenakshi was show offing. And you know Kittu. He has learnt all Delhi-type cleverness. He ran to the boy's house. It was his luck that boy also liked this girl. She spoke some English sahityam or something to him.'

'So that is why Meenakshi has not come. She has no luck only now. After that child died.'

'So much they said about that child. She was Devi. She was Bhagavati. What proof there was?'

'You do not remember? Kittu's first daughter-in-law, cripple she was. Now she is walking like a deer.'

'I heard also many sick people in these parts became all right after they saw the child. Somebody even got money back from that bank.'

'That bank that broke? That is something. So there was some power I believe.'

'Something there was. That first daughter was loving the baby so much. Now she has own boy. That fat one, shaapaat Raman. Always eating. His mother never says no . . .'

'Ssh. Ssh. She is coming this side. She is calling us for tiffin.'

From Prof. Seshan

Dear Rapa my girl,

I enclose an English translation of the lines spoken by the
bride and the groom as they take seven steps around the sacred
fire. This is called Saptapadi, the Seven Steps, and is done
after the maangalya dhaaranam when the groom ties the
sacred marriage thread around the bride's neck. This takes
place at an auspicious time, the muhurtam. The couple is
now considered companions for life and this is what the
Saptapadi ratifies. At each of the Seven Steps, the bride and
groom make a vow to each other. The vows are very beautiful
and immensely practical in that they encompass the everyday
issues of running a household with spiritual concerns. My
translation can give you only a bare sense of the original
Sanskrit but with your sensitivity to the written word, you will
be able to comprehend the deeper significance.

This comes to you with all my blessings. I know the young
man well. He is a fine fellow and a fit companion for you. The
Lord bless you my dear. Do not stop your reading and if you
can, employ a tutor who can teach you Sanskrit or Malayalam.
Since Padmanabhan belongs to Madras, he will be able to
arrange a Tamil tutor also. Tamil has a tradition of fine
literature but my own knowledge of the language is poor. As
you know, the Tamil we use as Palakkad Brahmins is a
fascinating combination of Malayalam and Tamil and horrifies
both our Malayali and Tamil friends. Rightly so.

Bless you my dearest girl.

Yours as always,

Seshu

P.S. You will be pleased to know that though Padmanabhan
is called Paddu by the family, his friends know him as Paddy.

The Irishness should appeal to you immensely. However take care you do not call him by either name when his mother is about. She is rather a dragon.

SAPTAPADI

With this first step you take, may Lord Vishnu who is everywhere, provide you with plenitude and protect you.

With this second step you take, may Lord Vishnu give you excellent health and the energy to live your life with high values.

With this third step you take, may Lord Vishnu help you perform your spiritual tasks.

With this fourth step you take, may Lord Vishnu bestow upon you joy and happiness.

With this fifth step you take, may Lakshmi, the Goddess of Prosperity, keep your cattle in good health and increase your wealth.

With this sixth step you take, may Lord Vishnu ensure that all the seasons are beneficial and may He lead you to fulfilment.

With this seventh step you take, may Lord Vishnu help you attain such rewards of noble acts that the Seven Sages have accrued through their penance.

The groom says:

With these seven steps we have taken together, we are now lifelong companions and best friends. We shall never forsake each other. We shall share the same strengths, the same tastes, the same food. We shall be of one mind. I shall be the upper world. You shall be earth. While I am the life source, you shall be the holder. While I am the lyric, you shall be the music. While I am the thought, you shall be the speech. While you are the word, I am the meaning.

You and I, my sweet-worded girl, we shall live a life of purpose and prosper with children and other riches.

Journal

I walked the seven steps not with the tall man, the Accordion, who was in front of me; I walked them with Inga.

With this first step I take with you Inga, I shall protect you.

With this second step I take with you Inga, I shall provide for you.

With this third step I take with you Inga, I shall give you happiness.

With this fourth step I take with you Inga, I shall bring you laughter.

With this fifth step I take with you Inga, I shall fill your lap with flowers.

With this sixth step I take with you Inga, I shall braid your hair with jewels.

With this seventh step I take with you Inga, I shall build for you a seven-pillared worthy house, where your eyes shall shine for me.

You who have walked with me these seven steps, become my best companion, my dearest friend. We shall share the same gardens, the same sunlight, we shall cross the same threshold, we shall share the same hearth. We shall welcome the same days and the same shy nights. I shall be the sun, you shall be its light; I shall be the light, you shall be its brilliance. I shall be the moon, you shall be its silver. I shall be the earth, you shall be its patience. I shall be the waters, you shall be its sanctity. I shall be the sky, you shall be its stretch of stars, I shall be the wind, you shall be its centre, I shall be all the seasons, you shall be their promise. For you, I shall be the lamp flame, you shall be my stillness.

Together, my sweet-worded girl, we shall live a life of fragrance. There shall be no third that walks beside us. There shall only be you and I, Inga. There is always only you and I.

Letter from Inga

Dear Rapa,

I am sending this letter by hand in a cover, because there is twenty-one rupees from Mother as ashirvadam for your marriage. It is only a small amount but her blessings are big. I was really wanting to see you dressed up like a bride but what to do. I hope this letter will reach you safely. From now, I do not know how we will write letters. So I shall stop until you say.

I came first in my shorthand typing class. My teacher is saying he is going to find a good place for me, somewhere nearby only. Then I can go and come by walk. Let us see.

Yours,
Inga

Journal

My blighted day came to an end at last, but when I was escorted, still in custody, to one of the inner rooms, beyond

Great Aunt Kuppai's sanctuary, I realized there was worse to come, much much worse. The room had been tarted up and stank of flowers that were already browned and wilting. These were looped and hung like so many nooses over a large bed covered with a white, lacy shroud. I recognized this as Sister-in-law One's contribution; she had lately begun to send for bedroom linen and embroidered petticoats from some relative in Calcutta. She pointed it out to me too, as she sat on the bed with much giggling and saucy smiles. There were several women with her who kept asking if I was hungry and thirsty and laughed like hyenas at whatever I said and whenever I was silent. Then Accordion came in, followed by gales of hideous laughter. There were more strange rituals, with more women howling songs that sounded utterly vulgar and bawdy. We may as well have been in an Elizabethan public house, some notorious tavern. When they finally left and the door was closed with great significance, I found myself trembling. I remember my armpit wet with sweat, my head throbbing. Accordion, Paddy as I learnt to call him, took off the heavy flower garland around his neck and hung it on the bedpost.

'Shall I take yours too?' he asked. I gave him mine without saying anything.

Then before he could touch me or do anything more, I burst out with the speech I had rehearsed for the last several weeks.

'I want us,' I said, I whispered, 'I want us to be like brother and sister. Like sister and brother. Like that.' Then I wept. Frightened. Stupid.

He said nothing for a long time. Then, very gently, he spoke. 'Don't cry,' he said. 'I won't do anything. But I want you to look at me.'

I turned and lifted my head. He stared silently, steadily, at the face before him, till I began to feel uncomfortable. Then, finally, in a voice I could hardly hear, he said, 'Your mind is written all over your face. What is a man to do?'

Then he turned away and I did too and we lay down as we were, each to each, at the opposite ends of a very wide, white bed.

16

Did Paddy look elsewhere for satisfaction? I never asked him and often I felt a great pity for him. This was usually in the middle of one of our long conversations where we both had so much to say and found that we thought so much the same way, not always, but often enough. He would suddenly stop and look at me as if he had a question. But he wouldn't ask it and I would not ask him to ask it.

I wonder now, when I have time to think, I wonder whether Paddy is a bit of a saint. If he is celibate, which he perhaps is, does that qualify him for sainthood? Is celibacy enough? But Paddy has other qualities. He is immensely kind, not just to me but to his subordinates at the office, to his jeep driver who seems to think that public roads are his private property, and to all the plaintiffs at court. Even now, when he visits, he has a store of stories to tell me. As he sits on the only chair in the room, and talks of his day, I see how hard he works, how long he works; he genuinely believes he can help make living better for the people in his division. He has set up a milk co-operative, he, a pure vegetarian, is introducing fingerlings into small water bodies so there is at least some fish for the poor to be had with their rice. I wish very, very often, that he had chosen another wife, a proper wife, a prettier wife, and not me who is no kind of wife.

But he has stayed married to me, has Paddy, and shared his thoughts with me as he has not with anyone else. That is what he once told me. I am the wrong one, not he. If there are saints here, in this world, to whom god has turned his back, then Paddy is a saint in spite of his occasional glass of beer, two cigarettes a day, and some bursts of anger. But I could not ever tell him this, nor that I always thought of Inga and of death, the ways of death. Paddy and I only spoke of things larger than ourselves, of our still young nation, of civilization, of the human race and its evolution, its refinement of language to become literature. 'How breathtaking human languages are,' he said once. 'How much they express our rational and irrational mind, and in what wondrous ways! Think of all the poetry we have read together. I really wish I had the time to read the literature, at least the poetry, of other languages. I can read and write Tamizh but I know so little of it. You will laugh at the way I speak it in court.'

I agreed only partly with him. I did not tell him so, but language is employed as much to hide as it is used for expression, it can camouflage as expertly as it can reveal. I know well, that what is secret is hidden, that which is hidden is sinister. I know that, but he doesn't, this smart, worldly-wise, immensely intelligent Sub-Collector.

It was during one of our conversations in the verandah of the Sub-Collector's bungalow, that I realized that Paddy's fields of knowledge, like mine, were unevenly tended. He had not wandered into the dark alleys of the mind (though he had read Freud), but he certainly knew much more about music than I did – Western classical as well as Indian. He has a large collection of long playing records through which he introduced me to music I had never heard. I remember how unrelated it seemed to what Inga and I had learnt, but when I grew more familiar with it, I saw the same stateliness in Beethoven and Bach, and some of Tchaikovsky, that I had found in south Indian ragas, the broad avenues and colonnades, the same orderliness. I felt Mozart frivolous and Brahms disturbing. There was something dark in that music, something too like me.

How I digress. How uncontrolled my thoughts. I must return to Paddy and to that Sunday morning which I remember vividly, even now, with pain. Paddy had brought me a book on Charles Darwin and his thesis on the origin of man, telling me, 'This book made the Christian world shake and tremble, they lost their God. But strangely enough, our Hindu mythology tells the same story.'

'Hindu mythology?' I remember asking. Those many-armed, languid-eyed gods and goddesses, what did they know about the human race? I suddenly realized that Paddy knew much more about them than I did.

'The *Bhaagavatam*,' Paddy replied. 'The story of Krishna, one of the avataras, the incarnations of Vishnu, narrates the circumstances of the other incarnations. There are ten in all, which includes the last one, Kalki who has not appeared yet. He is supposed to come on horseback, very much like the description in the "Book of Revelations", the last book in the Bible, about the four horsemen of the Apocalypse. Anyway, the other nine avataras of Maha Vishnu, who is worshipped as the Protector of Creation, have come down to the earth in the form of a sea creature, the fish, then the amphibian tortoise, then the land animal, the boar, next a half man-half lion, the vertebrate. After that, a midget, perhaps prehistoric man, next the hunter with early hunting tools, then the administrator, followed by the agriculturist, and finally the philosopher-king. If you take away the religiosity, the progression is uncannily similar to Darwin's thesis.'

'You speak so much like Inga,' I said. Without thinking. Without even a moment's consideration. How could I have been so off guard?

'Inga?' Paddy asked. 'Who is Inga?'

'My cousin,' I answered as carelessly as I could. 'We write to each other sometimes. She also knows a lot about Hindu mythology and Tamizh folk stories and all that.'

'Oh! So those are her letters in that packet.'

'There are others' letters also in there,' I lied, and went on lying. 'I keep her letters because she is not good in English, so she writes quite quaintly. I thought I could use that style for one of my characters in my book.'

Paddy looked at me with a face all lit up. 'Are you writing a book?' he asked.

'Trying to,' I said. 'I haven't got a good plot yet. I'm still gathering characters together.'

'That's like Dickens!' he exclaimed.

He was still looking at me with a kind of wonderment. Of admiration too perhaps?

'I have never been able to think like you do,' he said ruefully. 'I can only see the world as it is, through my senses, almost in a kitchen-maid kind of way. Perhaps my having to deal with ration shops has something to do with it. Rice is something to eat, it cannot be eaten raw, it needs water and heat to cook it and if there is too much water, it gets sticky . . . etc. etc. etc. But writers dazzle me with what they can see – that each grain of rice is a morsel of life born from water, soil and sunlight. They bring the marvellous into the mundane. And they never use "etc.". It is such a lazy word.'

I agreed with him about the laziness of the 'etc.', it is a word that yawns constantly, as if always in need of oxygen. But I was not sure of the rest of what he said; the philosophy of his thinking was more Inga's than mine. I did not speak further, the thought of Inga pierced me. I had mentioned her. I had slighted her. I was miserable. I was relieved when Paddy was called away and returned home much later, tired and cross, to a very late dinner.

I sat alone the rest of the evening, cursing my unruly tongue, my ill-disciplined mind. So far, nobody had spoken to me like Paddy did, with a sense of seriousness, of comradeship. I had to be watchful of myself with him; his gentleness was persuasive, it could undo me. It was dangerous. So, I began reading about Darwin. I needed the 'rice is a staple' kind of scientific discipline to anchor my mind.

Letter from Inga

Dear Rapa,
This writer Darwin is very very learned. But it is so sad that he was feeling he was going against God. He was not doing that. He was writing in English in scientific way, about what our rishis said only. This we are calling as Dasavatara or ten incarnations of Maha Vishnu. God became many different

things when he came to our world. First He was Matsya or Fish living in water only, then Kurma or tortoise, living in water and also land, third was Varaha, only land, then Narasimha, half-lion and half-man, then Vamana, small man, then Parasurama, the angry man, then Sri Rama, the best king, then Balarama with the plough, then Bhagavan Krishna, diplomat and also best lover. The eighth avatara some people say is Lord Gautama Buddha, not Balarama. The last one is Kalki who has not come.

I am not understanding this rice, water etc. But if you go to see, rice is not rice. It is mud, it is plant, water, sun, rain, then fruit of plant with cover. After cover is taken out, it is cleaned and then it is put in sacks, then we buy it. The life of rice is much like Dasavatara only.

Hoping you are all right,

Inga

P.S. Sometimes I am saying so many nonsenses. I am sorry for that.

Journal

All this happened much later. I have come too far ahead in my last entry and have to go back to what happened immediately after the wretched marriage ceremony. The 'bridegroom party', which now included me, was given an elaborate send-off. There were steel containers that seemed to run into their thousands, packed with sweets and snacks; there was a consignment of a special sweet made for weddings, small yellow cones encrusted with sugar. Then there was furniture and mattresses and an entire, enormous crateful of kitchen utensils. I remember Paddy looking dismayed as he saw the lorry being loaded, and remonstrating with his parents. His mother said very loudly, 'They only are giving it. We said no, no, one hundred times. They are only showing how much she is for them, one and only daughter no?'

At this point, my mother who had been supervising the freight, suddenly burst into tears. She ran up to me with loudly proclaimed sobs, crying, 'My daughter! My one and only daughter! She is going! She is going! How will I bear it? How will I live without her?' She then clung to me like a parasite creeper and sobbed some more on my shoulder. My blouse remained dry. After some time, while everybody watched, Sister-in-law One pulled her gently away with many false words of comfort. 'We are here no, Amma. Your son is here. I am here. Where is Rapa going? She is going to a big house no? She will be Collector's wife, so many servants, so many cars . . . Come Amma, stop crying. Wipe your face.'

There were no tears to wipe away but my mother meekly dabbed her face with the end of her sari. My father used the back of his hand. I noticed Prof. Seshu turn his face away and Mikhale's wet eyes. Brother One merely looked grim. I climbed into the flower-decked car and turned to look back at Komala Nivas. There was the house of my growing up and there, standing on the sun-scorched steps was Great Aunt Kuppai, her eyes streaming.

Nobody from my father's house accompanied me to Madras. The train journey was hot and dusty, and unquiet. My mother-in-law had insisted on a four-berth first class coupe because she 'cannot be left alone with all the jewellery'. So what did she think I would do? Run away with all of it and her son tucked under my arm? God! So there was my father-in-law, my mother-in-law, Paddy and I in the one compartment where my mother-in-law launched into a blistering attack on me, her son's choice, on my father and mother, on the miserable arrangements made and so on. She spewed forth. Her husband said nothing at all; her son tried but gave up after a time. Instead he helped me up to an upper berth and asked me to sleep if I could. I did. The train picked up speed and drowned out much of what she was saying.

However there was no such escape when we reached Madras. As long as Paddy was around, she could not say or do much. Besides, he still had a few days' leave left, and took me out to the beach, the cinema, to friends' houses. My mother-in-law resented all this, I could see that, but she could do nothing about it; after all her son was only doing what any newly married man is expected to do, spend time alone with his bride. Unfortunately for my mother-in-law, the visitors who came to examine me were very appreciative of her broadmindedness and modern attitude towards me. The women, while calculating the money value of my sari and the jewellery I was wearing, would tell me, 'You are so, so lucky. You have one IAS husband, and such a good, kind mother-in-law. She does not let you even enter the kitchen.' Of course, their thoughts said quite the contrary. 'How did you, so black, so ugly, manage to catch this fine IAS man? How much dowry did this greedy old woman ask for and get?' My mother-in-law simpered when she heard the spoken words, and smiled horribly when she was told how Paddy and I had been spotted on the beach, talking animatedly to each other.

However, a woman's sense of resentment is like a river in early monsoon, it is unpredictable. On a hot, airless night, when we were getting ready to sleep, there was a sudden sound of wailing outside our room. 'O! O! I cannot sleep. I cannot close my eyes. It is so hot! So hot!' It was my mother-in-law. When Paddy opened the door, there she was, clutching the wall and swaying as if drunk. She had a rolled up rush mat under her arm and a small pillow. 'I cannot sleep,' she wailed 'I cannot at all even close one eye. Your father is like stone, can sleep anywhere where there is fan. For me, in these kind of days, I can sleep only here.' She unrolled the mat over the threshold of our room and with a thump sat on it. Paddy looked at her and said nothing. Instead, he turned to me and said, 'Pack a suitcase Rapa, with a couple of days' change of clothes for us. We will take a room in the government guesthouse.'

Within five minutes she retreated, the room was ours once more.

When his leave was nearly exhausted, Paddy asked whether he should escort me to Komala Nivas. It always struck me as curious that Paddy never spoke ill of his mother, yet tried consciously to keep me from her harm. However, this time, a phone call to my father squashed all hopes of refuge. My father and mother, along with Great Aunt Kuppai, were starting on a long pilgrimage, visiting various temples and relatives. They could not say how long they would be away; there was nobody in Komala Nivas but Mikhale. They had got rid of me, why would they want me back?

Paddy left me with misgiving but there was little he could do except leave me his postal address. He was to be gone for more than three months, finishing the last phase of his training at the academy in Mussoorie before joining his post as Sub-Collector. In the event, I did not have to stay in Madras for as long as that.

Paddy had promised to phone and write often. He did both, but I was not allowed either to speak to him or have any of my letters to him posted. My mother-in-law kept a grim watch on the phone and answered all calls herself; Paddy was told that I was either in my bath or fast asleep or simply not available. Once, I was lucky to have my father-in-law in the drawing room. After he spoke to his son, he gave me the phone. But what could I have said to Paddy, with my mother-in-law listening in cold fury? Afterwards she mocked me savagely for not being intelligible or tender on the phone when speaking to her son.

My mother-in-law baffled me. Apart from her total anger against me, which I dimly understood, I detected a great fear of me as well. It was as if she saw me as a kind of wild animal, or a vicious snake, which she had had trapped, but which might break free if her guard slackened. In a perverse kind of way, she also boasted to her friends of my felicity in English, of my father's position as Member of Parliament, and his wealth. When there were visitors, and there were many those weeks, she made me dress up in my silks and jewellery to be presented as the rich, highly educated daughter-in-law from a 'big family'. As soon as the visitors left, however, she would turn demoniac, accusing me of making eyes at the men and speaking in English to put her down.

I had not written to Inga since that day in March.

My mother-in-law had a worthy crime partner in the cook. This man had come with her when she married, was fiercely loyal to her and was probably better informed of her wishes than her husband or son was. Naturally, my inability to cook was a cardinal sin; apparently, one was either born a cook or wasn't born that way, cooking was not a talent that could be earned through the learning of it. Paddy had told his mother, lightly but with seriousness, that she would have to be my cookery teacher. She had glanced at me then, but said nothing. Paddy assumed that she had agreed. How little men know of women! I had known for a long time, that a woman's silence almost never means assent. So it was with my mother-in-law. She pushed me into the kitchen the morning after Paddy left, and in front of the sniggering cook and two rather frightened maids, asked me to make upma. I had no idea what I was supposed to do. I remember staring at the rows and rows of gleaming steel jars, the fierce-looking stoves, the trays of vegetables, arranged as if for a photograph and wondering what I should do. She stood there, hands on her hips, waiting for me to stumble and fall. I did. I said 'Amma, Paddy told you I don't know to cook.'

She chopped me up, using as weapon, my own remark. 'Paddy!' she shrieked. 'Paddy? You dare take my son's name like that? You know who is he? You know how big is this family? You raakshasi! You black face! You whore! You street-walker. To cook you don't know? But to open your legs for a man you know! You know very well that!' Then she began beating her head against the wall screaming, 'What sin did I do? What sin? Tell me Narayana! Tell me Srirama! Tell me Adisesha . . .' As she started on the divine roll call, banging her head at each name, I squeezed my way out and ran into my room. I got nothing to eat that day till Paddy's father came home late in the evening and asked for me.

My father-in-law, Paddy's father, was a rather strange

man. He was like Dorai Athimbiar in that he did not speak
much. Nor do much. Great Aunt Kuppai always expressed
her opinion of such men with a loud snort and a pursing of
her lips, but I could not dismiss Paddy's father in the same
way. Dorai Athimbiar I did not care about; my father-in-law
was different. I saw that he read a great deal, both English
and Malayalam, and though he did not seem as much a
scholar as Prof. Seshu, he knew enough to have conversations
with his son on present-day politics and 'yester-year' music
legends. He was gentle in his ways, and if he had been in
England during the war years, would probably have opposed
Churchill; the world, like Great Aunt Kuppai, would have
seen him as a weakling.

So it was that Paddy's father did nothing for me for a
time. This was also because he was away from home most of
the day and did not know what was going on. Apparently,
after his retirement, he had taken to spending the day at
one of the libraries in Madras. 'My father is rather old-
fashioned in some ways,' Paddy had told me. 'He has his
lunch about the time when we normally have breakfast. His
next meal is around seven in the evening. In between, he
probably has a glass of coffee and a dosai or something. I
used to laugh about Appa eating lunch at half past nine in
the morning, but at the academy, I was told it is the best
thing to do when one is touring. One never knows when the
next meal will be!'

Paddy's father could not have known how often I had
been denied food or that I was made to wash heavy, greasy
cooking pots out at the backyard tap, because the maid's
hand was 'paining'. Nor would he have known that, one
day, my books had been flung to the floor, stamped on, and
kicked out of the room. She had screamed, 'You read, you

whore! I am doing work for you sweating in that kitchen and you read? Sitting in fan wind? Let god kill your eyes! Make your eyes blind!' She dashed into the puja room and hit her head on the ground again and again shouting the most horrifying curses. 'Guruvayurappa! She must burn, burn for one thousand years. This house must rot! She must rot! Rot and die!'

After the storm had long passed and when she was lamenting her fate sitting outside the kitchen door, I crept into the corridor and brought in my poor suffering books. Some of them had been severely damaged. When I think of that time now, I must own that I was always surprised by the inventiveness of my mother-in-law; she could have been an Ian Fleming villain in the way she baited me, led me into false suppositions, in the quickness with which she changed stratagem. Fortunately for me, Dr No could not laugh the evil laugh forever, he eventually got his comeuppance and so did my mother-in-law.

What happened was this. I received an unexpected dinner invitation from a senior bureaucrat, a long-time friend of Paddy's. I suspected that the invitation, for me alone, was arranged by Paddy; later, I found I was right. My mother-in-law could not stop me from going, especially since the phone call came to my father-in-law. Nor could she refuse because I was to be collected and dropped back by my kind hosts. The evening was pleasant, I spoke to Paddy for a few minutes on a bad trunk line and, around half past ten, was dropped home in an official car. The house was completely dark, even the porch light had been switched off. I stumbled up the steps and rang the bell. No lights came on, no voice called out, the darkness and the silence continued even after I had rung the bell several times. Then I saw the intermittent light of a weak torchlight, and heard my mother-in-law's voice hissing at me from the drawing room window which opened to the porch. 'You whore! You charcoal strumpet! This house you want to enter? Never! Stay there only. Go to Mount Road go. Your body go sell.' The venom was as dark and as thick as the night. Then I heard a chair being pulled up to the door, and she continued muttering as she sat herself down. The torch was switched off.

The renowned Madras mosquitoes would not let me alone, and even though I wrapped myself tight in my sari, like an Egyptian mummy, they got me, biting my face, my toes, my elbows, my waist, they were vicious. Presently, I heard my mother-in-law's snores, but there was no sleep for me as I sat on the floor of the porch dodging those helicopter mosquitoes. Time passed, my mother-in-law snored, then I heard soft footsteps coming round the house. I stood up and tried to think of how best to protect myself. It was my father-in-law, whispering, showing a feeble torchlight down the porch steps, to the back door, past the sleeping cook and into my room. I caught a glimpse of my mother-in-law, her head against the front door, fast asleep and making noises like a steam engine. 'Keep a suitcase packed,' my father-in-law said as we made our way in. I did.

There was bedlam the next morning. There was much screaming from my mother-in-law at the cook whom she accused of betrayal; he, red-eyed, shouted out his innocence and declared his decision to leave immediately. In the middle of this, my father-in-law, dressed and ready, knocked at my door. I too was ready, my suitcase, my books packed. Without a word, Paddy's father escorted me out to a taxi waiting at the gate. He took me to Pondicherry, an hour's drive away, to Paddy's aunt's house by the sea. It was a masterly rescue.

17

Paddy's aunt was not his father's sibling but a cousin. She
had been married at sixteen to a much older man who lived
in an interior village in Madras State where the caste system
was iron hard and those not born Brahmins were referred
to as N.B.s when they were spoken about in English. Paddy's
aunt – named Lilavati but I was asked to call her Lily – had
to confine herself to the kitchen and the back regions of the
huge, sprawling ancestral house and not allowed to speak to
anybody outside the family. When she did not get pregnant
within the first six months, she began to be ill-treated,
denied food and beaten by her husband. Ironically, the
imprisonment also slackened as if it was no longer necessary
to treat her as a jewel in a casket. Within four months or so
of her little freedom, she developed a well hidden friendship
with a stranger, an artist who had been commissioned to
paint her father-in-law, and ran away with the man to
Pondicherry. She was declared dead by both her parental
family and by her in-laws; her husband actually conducted
her death rites and married again, after six months, a fifteen-
year-old Brahmin girl of a poor family from the same village.
Lily appeared to have led a happy life with her artist, he of
unknown parentage, and to have been devoted to him. She

certainly did not elope with anyone else. The artist died, thirty years or so later, and left her all his wealth, which was considerable. She stayed on in his house, looked after the estate and continued the pottery work and the painting she had learnt from him.

Lily's history was told to me by my father-in-law, and I made my own footnotes to it, as we drove to Pondicherry that dramatic morning. 'I am the only member of the family to stay in touch with her,' he said. 'We became very good friends when I was studying in Madras and she was still in school.' He paused for a minute and then said, 'She wanted to do so many things, become a dancer, learn music, study art . . . but they got her married to an uncultured fool living in some godforsaken village . . . If only . . .' he paused again, then murmured, 'If only they had waited.'

Lily was like her name, tall, slender and with a butter white skin. She was unlike any Aiyar woman I knew; she spoke excellent English and seemed to know French fluently. She was equally at ease with the Frenchfied Tamizh used by the locals and with the mix of Malayalam and Tamizh that is the language of Kerala Aiyars. She greeted my father-in-law with a degree of intimacy that told a tale; she met me with surprise. There was no unkindness there though; immediately on hearing the few words of explanation my father-in-law gave, she took me to a vast bedroom with a four-poster bed and other, delicately-legged pieces of furniture. A servant brought in my suitcase and a set of towels, and told me in strange-sounding Tamizh that breakfast would be ready in fifteen minutes. There was a huge tub in the bathroom but I was not sure how to use it; fortunately, there was a more familiar bucket and mug also provided. Lily told me later that the bathtub was a relic, a showpiece. 'I hate sitting in dirty soap lather,' she said. 'Besides, the tub uses up a lot of water. Ami loved it,' she added, 'so I have let it stay as a remembrance.'

Ami must have been her artist friend's name, but whether it was a shortened version of Amitabh, or Ameen, or simply the French for 'friend', I never knew and did not ask.

The first thing Paddy's father did after we arrived at Lily's house, was to book a trunk call to Paddy. We waited all morning but the call did not go through; we were then told by the operator that there had been heavy rains across the hills in northern India and the telephone lines were down. There was nothing we could do but wait; in the meanwhile I wrote a long letter to him, so did my father-in-law, and these were duly posted. Paddy's father stayed for a couple of days and in that time, he and Lily took me around the town and to the sea front. The sea here did not seem to have as much character as at Madras; though it was the same waters, it looked smug and aloof as if it did not quite approve of dark skin. Lily laughed a great deal when I told her this; perhaps the sea found her more appealing. The town itself was a curious mixture of the Indian and the non-Indian, the French. In some areas, I could almost see Camus walking down the street with a pile of books under his arm, and knocking on one of the small wooden doors set in a wall. Or find Sartre holding forth at a street corner with a gaggle of women wearing caps, gazing adoringly up at him. How would it have been if the French had won the battle for India?

'We'd all have been more elegant perhaps,' remarked Lily, 'but also more confused than we already are. I believe this country is being governed with some efficiency because we adopted the British system of administration.'

'That's what my son always says,' murmured Paddy's father.

I remember we were walking down the promenade at the time; I remember Lily looking out at the sea and after an unmistakable pause, saying in a low voice, 'I wish I could meet your son.'

Paddy's father made no answer. I was about to burst out with, 'Of course you can . . .' when I realized that he had not spoken and I fell silent too. How could I, even for a moment, have forgotten that Paddy had a mother, and such a mother?

After my father-in-law left, I got to know Lily better and to observe her more closely. I began noticing that she never passed a mirror or a pane of glass without pausing to look at herself, much like Sister-in-law Too. Again, like Sister-in-law Too, this was not to smooth her hair down or arrange her sari. She liked seeing her reflection, she smiled at it as if it were a friend she missed. Lily also had a curious trick, during a conversation, of stretching open her hands and gazing admiringly at her pink-tipped fingers and the finely-etched lines on her palms. However, unlike Sister-in-law Too, she cast no sidelong glance at my own dark skin, nor did she ever allude to it. Instead, Lily treated me with a respect, almost with an affection, that I had not known from any older Iyer woman. She was always tastefully dressed. At home, she wore slacks and a loose tunic but when she went out, even for a walk, she wore a sari, tied her long hair into a mild bunch, and insisted on applying the vermilion mark on her forehead.

During the two-and-a-half months that I stayed with her, I

discovered how widely read Lily was, and in many ways, both astute and wise. She was a true Renaissance woman, if such a term can at all be applied to an Indian, and to a woman.

Letter from Inga

Dear Rapa,

It was nice to get your letter after so many days. But I am not feeling nice that you went away from Madras. Your husband's mother is just like your mother only. Why your father-in-law took you off I am not understanding. Mother is not agreeing with me. She is saying it is better that you are safe. In that way, I agree also. But I am thinking so much about why we are born as human beings. Is it not for doing good to everybody? Must not we be making peace like Gandhiji? We all have God inside. Even your mother-in-law. Please remember that.

Inga

Journal

Inga's little scold set me thinking. Was it wrong for me to have come away from Madras when it seemed, at times, that my life itself was in danger? It was, after all, Paddy's father who had brought me away. Inga was still young, inexperienced, protected. She had a capacity for trusting people that seemed to me to be naïve, sometimes even stupid. Was trust a virtue or did it come out of ignorance? I put the question to Lily without mentioning Inga.

'Do you trust people?' I asked her on one of our evening walks to the sea. It was hot and sticky and the sky was almost blotted out by dark clouds. Lily was saying that she expected a storm to come up in the night, when I blurted out my question. She stopped walking and looked at me before she answered. I wondered why. Did she realize that it was far from being an idle question?

'Trust is not an instinct I think,' she said slowly. 'I feel it is a talent. I use the word talent in both ways, as in the parable, and in its modern sense. It has to be spent, so it can grow. Of course,' she continued but now with great bitterness, 'a child who trusts is looted by the parents themselves, then by the family, then by teachers. By the time the child is ten or eleven years old, there is precious little of the talent remaining.'

'Then what happens?'

'Don't you know?' she asked sharply. 'You and me happen. Paddy's father happens. And thousands of others, millions of others are betrayed by family, by friends, by those in authority. Sometimes by life itself.'

As she said this, the storm broke suddenly over our heads and the rain pelted down. We had wandered away from the market and we now found ourselves in a deserted area with only a small shack ahead of us. 'Come on,' said Lily. 'Let's get there. Run.'

We ran, bunching up our wet saris that clung to our legs like fetters and made it to the shack, soaked to the bone. It was a tiny shop selling tender coconuts, lit by an unruly hurricane lantern and crowded with rough-looking men, who had also come in from the rain. They fell silent as we entered, then the shack owner said sharply in Tamizh, 'Ay! Ay! Move da! Move!' The men moved to a side, there was a small wooden bench behind them. Lily and I sat down with a loud squelch. The coconut seller said something to us in what seemed to be French. Lily answered, in the same language. Then they held a small animated conversation and at one point, all the men burst out laughing. So did Lily. The coconut seller, 'Senthil by name', then picked two large green coconuts, sliced off their tops expertly and offered them to us. In Tamizh, he said, 'Drink, drink, I am giving you more water only. But drink!'

The coconut water was sweet and warm. After we had drunk up the water, Senthil cut out slivers of the white coconut meat and gave them to us on strips of palm leaf. They were delicious. The rain stopped as suddenly as it began. We got up and Lily brought out her purse. But the man waved his hands in mock horror. 'No! No!' he shouted. Then switching back to Tamizh, he said, 'I am new to this place. Just starting this business. You came like goddesses to bless me. How can I take money from you?' Then he asked, 'You will be all right? Shall I send my boy with you?'

We declined. As we made our way home, our wet saris still clinging to us like seaweed, Lily laughed a short, bitter-sounding laugh. Then she said, 'That sanctimonious drivel I delivered on the topic of trust? Forget it!'

I remember that I asked Lily the next morning what her conversation with the coconut seller had been about. 'Oh, it was about you,' she replied cheerfully.

'About me?'

'Yes, He asked whether you were my daughter. He felt sure you were, because you looked so much like me except for the colour of your skin. I told him you got that from your father who was dark and handsome.'

'So you told him I was your daughter?' I asked, not being sure.

'Yes. Yes I did,' answered Lily.

Letter from Inga

Dear Rapa,

I am really sorry about last time's letter. Now you told me all in detail, it is good you went off from Madras. What you are saying about trusting is also very correct. If you go to see, who you can trust? Even milk is mixed with water in these days. But I am also finding that if you are trusting God, then nothing bad can happen. But we must be doing our duty also. Everyone we must give respect to, even small children and sweepers and all, because they have God inside. We must not laugh at ignorant people. How they can help it if they are ignorant? We only have to teach them no?

Inga

Journal

My conversations with Lily were very unlike the women's gossip sessions I had heard in Komala Nivas and Madras. Considering that Lily's vocabulary was often as colourful and intemperate as theirs, I wondered what the difference was apart from the fact that we discussed literature and music too. The difference was that Lily held many things sacred, not the rituals of daily worship and the chanting of divine names which she scorned, but things like restraint, etiquette, privacy. As I write this, I feel they are all related, and that they were not important to anybody in Komala Nivas. Lily could have asked me about my parents, about my marriage, my mother-in-law. But she never did.

For the next six weeks or so, I lived with a happiness so complete that it felt unreal. There was a regular flow of letters from Inga and Paddy, there was a huge collection of books in the house, Lily and I walked down to the sea in our saris every evening, we talked, she more than I, and my father-in-law visited once. He looked beaten, tired and hardly spoke to me except to say I looked well, and to ask whether I had letters from Paddy. He did not tell me anything about the situation in Madras, and I did not care to ask him how his wife was. Whether he told Lily how it was there, I don't know. We talked of other things, Lily and I, of books, music, art, clothes, her life with Ami, mine at college. She did not speak of her parents' or her husband's family, I did not speak of mine.

There was something that Lily did for me, for which I was grateful. She had her Muslim tailor sew a few pairs of light linen slacks and pale-coloured shirts, which I wore in the house, just like she did. She warned me against wearing them when we went out or when my father-in-law was around. How free I felt when I wore them, free, able and totally myself.

Lily was very decided in her views and I felt her range of reading entitled her to it. But what struck me as inappropriate was the way she expressed herself. She used inelegant words unexpectedly, which she applied to anyone who offended her with inattention, laziness or rudeness. She held strong views about people and systems that were completely opposed to accepted thought. I still remember some of them, mostly because I discussed them with Inga. I found her anger curiously contradictory, as if she did not know where her rage should be directed.

'This Brahminism! What a bloody imposition it is. To have to eat only what is cooked by another Brahmin. To bathe if one touches a non-Brahmin even by mistake. What nonsense! And what happens when these upper-caste fellows lust for a poor fisherwoman and rape her? A bath cleanses them, is it?

'Do you know Rapa, that a Brahmin is only expected to eat as much as his closed right palm can hold? Close your fingers over your palm and tell me how much space there is. Enough to survive a day? For god's sake, why this punishment? Eat well, but with moderation, and treat your women with respect. That will make any man a deva. Sure to.'

Once, we went past the Aurobindo Ashram on our way to the sea front. 'Have you read Aurobindo's work?' she asked. 'No? Believe me, you have missed nothing. Such ponderous writing. But he had ideals, I grant you, and he worked to make them real. But that woman Mirra Alfassa! Who does she think she is? I cannot stand foreigners who come to our land and tell us what is good for us. Will they let us into their country to teach them about life? About how to use fingers to eat instead of badly-washed forks and knives?'

I wondered whether Lily, and perhaps her artist friend, had had some kind of collision with the residents of the new township near Pondicherry, which apparently strove towards self-sufficiency in all things; they farmed and baked and made pottery and paper. I would have liked to have gone there but Lily did not ever propose to take me. She was bitter about it, as she was about her 'spineless' countrymen and women.

One day, as we were discussing Jane Austen's *Emma*, she suddenly got up, took a book out of the drawer of her desk, and thrust it at me. It was a notebook, its pages covered with quotations written in her fine hand. 'Read the Macaulay one. That disgruntled oaf. The villain who is responsible for the disfigurement of our country.'

I began to read.

EXTRACTS FROM THE 1835 MINUTE ON INDIA'S EDUCATION WRITTEN BY LORD MACAULAY.

'I have no knowledge of either Sanscrit or Arabic. But I have done what I could to form a correct estimate of their value. I have read translations of the most celebrated Arabic and Sanscrit works. I have conversed both here and at home with men distinguished by their proficiency in the Eastern tongues. I am quite ready to take the Oriental learning at the valuation of the Orientalists themselves. I have never found one among them who could deny that a single shelf of a good European library was worth the whole native literature of India and Arabia . . . English is better worth knowing than Sanscrit or Arabic; that the natives are desirous to be taught English, and are not desirous to be taught Sanscrit or Arabic; that neither as the languages of law, nor as the languages of religion, have the Sanscrit and Arabic any peculiar claim to our encouragement; that it is possible to make natives of this country thoroughly good English scholars, and that to this end our efforts ought to be directed . . . it is impossible for us, with our limited means, to attempt to educate the body of the people. We must at present do our best to form a class who may be interpreters between us and the millions whom we govern; a class of persons, Indian in blood and colour, but English in taste, in opinions, in morals, and in intellect. To that class we may leave it to refine the vernacular dialects of the country, to enrich those dialects with terms of science borrowed from the Western nomenclature, and to render them by degrees fit vehicles for conveying knowledge to the great mass of the population.'

I decided to enter the extracts into my own journal. I wanted to discuss this with Paddy and perhaps with Inga too. When I had finished and returned Lily's notebook to her, she said, 'You see how it is. How this "English" education has emasculated our country. We now have one set of Indians, traditional, mostly poor, who know the value of using cow dung cakes for fuel. And we have a small set of important, westernized people who are repulsed by cow dung and have afternoon tea at four with crumpets and cake. So tell me, Rapa, where do you belong? Are you an Indian who pats cow dung into cakes? Or a genteel, brown English woman? An Ammu or an Emma?'

I did not like these questions. I still don't. Could I have chosen where I was to be born? And my marriage . . . did I have a choice there? My schooling taught me to think in English; am I not Indian therefore? I have been brought up on green mangoes, rice and rasam. I am sustained by the Indian monsoon, by Komala Nivas in a small Kerala town, by Inga. So am I to be divided in myself? Can I not be an Ammu as well as an Emma?

O god! Inga!

Letter from Inga

Dear Rapa,
You can be whatever you want. Our holy rishis say we can even choose in what type of family we want to be born. It all

depends on the actions we did in our previous birth. If we have much of sadness in this life, much pain, we will not be born again, we will burn all our karmam and become part of God himself. But we should not ourselves hurt anybody or think bad about them. We must always help people. Anybody can be what they want to be. Only thing is they should know what they want.

But why you are thinking about all this? Lily Aunty must be a good lady. I think she is also sad. She is always thinking about God, is it not?

Inga

Journal

Six weeks into my stay in Pondicherry, something unexpected happened. I had not spoken to Lily about Inga, except to say she was my cousin because she knew I was getting letters from someone other than Paddy. She did not ask me about it though, which was decent of her. But I could not resist telling Lily that Inga had supposed her spiritual. I assumed that Lily would laugh caustically and call it much fanciful thinking. Instead she stilled for a moment, then turned to me and asked, 'Your cousin? What exactly did he say?'

'She,' I answered. 'She said you were always thinking about god.'

Lily fell silent; then, in a tone that was almost a plea, she asked, 'Would you allow me to read the letter please?'

I saw nothing untoward in the letter to keep it away from Lily, and it would have been impolite not to show it. I believed, then, that Inga and her thoughts were as unvarnished as leaves on a tree, but now . . . I fetched the letter from my room and handed it to Lily, who read it with the concentration of a first-time reader. Then to my utter surprise she kissed the inland form, folded it carefully, and gave it back to me. Her eyes were brimming with tears.

'Whatever's the matter?' I asked.

She did not reply. Instead, she said, 'Your cousin must be much older than you.'

'Oh no. She is younger, she is about . . .'

Lily cut me short. 'Rapa, have I ever talked to you about . . . about . . .' she paused, then whispered, 'about god?'

'Never,' I said stoutly. 'In fact, I thought you would laugh at . . .'

Lily said, more to herself, than to me, 'How did she know?' After a moment, she asked, 'Where does she live? Will you take me there? To meet her?'

Letter from Inga

Dear Rapa,
Surely, Lily Aunty can write letters to me. But she must use only the post box number like you are doing.
Inga

Journal

Suddenly, even before the week was out, Lily had become another person. Her autocratic ways, her sarcasm, her anger, her cynicism, all fell away like clipped fingernails. She was more considerate with the servants, much less impatient and fastidious. She began planning a small school at home for poor neighbourhood children, where she would teach basic English, French and arithmetic. There was a quickness in her step now, and an eagerness in her voice that bewildered me. Was all this because she was corresponding with Inga? My Inga? I knew there was a regular crisscross of letters between them; what they said to each other, I was never told. During our walks, which continued, Lily talked incessantly about the school she was getting ready; her monologue on chalks and dusters sickened me, she did not mention Inga even once.

Why did I not ask Lily any questions? I could have, she was as courteous, as affectionate with me as she had always been, but I could detect a singing bird in her, whose melody she kept from me. I began to have misgivings, deep misgivings.

Letter from Inga

Dear Rapa,

Why you are asking such questions. Yes. Lily Aunty is writing quite a lot of letters to me. But I am able to reply not so many times. She discusses religious things with me, that is all. What else it can be? If she does not want to say anything, let it be. Matters about God etc. are private matters. Whatever is private is kept as a secret. A secret is not always a bad matter.

Sometimes you are so funny Rapa. Stop thinking so much nonsense.

Inga

18

Journal

I was clearly not relevant anymore in Lily's house. I felt gauche, unwanted, a house plant that had grown too large, had lost its rightness. Fortunately for me, Paddy's period of training was over and his posting as Sub-Collector had come through. I could leave Pondicherry. Paddy called from Madras to say that he was coming to fetch me. We were going to Pollachi.

'Where is that,' I asked.

'Near Coimbatore,' he explained. My heart gave a leap. Inga's post box was in Coimbatore.

I packed the pants and tunics that Lily had got tailored for me along with my other clothes, and dressed in a sari to wait for him. That first meeting between Paddy and Lily was not what I had thought it might be, considering the sentiments Lily had expressed to his father. Once, nearly three months ago. She was kind to Paddy though, had an elegant lunch ready, and insisted on our taking neatly-wrapped packets of sandwiches and plenty of water. She did all this with great affection, but it was obvious that the singing bird was very loud in her, and often, she did not hear what we said to her. Just as we were about to leave, she called me into her room and pressed a small envelope into my hand, she was almost the old Lily at that moment. 'No, it's not money,' she said with a little giggle, 'it's something more precious. I don't need it anymore.' Then as I moved away from her hug, she said in a whisper, 'I have not thanked you Rapa. You gave me great delight by staying with me. But more than that, you gave me . . .' I was at the door, I could hear Paddy calling, Lily's voice had sunk, but I knew the name on her lips and on her tongue.

Paddy made no comment on Lily except to ask, as we drove away, 'Is she always like this?'

'Like what?'

'Distracted. As if her mind were elsewhere.'

Only in the last few weeks, I assured him. 'She was quite normal before this.'

We stopped for the night at a small divisional town, and stayed in the Inspection Bungalow. Paddy was most apologetic about the food that was served us, with a great deal of fuss but quite uneatable. The tahsildar, the cook, the peon, the smaller satellites, could all have been different forms of Miss Bates in their effort to please and being woefully foolish in their attempts. Fortunately we had Lily's sandwiches, they were excellent, yet all the sandwiches eaten at Pickwick picnics could not reconcile me to Lily's betrayal. Nor Inga's neither. But was Inga's a betrayal at all? What could she do if somebody wrote to her after I had given the address? And yet. . . .

We reached Paddy's revenue division headquarters the next day and again stayed in an Inspection Bungalow. It took us a week to move to the Sub-Collector's residence, by which time Paddy was able to arrange for a cook who used less oil and fewer spices and made sure the food did not smell suspicious. It turned out that this person was a Brahmin and this caused Paddy much difficulty later. Poor Paddy! He is the least caste-conscious Brahmin I know, but when it comes to food, he is extraordinarily fastidious. He would rather starve than eat anything smelly, over-spiced or greasy. I remember Prof. Seshu once saying, a trifle sadly, that a Brahmin's life was greatly restricted because he could eat only that which is cooked by another Brahmin or by himself. 'It is not a matter of caste,' he assured me. 'It is a question of food habits and taste. I am afraid there is such a thing as a Brahmin rasam.'

I understood this when, before we moved into the residence, I saw Paddy pushing away, meal after meal, a sambar ferocious in its colouring, a rasam reeking of garlic and vegetable curries that looked like a ship's wreckage in a sea of oil. Finally, the two of us settled for curds and rice at every meal. Paddy taught me later to make strong filter coffee. I became quite good at this, but never did master the art of rasam making.

The cook that Paddy found was efficient. I should have known right from the start that she was a Brahmin because the food was so much like what we ate at Komala Nivas. But I never thought of the caste she belonged to; that did not occur to me at all. I learnt later that she was a widow from a very poor family and had been allowed to work for us because we were Brahmins too.

However the cook's deference to us for being Brahmins was nothing as overpowering as the initial adulation offered to the Sub-Collector and 'fly'. I was never referred to as a wife, only as 'family'; written invitations were sent to

Mr Padmanabhan, IAS and 'fly'. Paddy was treated as a god and I his consort. I was only half divine, I gathered, but that status itself was so overwhelming, that I felt almost afraid. Everything we said was taken as gospel truth. I did not say much to anyone, because my Tamizh was not good enough. But Paddy's smallest murmurings, mere trifles, were considered a Declaration, never to be disregarded, not ever to be contradicted. I remember Paddy once whispering to me, while one of his clerks was looking through a file, that sometimes the journey to the district headquarters could be tiring, even though it was about thirty miles. The clerk immediately spoke up in agreement. 'Yes sir, yes. Only thirty miles, yes sir. Very, very bad journey sir.'

The next moment, Paddy, out of sheer mischief, whispered to me that the travel was comfortable, even though it was a drive of thirty miles.

'You are right sir, very much right. Thirty miles, sir, but very, very good journey sir.'

Being divine or royal, and probably both, Paddy and I had no privacy. The house was next to the office, within the same compound, so when the office was working, the house was open too. During the first weeks, I could not sit in the verandah, or near a window, because men and women came by to stare at me. Children peeped through the windows all times of the day, while the house staff stood around eternally. I could not stand or sit or read or yawn without evoking a question or a comment. Amma is tired? Amma is tired. Amma wants to see out? No, Amma wants to read. Amma reads so much no? Amma wants one other book?

In trying to cope with the trials of being the squire's lady, I had completely forgotten about the envelope that Lily had pressed into my hand as I left her. It was still in my handbag and now, three weeks later, I opened it. The envelope contained a letter from Lily and a newspaper cutting. I remember the distaste I felt as I opened Lily's letter, I was quite sure it would be about some 'profound' relationship she shared with Inga and I wanted none of that to be told to me. But the letter surprised me, the newspaper report even more.

Lily's Letter

Dear Rapa,

i know you have been deeply distressed about the great change that has come over me. It was a transformation that i have been awaiting a long time. That it happened because, thanks to you, i was enabled to express myself to somebody like Inga, is incidental. Anybody like her could have done as well. i have heard of a man who searched everywhere, and for many years, for a guru and then found his spiritual teacher in his own cook. All these years, i have lived a life of near duplicity, projecting myself as a foul-mouthed old woman with her mind always on sex and the want of it. It was a miserable time. i was like a young bride who is left behind when her husband goes to war; her consciousness is always with him, but she plays the role of an obedient daughter-in-law to perfection. i was playing a role too, that of an embittered, deprived woman. Is it not significant that many religious texts refer to the Maker as a bridegroom, a lover?

i use the small i for myself because it is only now that i also realize that my face is a tenant, my personality rented.

Enclosed is a newspaper cutting. i treasured this through the last year, reading it over and over again, cherishing its

contents. i have no need for it now, it may interest you. Do be
kind to yourself my dear. May you discover the niche that is
yours, just as every leaf finds its perfect home in this unruly
world.
    Lily

The cutting seemed to have been taken from a local
newspaper of the four-page variety. The paper was fibrous
and the printing smudgy.

MIRACLE WORK OR DUPE?
By a staff reporter

There are reports of some strange goings-on in a small
township on the outskirts of Coimbatore. The reports
indicate that there are many events of a miraculous nature
that are taking place there. Sick people have allegedly been
cured, some disabled persons are healed, and a child who
could not speak is now doing so. The sick persons who are
now well include Rajamma who had been diagnosed with
cancer of the mouth due to betel chewing, one Aziz who
suffered from acute stomach pain, Senthil who had a
damaged right leg (he is now walking albeit with a slight
limp), and a child Mary, who did not speak even at age six.
The inhabitants of the locality are attributing these so-called
miracles to the actions of a mysterious lady who seems to
appear from time to time and disappear again. The lady is
always heavily veiled and covered from head to toe in a dark
garment. However people are reported to have seen her
hands which they say are as white as a foreigner's. This staff
reporter went to the area and personally interviewed many
of the beneficiaries but was unable to sight the strange lady.

Journal

I showed Paddy the paper cutting some months later, not the letter. I handed it to him as casually as I could. But Paddy did not smile. He read through the article twice and then he said, 'May I keep this? I would like to find out a little more about it.'

He said exactly what I had wished him to say.

Letter from Inga

Dear Rapa,

Yesterday evening I got a little afraid. Mother suddenly got some breathing problem. She could not drink water. I did not know how to leave her and go for the doctor. Luckily, the next door lady, Kanaka Mami, came with the glass of sugar that she borrowed some days before. So I ran for the doctor. He was in his house and came immediately. He said it was only some stomach trouble, and he gave some tablets for gas. She is all right now. We are so lucky to have such good people here.

I hope you are learning good Tamil and hearing good concerts on radio. Tamil and Malayalam are very good languages, like English, maybe more better because they are languages of our country. You will get angry about this I know. But what harm learning more?

Inga

Journal

Since the day I gave the paper cutting to Paddy, I floated every moment in hope. It was honeyed hope mostly, but now and again, there was a lash of vinegar that burnt. For nine months and a little, I did live a life of quiet contentment. Paddy brought me books from the local library, some of which had never been opened. He was away most of the day, but late in the evenings, we sat together. Husband and wife, yet not husband and wife. Companions, friends coming close.

Through all this time, though, there was the daily anticipation that Paddy would give me news of Inga. My heart beat hard and quick, whenever I saw Paddy, for the news he might bring; I had to guard myself from showing any eagerness. All through this time, I continued to write to Inga in the old way; I gave no hint of a whisper that I might, very soon, be at her door. Her letters arrived regularly, within a couple of days. She laughed at having had to keep pace with my frequent change of address when she had stayed with the same post box for years. I could not laugh about that. Instead, I thought bitterly of that unknown reporter who did not even give a name to the place that he had visited. So close to where I was now. Where Inga hid from me.

During this time, I was struck once with a high fever, and I who had never fallen ill, had to take to bed for a week. Paddy was worried but the doctor murmured that it was 'bridal nerves', whatever that meant.

Then came news from Komala Nivas, from my mother. She spoke to Paddy at his office to say that Great Aunt Kuppai was critically ill and wished to see me. I should have known. It struck me even then but faintly, that it should have been my father who ought to have made that phone call, not my mother. But I did not have the time to think. Paddy wanted me to pack quickly, he had already arranged a car and an escort for me, and so I left. I should not have gone.

Komala Nivas was dark and silent when I arrived in the gathering gloom of a hot and humid evening. Mikhale opened the big gates and took us in, my bags, my escort and me. I noticed there was no lamp at the tulasi plant and no fragrance of incense wafting out through the open, front door. Mikhale did not say a word. I found it strange that he should enter the house and walk me straight through to Great Aunt Kuppai's inner room. There was a low light burning there, I could see my mother, a faint shadow, sitting on a stool by a bedstead and working a hand fan. She did not greet me. I stood uncertainly, then walked slowly towards the cot. A harsh voice rasped, 'Mikhale?'

It was my father. He could not make me out.

I should have known, isn't it? I should have known and I shouldn't have left the small ugly house that was the Sub-Collector's bungalow.'Twas a poor thing but mine own. And now I had been lured back into my father's lair; I had been shamefully tricked, I had been duped. When I saw it was my semen-spreading father on the bed, I turned to leave, I would go straight back, bags unopened, back to my own home. But my mother roused herself to scream at me and I found that Mikhale had disappeared.

'What I can do?' my mother shrieked. 'Your father only made me to phone. He only told me to tell that lie. He only told.'

'Lie, it was not,' my father mumbled through a storm of cough. 'She wanted to see you, called your name. Five minutes afterwards, she closed her eyes. Ayyo! Ayyo! She just went!'

The Malayalam stage lost much melodramatic bombast when my father decided to wear the Gandhi topi. What an actor my begetter was! There was not a tear in his eyes save what his coughing brought on and yet he mourned and wailed his mourning as if his heart would break. So Great Aunt Kuppai was gone. I had come for nothing.

'You we wanted to phone,' my mother said in a high-pitched voice, nervousness in every word of her lie, 'but your father only said . . .'

'Why disturb?' my father cut in. 'What she can do now when all is over?' He began sobbing loudly again.

'Small ceremony only we held,' my mother continued, like a Greek chorus learning its lines. 'Even thirteenth day we gave rice and bananas to temple. Just did shaanti poojai here.'

'Purification of house,' my father explained. 'I only did everything. Your brothers did not even show their heads.'

The Greek chorus was silent.

'All they want is money,' the chief actor spluttered on. 'Money. Money. Money. The second fellow also appeared. His share he wanted. Everything. They have both looted me. Looted.' His wails began, whether for Great Aunt Kuppai, or for the perfidy of his sons, or his lost wealth, I could not tell.

'Your father is destroyed Rapa,' he wailed, now in English. 'He has nothing! His sons have crushed him beneath their feet! You see a ruin of a man Rapa! What I was. What I have become! Your father is a Shakespeare tragedy Rapa! Hamlet or Macbeth.'

'Lear,' I told him.

'Yes. Yes. King Lear. Yes. You see before you,' he was sobbing now, 'King Lear!'

The Greek chorus intruded suddenly, 'Your sons are good boys. Surely, they will come back, you go on seeing.'

'They are rascals,' King Lear mumbled. 'Rogues. Rascals. Give the girl some food.' He turned over and fell silent.

Rukku Paati grumbled like a coffee grinder as she served me rice and curds. She had obviously been lying down on Great Aunt Kuppai's long swing and did not relish my arrival. My mother came to speak to me as I was washing my hands in the back verandah. 'In the west room you can sleep for today,' she said. 'Tomorrow, your father will use office room.'

'Tomorrow, I leave,' I told her. 'I am going back.'

'Go back?' my mother asked. 'Where you will go?"

I remember I was rinsing my mouth at the time; as I spat out the water, I wanted to say, 'To my lawfully wedlocked husband', when she said sharply, 'Your mother-in-law is going to be there'. I stared at her, my mouth empty of water and words.

'Your father wrote no, to say we called you. She should also know where where you are going.'

I had fallen into a trap, a devilish trap of my father's contrivance. I cursed him then, and every moment of every day thereafter. That is when he began to rot like a mangled pumpkin, a banana pulped by the anger of all those he had humiliated and destroyed. And yet, I did not know then of the greatest crime of all, his most monstrous sin.

That night I fell ill again, with a high fever and sweating. I was in bed for ten days.

Letter from Inga

Dear Rapa,
This is to inform you that my mother passed away when she
was sleeping yesterday night. I sent wire to Komala Nivas and
Brother One. Somebody of them will inform your mother.
  Inga

Journal

Paru gave me this letter after I got better. I had told Inga
that I was going to Komala Nivas, but I do not know who
informed my mother of her sister's death. I certainly didn't.
She said nothing to me, but I knew she knew when I saw her
unguarded face one morning, a few days after I had got
Inga's letter. There was triumph there but there was also a
faint flicker of fear as if somebody had whispered to her
from beyond the unkempt hedge of the everyday. I saw this
face only for a moment, then she saw me and in an instant,
she was again the ex-MP's Wife of Comely Aspect, Dispenser
of Comfort to him and his Sons, and Co-Sufferer.

The suffering was mine; my mother had not the faintest
notion of what I was going through. It was many weeks
before I could get a night of rest, my aunt's face loomed over
my pillow, Inga cried into my face and sobbed in my ears. I
tried to gather her into my arms, I murmured words - no,
not words but sounds - of comfort but I opened my eyes
always to a lumped up pillow snuggled close to me, inert
and damp. I had a fever most nights, my sweat, when the
fever broke, smelt ill. I felt stronger during the day, I wrote
to Inga, begging her to give me her address, just a hint of

where she lived. Please Inga, please. Tell me. I want to be with you. I don't want you to be alone. Please. I wrote every day, I spent recklessly on postage, I went across to Paru with none of my customary caution, she caught my worry but had no help to give. My mother waylaid me more than once but I wriggled out of her interrogation almost always with rank incivility. I did not care for her suspicions.

Inga did not write. There was not a word from her. I was wild with worry. My mind filled darkly with the most inauspicious of thoughts. Was she paralyzed with grief? Was she ill? Or much worse, was somebody else comforting her? Lily? Or may be . . . may be Paddy? He might have located her, not told me, and then . . . The bile surged up into my throat as I imagined them meeting. Paddy and Inga. Inga and Paddy! My Inga! You are mine, Inga. You belong to me. Remember that! Oh god Inga!

In my desperation I felt it may not be too imprudent to write to Brother One for news of her. They would surely have been informed of her mother's death, a postcard would have been sent as is usually done; such a message would have come to my mother too. The community was very particular of being told of deaths, they would have to observe periods of ritualistic mourning, not go to the temple, be available for condolence visits, specially on Thursdays and Sundays. . . . Of course, there would be talk of Great Aunt Kuppai having called my aunt to her, since the two deaths occurred so close to each other. So talking to Brother One might help. However, I could not telephone him even if I had had his number, which I didn't, because my father had taken to locking the telephone as an 'austerity' measure.

In any case, it was better to send a letter, a telephone call gave the matter a sense of urgency, which I did not want. A letter could amble along and bring in an inquiry about Inga as a casual question. But how was I to get Brother One's address? Ask my mother for it? When I thought of the consequences of such an action, my blood ran cold. Everything would be discovered. My bags would be searched, the locks smashed, my diary, Inga's letters, all ruthlessly exposed.

No. I could not ask my mother for the address, I could not take the risk. I would suffer the silence and the wait. In the meanwhile, I snooped around for abandoned letters, for envelopes that, perchance, carried the sender's address, and eavesdropped on conversations, telephonic and otherwise. I learnt nothing. I was only certain that my mother was in clandestine contact with her beloved stepsons, Brothers One and Two. My mother behaved as if all the grief she had was for my father's illness, his fall from power and his loss of wealth. She had no sister to mourn for, no bereavement save that of a tyrannical aunt-in-law, who, at the point of death, had heaped the final insult of asking for me.

That was not all. I soon found out why I had summarily been called to Komala Nivas. One morning, Mikhale told me that my father wanted to see me. It was clearly an order. When I appeared at his bedside, he was sitting up, with a notepad and a pen beside him. Mother was standing in her handmaiden pose by him.

'You, girl,' he barked in English. 'Write here on this paper that Komala Nivas belongs to me, to Krishnan Iyer.'

I stared at him. So Inga was right. Komala Nivas was mine.

'Why should I?'

'You do not need this house,' he burst out in anger. 'I got you married to a big Collector. For what?'

I turned and walked out of the room.

A month and five days after her last letter, Inga wrote. In this time, Paddy had written, brief notes about his work, and had mentioned that he was trying to get his mother to return to Madras. But he had not come to see me.

Letter from Inga

Dear Rapa,

Please forgive me for not replying for so many days. I collected all your letters and thought I will write, I will write but was not able to. Many things have happened. But do not worry. I am perfectly all right.

What has happened is I have got a clerk's position in the office of Bhagavati temple which I always used to visit along with Mother. The temple has also given me a small one room kitchen quite near to it. There is no rent because the room belongs to the temple only. The work is quite easy, writing daily accounts etc. and when I have periods I do not have to go for three days. With the temple salary I am getting, I am quite all right. Yesterday, I bought a sari, a red sari with small checks. It is the first sari that I have bought, otherwise I wear Mother's old saris.

I also want to start music classes for small children. The temple people say they will give me a room in the outside compound. That will be nice.

Hope you are well.

Inga

19

Journal

I had to read Inga's letter over and over again to take it in. This was not the letter I had expected. Where was any sorrow for a dead mother, any morsel of fear for suddenly being left alone? Did she not know she was now an orphan? So young and so tender. These were my thoughts then, as I held her letter in my hands – there was not a creature in the world she could turn to, nobody at all to offer her solace, to manage her affairs. Did she not realize that I was the only one who would take charge of her, be her guardian, her . . . her friend? Her companion. Her fellow traveller. I would be the other that walked beside her, hold her close through shallows and deeps, over formidables, around marshes of helplessness, to arrive at last, to the glad light on the bank where the honeysuckle blooms. And there, Inga and I shall . . . But then my thoughts jerked to a stop. Was Inga not alone, not as helpless as she ought to have been? Her letter was that of a giddy girl, giggling with somebody equally silly. So was there somebody else? Somebody else more important, more close than I was. Lily? Had she found out where Inga lived? And met her? I had pleaded with Inga, several times, to tell me where she was, so I could share her mourning, settle her living arrangements, move in with her. But Inga had never answered that part of my letters, not even if they comprised just that one question. Where in a maze of unpronounceable names of townships and villages could I find Inga?

Lily was clever. She would have found a way. She knew more about this part of the world than I did, she would have asked anyone who could help, perhaps the local government officials, perhaps . . . Then my mind gave a sickening jolt.

Had Paddy found Inga? And not told me?

Letter from Inga

Dear Rapa,

Why are you writing like this? Yes, I have many people who are looking after me quite nicely. The priests, especially the old priest, the manager maama who does puja on Sunday and public holidays, neighbours from our earlier house. Many people who visit the temple even otherwise, come to talk to me. I feel so nice at that time. Their name, house number and all I do not know, but they say nice things and their children sit on my lap. You think I do not think of my mother? She is always inside my mind like a flower sleeping. That is why I did not cry after the first day. That is why I am not at all afraid or sad.

I think maybe you are angry because you are worried about me. Please do not be. I am very much fine.

Inga

Journal

My anger diminished a little but my suspicions did not abate. How much did I know of Lily? Or of Paddy? Lily was a clever woman, she was capable of engineering things, of manipulation, to get what she wanted. And Paddy? He was more difficult to define. Was he also adept at disguise and deceit, as I was sure Lily was? Disguise and deceit. I saw them always as being connected. Was I wrong?

Then came a brief call from Paddy to ask how I was and when I asked about him, all he said was, 'Remember the Chancery fog in *Bleak House*? That is where I am at present. I'll write to you tonight.' I did remember Dickens' description of the fog, and recollected vividly a winter morning in Delhi when Inga and I crossed a road swathed in white mist, to catch our school buses. We need not have done it at all, because the buses did not appear. I remember how Inga giggled and how small her hand felt in mine and how the fog climbed into my nose, smelling of peppermint and petrol. Half an hour after we returned home to my very anxious aunt, the fog had cleared. Quite unlike Dickens' fog which lay up the river and down the river and all around it, like a white swirling curse.

The letter from Paddy arrived three days later. It was a letter written hurriedly by a very tired man and I realized how thick and unhealthy the fog was. Paddy had been accused by a local political leader, the MLA, of being pro-Brahmin, of protecting Brahmin interests, of even having employed a Brahmin cook. 'I had refused this man the use of the official jeep for private purposes,' Paddy wrote, 'and since then, he has been extremely hostile. The situation got worse when my mother came to stay, she was a little highhanded with some of the staff. It is possible that I shall be called to Madras to push files. This would be disheartening because I have begun work on bringing electricity and drinking water to some of the Harijan villages in my division, and I would like to have seen that completed. But the fog is heavy and clammy on me. What am I to do? I certainly did not ask to be born into a Brahmin family. This entire caste business is deplorable and all of us are forced to bear the cross of history, that of using a man's caste as a bloody weapon against him.'

I had never seen Paddy this angry, though it was possible that he had used the word 'bloody' in its literal sense. Nevertheless, it was all baffling. Here were my parents and others of their ilk, who treasured their Brahminism as if it was a high award, a medal for good behaviour in past lives, and then there was Paddy who saw it as a sword poised against him. There was Lily who squashed it out of her life, and then there was Inga. And me.

In a postscript, he added, 'I am sorry I have not been able to trace the journalist who wrote that piece. Let me see if I can, in the next couple of days. I had told one of my office boys but I have not been able to follow up the matter. Sorry about this.'

I read Paddy's letter more than once, like I had Inga's. There was nothing in what he wrote that aroused suspicion and yet . . . Then curiously, my mind travelled across and towards what we had all inherited, Inga, Lily, Paddy and I. I suddenly found it all absurd, And so very childish.

A is for animal
B brands it Brahmin
C canonizes it
D damns it
E examines it
F frames it

G garners it
H hides it
I indicts it
J jibes at it
K kisses it
L lampoons it
M moans for it
N nips it
O oblates it
P pampers it
Q quakes before it
R ravages it
S spays it
T taxes it
U ulcerates it
V vindicates it
W worships it
Y yawns.
Others have learnt the alphabet in a different way
A is for apple
B bakes it
C craves for it
D is devilish about it
Eve with Adam eats it all up.

Letter from Inga

Dear Rapa,

It was so nice to see your poem. It was nice. Funny also. But why did you tell not about X and Z? X can be for X-ray, no? Z has no doing word I think.

I am not any more staying in that same room given by the temple. It was very noisy and people going to the temple kept coming to my place also. Now I am staying in outhouse of a big house where there is just one old man and his servant and servant's wife. I can make out that you are worried about me. You want me to tell you about my home? There is very big garden with many trees and flowers. Every day I take flowers from here only, for the temple. Because of so many trees, nobody can even see there is outhouse here. The big champaka tree I can see from the kitchen, and can smell the flowers. Some people are saying that there are yakshis living in champaka trees but I have not seen even one. It is so so safe, I even keep the back door open many times and nothing happens. At night only, I lock it.

Just fifteen days before, one new manager came. He is all right till now. Hope you are all right.

Inga

Journal

I did not realize how important this letter from Inga was, but even when I received it, I found it unusual. Inga had said much more about herself than she had ever done before. I had not understood her need for such iron privacy, almost a secretiveness, particularly with me. Was she freeing herself of this burden at last? Now that her mother was dead, would she be less hidden, less reserved? Less private? Would she now tell me where she lived? Allow me to see her and . . .? It was a prospect that made my feverish nights bearable; I had had another bout of fever that kept me awake. But these were passing things and I did not bother to say anything to my mother and father. I hardly spoke to them now, my father's growing blindness had made him ungovernable, my mother had ascended to being a Brahmin Florence Nightingale. She wore the habiliments well – the soft voice, the occasional sigh, the sari tight around her breasts and hips, 'so many medicine bottles, I have to be careful no?' And of course, the head bent sideways as she ate to show grief, fatigue and unconcern for her own welfare. Her audience was sparse. Rukku Paati went about declaring that destiny and daughters were to be condemned for selfishness and emitted dry sobs whenever she saw my mother. Paru, who was now allowed into the house, did not show much sympathy for anyone, but clearly enjoyed the authority she held in Komala Nivas over man, woman and beast. Rukku Paati and the cows alike were to take orders only from her. As for Mikhale, his suffering was muted but very visible, and I could see that it was on account of his master, not for my mother.

But none of them was a friend to me.

Then, the very next day, came another letter from Inga with some startling news.

Letter from Inga

Dear Rapa,
I got a letter from Lily Aunty yesterday after a long time. She is wanting to go to some ashram for a few days, just to see. She has found a place somewhere far away. I think it will be good for her.
Inga

Journal

Shortly after I received Inga's letter, I heard from Paddy. He first gave me the news that he was not to be transferred after all. He wrote, 'I could sense a wave of support for me from the citizenry. I have heard that some people even went to Madras to speak to the Chief Minister. The MLA has received a letter from the CM advising him to desist from making allegations of a personal nature against honest and hardworking officers. His office has sent a copy of the letter to me. It says, "IAS officers are not born. They are made. You must realize that the officer has been doing his duty well and should receive your support." I can now work in peace. I am also mightily relieved that I managed to send Amma home, finally. She has an unfortunate Brahminical way with her, and, I suspect, was also glorying in the status of being an IAS mother. It seems to me, that the mothers and wives of IAS officers feel their positions much more keenly than do the officers themselves. Thank the good Lord you are different, so rare.

Before I close, I have to give you some news about Lily. My father has written to say that Lily has left her house and properties to the Trust she had started, and appointed him sole trustee to manage the affairs of the school. She has gone on a retreat for a fortnight to consider her future. A life of renunciation perhaps? She sends her affectionate regards to you and prays for your speedy recovery. Something tells me that she will not return to Pondicherry and to her old world. My father's life is also changed, he is often away from Madras.

When can I come to bring you back home? Do let me know.'

Paddy's postscript said, 'I have lost the trail of our reporter, I am told he has moved to Bombay with his family. I am sorry, my chaps were not of much use. Stay well.'

My unhappy thoughts about Inga evaporated as I absorbed the contents of the letters. I was fiercely glad that Paddy's position had been vindicated; nothing is more unforgivable than being punished for one's birth. Can anyone be untouchable? Because he is of a 'lower' order, do you deny him his talent? Is a man to be condemned because he is born a Brahmin? Is his work to be counted for nothing? Am I to live without grace because I am a woman? And yet, despite what I write, I feel myself untouchable. I am to be shunned. I am not fit for grace.

However, at the time, when I read the news of Lily's renunciation, I was hugely relieved. She had assumed the shape of a formidable rival, almost a foe, but now she was gone. Inga was safe. She was safe, safe from other attentions, safely mine. We could never be divided or torn asunder. We were rivers that met and merged, we translated into the same map.

~

KOMALA PARK

Shri Kittu Ayer had been long settled in the district of Kulam. His estate was large and his principal seat was Komala Park. By a former marriage, he had two sons of unsteady character and by his present wife, a daughter, with an elegance of mind and a sweetness of temper whose true value he did not comprehend. Shri Kittu was a lawyer who for his edification never took up any papers except his horoscope. There, he found a satisfaction in reading his own history that never failed to delight him . . .

Notes:

How do I continue? Find out more about ancestral roots? Where did Tamizh-speaking Brahmins come from originally, before settling down in Kerala? Why did they move? For better employment? For safety? Were they persecuted? (How do I get all this information? Prof. Seshu? Paddy's father?)

Can I sustain the Austen style? It seems suitable now but if I discover blood and gore in the family's history, how will I maintain Austenesque gentility? How will I cope with sex? By implication alone? Austen's married men seem to have stayed faithful to their wives. My father has had several mistresses, perhaps his father did too. How do I bring this in? What would the vocabulary be? The word 'mistress' had a different meaning then; shall I use 'his keep'? Ugh! What would the plural be anyway?

May have to abandon Miss Austen. What do I do now?

Journal

I was mulling over how I was to continue with this rather mischievous piece of writing, when I heard a huge commotion below stairs. It seemed to be coming from the direction of my father's sick room and was made up of screams and shrieks and sobs in several female voices. Rukku Paati. Paru. My mother. My father had probably hurled indescribable words of abuse at them. He had lately taken to showing off his extensive vocabulary of foul language, most of which targeted women, legendary, historical, fantastical, those alive around him in the present time. It was a comprehensive list and would have impressed any social historian.

'That Panchali,' I had heard him yell, 'she needed five men to satisfy her. All at one time. Five. All soldiers with strong thighs and big instruments. Is that fool of a girl hearing? All of you, you hear, all of you want only that one thing. All sluts. Whores. That Meenu! You think her half-man husband Dorai can do anything? That fool. She . . .' He burst into loud weeping. 'She took my riches away, my bhagyam. My goddess. Ayyo! Ayyo! Meenu plundered my house. Her hands should rot. Her breasts should be . . .'

The din this time too, I thought, was a similar rant, and perhaps specifically aimed at the three women attending to him. I ignored the high noise and went back to my writing. I had barely written half a sentence, when I heard someone call up to me quietly from the foot of the stairs. I peered down. It was Mikhale.

'Molay,' he said in a voice thickened by tears, 'child, it is your father.'

He was not dead, my begetter. He lay stretched on the bed, in a grotesque imitation of da Vinci's sketch of the Vitruvian Man, his eyes open and staring without purpose, his breath harsh and rattling like a frenzy of stones in a tin can. The room stank. My mother had thrown herself on the floor and was wailing like a banshee, Paru, sobbing, was trying to calm her and Rukku Paati who could hear nothing, was holding a steel glass, shaking the side of the bed and screaming, 'Kitta! Get up! Get up! Some rasam I have made. Taste and see. Come! Get up!' Nobody took any notice of me. I came out of the room to where Mikhale stood, his face streaked with tears. I asked him to send word to the doctor and to Brother One. 'Doctor is coming just now,' he told me. 'This morning only, Amma said to Elder Brother to come. She was feeling somewhat about him from today morning. But molay, what about our Collector sahib?'

I booked a trunk call to Paddy's office number. As usual, I was told by the telephone exchange to wait. I could not get away upstairs to my books. I sat on the hard chair near the telephone, hating the wait, hating what the day was to bring. Mikhale stood next to me, whether as protection, or to prevent my escaping, I could not tell. The telephone was in the front hall, placed on a table close to the famous window. This was where Inga and Brother One had stood, holding Goblin up to the open-mouthed crowd in the courtyard as if she were some kind of an infant pope. Now, through the same window, I saw to my astonishment, a stream of people coming into the house. I found I was expected to greet them while displaying great grief at the same time. Many were neighbours, some were relatives, some both, but there also were a great many who seemed to be tradespeople and kitchen maids. I did not notice any of my father's party workers. I supposed they would only appear when he was properly dead and someone high up sent them with wreaths. How the groups streaming in had heard the news I did not know, but I could see that they had come prepared to exhibit grief. Their sari and dhoti ends were ready to sponge off quantities of tears when required, but till then, their eyes darted about, taking in every detail of the scene and of the main actors. These were tattlers, gossips; they would prattle of this day as the Goblin watchers did years ago. Fortunately, this lot seemed to have forgotten that earlier piece of absurd drama. Suddenly, however, an old woman, who was leaving after she had had her view, stopped and looked towards the self same window. 'O! O!' she wailed. 'My Bhagavati! My little Devi! You I saw from that window! You made my legs to walk. O Bhagavati, why you went? Wretchedness has come to this house! Why you went away Devi?'

Immediately there was a babble of voices. 'Yes. Her son only carried her that time . . . My aunty also same thing happened . . . Remember that old school maasha? Like stone his ears were. He did not have belief. But he came for some other work and saw Bhagavati Molu. After that everything he is hearing . . . But now . . . the bhagyam, the luck of this house is all gone . . . Yes. All is gone . . . That holy face, we cannot see any more . . .'

A slightly scornful young voice piped up in the middle of this moaning drivel. 'Why they did not keep photo of that baby?'

Mikhale turned to me abruptly and asked, 'Photo of Inga mol you have got molay?'

I stared at him. The phone rang. It cut through any reaction. It splintered all conjecture. For that moment.

I did not need to explain the situation to Paddy; he could hear the bedlam in the background. Perhaps, he heard the strain in my voice too, though he would not have known the reason for this. He spoke briefly and succinctly, saying he would set out as soon as he could. 'And Rapa,' he added, before he rang off, 'do please stay well.'

I put the phone down and turned to Mikhale. He had gone.

It was then I noticed that a hush had fallen on the crowd, broken by a few whispers and murmurs. I caught the word 'doctor'. I pushed past those still standing around, and made my way to the stinking sick room. Mikhale was at the bedside, rolling up his master's vest, as a tall thin man with bony wrists placed his stethoscope on the chest. He then peered into the eyes and looked grave. Then he said in Malayalam, to no one in particular, 'Let him stay at home only. That is better.' Right on cue, my mother let out a long wail, followed by Rukku Paati, who dropped the glass of rasam that she had been holding and began banging her head on the wall nearest her. The doctor put away his stethoscope and left without another word. I did not detain him. Mikhale went out too, stumbling like a blind man. I followed, calling out to him but he heard and saw nothing as he suddenly picked up speed and ran to the gate, and out of the house. I had to stop where I was. The crowd broke its hush and started a loud, mournful dirge.

Strangely, but perhaps not so strange, it was Paru who took over command. She shushed my mother, made her take a sip of water, then stopped Rukku Paati from further damaging the wall, and made her clean up the mess of rice and rasam on the floor. She went out to the moaning crowd and requested them to leave. 'Nothing you can do now,' she said crisply. 'Bhagavati's will it is. Show kindness and go. For him, send up prayers. Go now.'

They did. The house quietened. I asked Paru, 'Mikhale, where is he?'

She treated my question with some disdain. 'To church he will go now. Where else?'

The day wore on painfully. The effigy on the bed breathed on like a ticking clock that had run out of correct time. There was nobody there on the bed, no former Member of Parliament, no landlord, no paramour, nothing but a stuffed, inefficient scarecrow that needed to be fed and cleaned and attended to. I went back to the attic but I was unable to write, no book could hold my attention either. I went through Inga's letters as I had done many times over but it brought no relief. When it grew dark, I went down to light the lamp and the incense sticks in the puja room but did not bother about the basil outside. When I stepped out of the puja room, I found Paru and Rukku Paati at the door of the kitchen, whispering to each other like conspirators; Paru having to speak right into Rukku Patti's better ear. They beckoned to me. 'Paru will sit there,' Rukku Paati whispered, as if the house had been surrounded by the Gestapo. 'You your mother bring here. Her face and hands she must wash, then she must tell prayers. Then eat. You also.'

It was a strange time of waiting. We ate, my mother, Rukku Paati and I, sitting near the kitchen in the dimly lit inner hall. There was no conversation, but Rukku Paati showed a gentleness I had never before seen. My mother was subdued, compliant and allowed this new aspect to flow over her. I could hear Paru's voice from the sick room, softly chanting, 'Narayana. Narayana'. The perfume from the incense sticks I had lit still lingered; was a setting for peace but of that there was none. We were like the Micawbers dreading the creditor's thunderous door knock. Like a poor scholar, hating the prospect of the post bringing examination results, certain of their inevitability. Komala Nivas was expecting a sinister visitor.

20

How does one wait for death? What does one do while waiting? Carry on the same daily tasks? Bathe, cook, eat? Bring the washing in when rain threatens? Read a book? Hold up a mirror to one's face? Write a letter, a diary entry? Death provides no calendar, no timetable, no clock to consult. No doctor, no acclaimed astrologer can say when it might come calling. Whatever mankind may do to bring about method, order, regulation, and use the astounding logic of mathematics, death will not obey. Death is most ungovernable, unmethodical, unruly, unreasonable. Death mocks.

It jeers.

Brother One arrived with his wife and brat, sometime after midnight. I had been unable to sleep, I wanted to wait up for Mikhale but was persuaded by Paru to try and rest for a few minutes. I did try but while I could keep my eyes closed, I could not, my mind. I felt the fever come on again, I saw Inga and Mikhale, each with a shimmering halo. But Mikhale also had a pair of horns under his halo and a long, hairy tail behind him. Suddenly, Inga pulled her halo off and flung it over my head, as if she were playing hoopla, and I was the prize she had won. Then she laughed. Her laughter echoed through me and woke me up. I thought she was in the room. Of course, she was not. It was Brother One's brat. He was bawling and his mother, equally loudly, trying to pacify him. But as my mind woke up fully, I realized it was not these two alone disturbing the night. My mother had started her shrill dirge again, alongside a high-pitched wailing from Rukku Paati. I heard Brother One say loudly, over the din, 'Why I should come? This house is my house or what? No. It is for that wretched girl. Let her itself do everything. Why I should?' I heard somebody, perhaps it was Paru, trying to quieten him. The curtain had risen for the last act.

I was wrong, Death mocked again, it was not the last act. My tyrant father's fondness for theatre made him stay centre stage. He kept death waiting at the door as he would have done to all those who came to him for help. Or for recompense. He lay there, hour upon hour, heavy, uncouth, smelly. Two men were engaged to clean him, not even Paru could turn him over. My mother sat at his bedside, Rukku Paati fed him, spoon after spoon. He dribbled but he also swallowed. So he went on, all day, securing all attention to himself, keeping everyone in suspense, waiting.

Komala Nivas continued to have visitors through the morning, as Sister-in-law One took over as official hostess. The Brat was stuffed with chocolates, and sent off with his nursemaid, a small, hollow-eyed girl, to a neighbouring relative's house with a thousand instructions from the mother. She seemed to think that every natural disaster, and all manner of kidnappers, dacoits and poisoners were lying in wait to harm her precious offspring. The Brat and his starved caretaker being sent off, she assumed the role she had been assigned, certainly by my mother. She did her duty admirably, with just the right tone of hush in her voice, a perfect angle to the downcast eyes and head, the occasional, barely audible sob. When she had to carry my mother's instructions to Rukku Paati, she did so near the cowshed and seemed to do it so well that kitchen operations ran smoothly all day. Visitors she discouraged sweetly, and relatives she sent away with reassuring promises of 'we will inform immediately'. Within hours, she cleared Komala Nivas of everything except her husband's loud and oft expressed bitterness.

In the evening, even as the house gradually became private and quiet again, my mother broke into a new line of martyrdom. Suddenly, I heard her say, from the sick room, in a deep, guttural voice, as if she were drugged, 'She only did this. She only is killing him off.'

For a moment, I thought she was referring to me. But she added, as if in a trance, like a psychic medium. 'She came. Two days before. He was all right. But she put her eyes on him. She put her eyes.' Then her style changed dramatically and she screamed, 'She put her eyes. She put her eyes. He was all right. She put her . . .' At this point, when she could have named a name, my mother decided to cheat. She fainted.

I heard whisperings and murmurings in the sick room and then Brother One's loud command to his wife to take my mother away. 'This is the time to be saying these things?' I heard him say. 'That woman to talk about?' I wondered what he knew that I didn't. Who was 'that woman'? I didn't have long to wait for the answer. I had always trusted Komala Nivas to give up its secrets to me. I trusted the house as a friend, like a candle relies on the wick to burn, like a gun an honest trigger. I knew Komala Nivas, in the manner of a master thief. I knew where the darkest corners were, where the most hidden of hiding places lay, where the night slept through the day. So it was not very long after Brother One's admonition to my mother, that I heard him and Sister-in-law One holding a low-voiced conversation, in the alcove next to the well. I was in the storage room opposite the well and could hear them clearly.

'Our child is happily sleeping,' Sister-in-law One said, with a trace of jealousy. 'Even once he did not call me it seems. Children become big so suddenly no?'

Brother One grunted. He did not show any interest in the Brat; my father would doubtless have said his son's mind was on some particular pair of female breasts.

Sister-in-law One sunk her voice. 'That woman your mother said about is who?' she asked. 'After I left for my delivery?'

'She is girls' school headmistress,' Brother One replied irritably, not exactly whispering.

'Ayyo!' his wife exclaimed with relish. 'She was always coming here. So much and all she was talking to your mother.'

'Yes, yes. But she was also going to my father.'

'I did not know at all,' whispered Sister-in-law One with great enjoyment. Then bringing her voice down to a subterranean level, she asked, 'But why your mother tell this woman put black magic on him?'

'You both are stupids,' he rasped. 'You both have no ears or what? All people in this place know. His body she was rubbing with some oil. All parts of body. This oil, some ayurvedam oil, it seems makes the body to go weaker and weaker. Lastly, there is death.'

'But why?' was Sister-in-law One's next question. 'He was giving everything to her no? Good money.' She was astute, this Sister-in-law One.

'Yes. Yes. Gold ornaments. Money. Coconuts. He was giving donation to that school also. There is a stone in that building with his name.'

'She was getting all this, then why she did this?'

Yes, why?

Brother One took a moment to answer. In the silence, I heard a car driving up the lane.

'It seems she was wanting this house – Komala Nivas.'

The car stopped. There was an impatient rattling at the gate, I heard Paru's voice, then the loud wailing of the Mistress of Keening. FishEyes had arrived. In full armour.

I kept to my room, my head on the pillow, while the hubbub mounted. There was more wailing, more howling, more pleading with the live corpse to get up and out of his sleep, to become 'my beloved anna' again. More stage scripts. More histrionics.

I waited desperately for release, for Paddy.

Paddy arrived as dawn was breaking, a few minutes before Prof. Seshu. He had taken a day to come via Madras, so as to bring his father with him. His mother had preferred to be too unwell to leave home. When I heard Paddy's voice at the front door, I wiped my face dry and ran out. I almost bumped into Brother One. 'O, I see!' he hissed. 'Well enough you are to meet your husband. Your Collector husband!'

I pushed past him. I flew down the steps into the half light of the courtyard, and towards Paddy. I think my father-in-law said something but I did not heed him. Paddy said, 'You are not well.' He dropped his bag and held out his arms. I ran into his hug, put my head on his shoulder and burst into tears. In doing so, I broke nearly all the rules in the Brahmin Women's Book of Decorum.

THE BOOK OF DECORUM FOR BRAHMIN WOMEN

1. You shall not go past your Elders without stopping to greet them. You shall touch your head to the ground before them wherever they may be standing.

2. You shall not greet your Husband with a smile or anything of a similar nature, in public. You shall always stand behind him, to his left, in silence.

3. You shall never, never address your Husband by his Name either in private or in public. His Name is Sacred and not for your use.

4. You shall never, never, never make any physical contact with your Husband either in public or in private. In the Private chamber, the Husband shall initiate physical intimacy.

5. You shall never, never, never display private emotion in public and seek sympathy from any Male, including your Husband.

6. You shall not give expression to any form of pain, especially during childbirth.

7. You shall not sneeze or cough in public.

8. You shall not laugh in public. In the privacy of the bedchamber, you are to laugh moderately in the presence of your Husband.

9. You shall not wear flowers loosely in your hair. Flower strings have to be fixed firmly to the hair plait.

10. You shall not have knowledge of matters more than your Husband.

11. You shall not discuss matters pertaining to your sex with anybody other than your mother or sister. In their absence, you shall bring up such matters with your sister-in-law. Provided she is married.

12. You shall, at all times, remain quiet, submissive and obedient. The mark of a true Brahmin woman is her ability to suffer in secret.

Additional rules shall be imposed as and when they are found necessary. Women who faithfully observe these abovementioned regulations will be endowed with wealth, their cattle will increase and the coconuts will be tender. Such women will be blessed with male progeny and their Husbands shall rise and call them virtuous.

Nobody had anything to say, not my father-in-law, not Prof. Seshu. They gathered around the bed where lay the Vitruvian Scarecrow, looked at him, looked away and went out as silently as they had gone in. In the front hall, FishEyes rolled up and down the length of the room, moaning and mouthing inarticulate sounds. When she found that the men paid no attention and walked past her, she sat up, patted down her hair and demanded a glass of thick, hot coffee.

Paddy refused to let me stay on in Komala Nivas. A few hours after he arrived and after the obligatory bath and tiffin, he told my brother that he was taking me away. They were standing in the side courtyard, close to the window of my room and away from other listening ears.

'She is not well,' I heard Paddy say in English. Then abruptly switching to Tamizh, he continued, 'Immediately, to doctor I have to take her.'

My brother's reply was rough and resentful. "What you think?" he said in English. 'You think I am not knowing this stupid foreign language? You are Collector no? Then speak like one Collector only.'

I could almost hear Paddy's temper rear up, he the most gentlest of creatures. I waited, holding my breath. Then suddenly, there was. Prof. Seshu's voice. 'What is it, my boy?'

It was Paddy who answered. 'I was saying that I want to take Rapa back with me today, if possible. She is not looking at all well, she has a high fever.'

'Then she must see a doctor at once,' replied the professor. 'Shall I send for the local man?'

'Local man and all our Collector does not have trust in,' Brother One sneered. 'District surgeon only must see.'

Paddy said quietly, 'I am worried about her. She has been getting these bouts of fever intermittently and she is losing weight.'

There was a small silence. Then I heard the professor say, 'Then of course you must take her away as soon as you can. You will take her to a specialist, am I right?'

'Yes. May I take her away right now?'

I could not hear the professor's reply because Brother

One cut in. 'Why you should ask me? This house is owned by her only. What she likes she can do.'

'I better leave,' I heard Paddy say.

Prof. Seshu suddenly spoke in a tone I had never heard him use; it was a knife-tone, sharp and serrated. 'Look Ambi,' he said to Brother One in crisp English. 'This house was built by your father. He did not inherit it; it is not ancestral property. Your father gifted it to his aunt Kuppai, a childless widow; she, in turn, left it in her will to Rapa. You have already taken what is due to you and a considerable amount it is too. How much more do you want?'

'That useless brother I have, he also got one share,' muttered Brother One. 'And because my father wanted some Collector to come as his son-in-law, so this house went to that wretched girl. You think I have no knowledge of that? I also have some brain.'

'What did you say?' I heard Paddy's voice. High. Enraged. I heard what seemed to be some kind of scuffle, several voices saying, 'Let it be . . . Professor . . . Maashe . . . let him go . . . this is house with sick man . . .' And over them, Brother One shouting, 'Your mother you ask what what dowry she got. Ask. Collector you are, you fool, you . . .'

I began to pack my things.

Paddy, his father and I left that afternoon. There was no opposition to my leaving, not from my mother of course, not even from Rukku Paati. The professor had obviously spoken to them. He had his arm around me when I went to tell my mother I was leaving. She was sitting with FishEyes, very subdued. Neither spoke to me. I went out and as I reached the gate, Paru came running to me. 'Molay,' she said, her face wet, 'Enday molay, my child what I am hearing?'

Paddy took me gently away. He and I, with Paddy's father, got into the car. As we began to move, I looked back. Paru was standing on the steps, weeping, as I had seen Great Aunt Kuppai weep, just a year ago.

I did not realize it then but I know now that I will never see Komala Nivas again.

I remember, as we drove away, how ragged Paddy looked, ragged and weary. He spoke little. His father tried to make conversation and, at one point, said, 'It will be all right, kanna. It will all be all right. God is there.'

A day later, I was taken to a specialist in Coimbatore. He examined me, took tests, asked me questions. He did not need to tell me what he feared. I could read it on his face.

After such knowledge, what forgiveness?

Letter from Inga

Dear Rapa,

What has happened? This address you are giving me is again c/o Paddy Anna. Why you are not in Komala Nivas still? Brother One said something to Paddy Anna? Please do not feel bad about that. Some people keep anger in their nose and have a wrong way of talking. Afterwards they feel bad. Brother One is somewhat like that only. Please tell Paddy Anna also this. Anyway, it is good you are with him. You can go to Komala Nivas when Brother One is not there.

I am all right. But this new manager in the temple is doing some wrong things I feel. Every day some money from what *people put in the hundi is not there. I count that money every evening after the temple has closed, write the total in one my register and I put that amount in a bag and give him. Next morning he is supposed to put in the temple's bank account. Now I am seeing that what money should be in the account is lesser. This is happening last three months. Till now, I have not said this to anybody. Our priest is also this manager's maternal uncle. So I am waiting to see what I should do.*

I hope you are all right.

Inga

Journal

When Paddy brought me home, to the Divisional Officer's bungalow in Pollachi, I told him I was not afraid but that I did hope I would be able to start and end my novel. This was my deepest desire, I said, ever since I was ten years old. He listened in silence as I described the various roads and paths and alleys I had travelled, had explored, yet not found the one that was mine alone. He smiled and said that I would find my way, if only I stayed still.

'Stayed still?' I remember asking.

'Yes,' he replied. 'I have never forgotten a story I heard long ago of a man who was afraid of his footprints. So he ran and ran as fast as he could to get away from his footprints. But the more he ran, the more the footprints. He did not understand that if he had stopped and sat still, there would have been no footprints.'

'What happened to the man then?' I asked.

'Well, he ran so much and for so long, that he . . .'

'. . . Died I suppose.'

'Yes,' Paddy said quietly.

But I could not stop running yet. I could not tell Paddy of the desire deeper still, immeasurable, unquenchable. I had to find Inga, I had to tell her about . . . tell her that she burned within me, sometimes like a lamp flame, sometimes like fire.

O Inga! Inga! What did you do?

21

On the last day of my first stint in the hospital, I had an unexpected visitor. He was ushered in by a nurse, who told me he had come from Pollachi. He staggered a little as he entered. He had come a long, very weary way, an old shrunken man, his eyes filled with tears. Those eyes helped me recognize him, they had held the same tears for my sick father. Mikhale.

'Molay,' he said as he stood at the foot of my bed, his hand clutching the rail, 'Molay, I heard only two days before.'

I said nothing.

'Mol is angry I know it,' he went on, 'Please forgive this sinner molay. Before itself, Collector I should have called. Mol was not all right. I did not see. My mind was sad about mol's father.'

'Where did you go off so suddenly?' I asked rather sharply.

He wiped his face with the back of his hand, and then said, 'To pray I went. I came out, my head went dizzy. I fell. When my eyes opened, in my nephew's house, all were crying. Three days had gone, I did not know that.' After a pause, he continued, 'When I went to big house, mol had left. Mol's father . . . he is still like that . . .' He broke into sobs. I hated the sound, hated their meaning.

'That day,' I said, 'that day before you went away, you said something. About Inga. What was that?'

He controlled the sobs and then spoke more clearly and firmly than he had so far. 'Molay,' he said, 'she . . . Inga is not one ordinary child.'

'What do you mean?'

I saw him hesitate, consider what he was to say, and then, 'How to explain? She . . . she can make people all right, make illness go. Some . . . some power she has . . . No name it has which I know . . . Hindu friends will say Inga mol is one yogi.'

Yogi? What nonsense! Yogis were naked men with long beards and sticking out ribs, who sat on mountaintops with their eyes closed. My Inga a yogi? Utter rubbish!

Mikhale saw my disbelief and said, 'That astrologer, he saw it also. To Inga mol, he bowed, not to that baby.'

I gave myself time to collect my thoughts, I was still extremely angry.

'Why did you keep quiet then?' I asked. 'Why did you not speak?'

'Who will have listened?' he said sadly. 'In that house, Inga mol . . .' He stopped. 'Only that baby they saw as Bhagavati, especially Master. Like rock his belief was.'

'I did not believe that,' I reminded him. 'Great Aunt Kuppai did not either.'

'Yes. But she . . . she saw enemy in Inga mol and her mother always. From before itself.'

'Why?'

He did not reply. He looked confused as if he did not know where he was. He gazed through the window at the darkening sky, then abruptly, hurriedly he said, 'I am to go. It is time. Her I have to see. Before I go, her I have to see. The sea she will help me to cross . . .'

'So you know where Inga is?' I asked. It was not a question.

He did not answer. He mumbled something I could not catch, and began to move towards the door. In my desperation, I shouted, 'Where is Inga? Tell me, where is she. Tell me now.'

The door opened and the nurse looked in. 'Madam is all right?'

'Yes. Yes,' I said, impatiently. But she did not go. Instead, she looked at Mikhale and asked him, 'You are going? It is time for her medicine.'

I could have screamed. But before I could do anything at all, Mikhale spoke to the nurse. 'You can tell me where bus stop is?' he asked.

'Where you want to go?'

'Devi temple,' he said.

She half laughed. 'So many Devi temples there are here. Which one you want?'

He beat his forehead with the palm of his hand, and said, 'Old man I am. Stupid also. It is Kamakshi temple. Station Road.'

The nurse answered and I memorized every word. 'There is straight bus from here,' she said. Nine number. You cross the road to that side bus stop. You will go in two minutes no?'

Then she shut the door.

Mikhale turned his face to me again. 'You must forgive me molay,' he said in the old way, as if I were still a child. 'I am not to say where she is. You just keep on writing letters all right?'

With an effort, I lowered my voice. I asked, 'What is the place Mikhale? How many people know where she is?'

Suddenly he stopped mumbling and a sly look glazed his face.

'Seshu Maish told me she will ask and ask,' he said. 'But you keep your mouth closed fully. So I never told. Money also he gave to them sometimes.' Abruptly, he fell silent. He turned away from me and went to the door again. 'I must go molay,' he muttered. Then he went out of the room, and out of my life.

I remember that after Mikhale left, I sat frozen, my mind congealed. I could not think. I stared at the door he had closed behind him, at the floral printed curtain hanging crookedly across the window; I stared stupidly and long, that was all I could do. Gradually, my mind unfroze. Slowly, I began to consider what I had learnt from Mikhale, and I found myself plagued with questions that buzzed like wasps. How did Prof. Seshu know where Inga was? What was his interest in her? I suddenly remembered the day he had first seen Inga and how intently he had looked at her. Was his interest fixed on Inga or her mother? And Mikhale? My begetter's apparently devoted servant? I was convinced my father knew nothing of these goings-on; he was too wide-mouthed to keep secrets. So was Mikhale working against my father? Betraying him? Betraying me? Why did the professor say nothing to me? Did he not know of my . . . my affection for Inga, my cousin? What was wrong with my meeting her? Why was Inga herself hiding from me? Why? Why did she never tell me that Prof. Seshu and Mikhale visited her?

My mind boiled. I took out Inga's letters and looked through them feverishly. I saw then, that she had sometimes let slip references to events that I had not mentioned or did not remember having mentioned in my letters. Fool that I was, I had not noticed these before. Now I did, and I found myself trembling. Was Inga a part of this dastardly plot? What was the secret that I was not to know? Why was it so imperative that this something should be hidden from me? Why was I forbidden to see Inga? Why did Inga herself not wish me near her? It was all like some banal gothic novel, full of ghouls and half presences and sinisterdom.

The only way I would get answers to my questions, was by tracking down Inga. I did not need the reporter anymore.

I resolved that I would do that just as soon as I could. I now knew Seshu was a conspirator, a traitor, a Cassius. In the meanwhile however, I had to prepare my face for Paddy. He would arrive any moment. Inga's letters were scattered all across my bed, I put them away in the large envelope I had purloined from my father's office. Then I slid it, as I always did, with my diary, under the mattress at the head of my bed. My most precious things were safe there, hidden. The slovenly nurses never noticed the lump under my pillow and even if they did, they never asked me about it. In any case, I knew how to freeze any questioning. I was a VIP patient. They had to be careful how they treated me.

I had cleared the bed but I had to clear my mind before Paddy arrived. He tried so much to spend some little time with me every few days. I forced myself to think of the nurses and their sloppiness; they did not seem to care that the window curtain was torn and hung crookedly or that the door creaked hideously. They slept every afternoon so deeply that not even Rasputin could have charmed them out of their slumber. They lay like logs on the floor of the verandah outside my room; I envied them their sleep. For the Sub-Collector's wife shall sleep no more, Rapa shall sleep no more and still they cried . . .

There was a quiet Paddy knock on the door and he entered. He looked tired as usual but he smiled. I did too.

'I hear you had an unexpected visitor today?' he said. 'He must have made you happy.'

'I was glad to see him,' I lied, 'but he looked very unwell.'

'Your father's illness must have affected him badly,' Paddy said. 'He is tremendously attached to him.'

Later that evening, after dinner, as Paddy and I sat in the verandah of the Sub-Collector's bungalow, he said, hesitatingly, tenderly, 'I have a request to make of you and yet I don't know whether I should at all.'

What could he mean? I felt a shiver of apprehension. I stayed quiet.

'You say nothing, you don't even ask what it might be,' Paddy went on, 'and I am daunted. Yet, I must ask it. Please do forgive me but can you let go Komala Nivas?'

My thoughts had been fearful for so different a reason that it took me a moment to comprehend what Paddy had said.

'Let go Komala Nivas?'

'Yes,' he answered, speaking very rapidly, as if he had memorized the words. 'My mother should not have insisted on it, I do not want it, I will build you a home, it will be ours, yours and mine. Please can you give Komala Nivas back to your mother?'

'It was never hers,' I told him.

There was now a note of strain in his tone. 'True,' he said. 'Legally, technically, you are the owner of Komala Nivas because your great aunt willed it to you. But Rapa, think of this – your father built the house, he did not inherit it. Yet he and your mother live there now as tenants. Your tenants. When your father passes away, whenever that may be, where will your mother go? Where is she to stay?'

There was a sliver of silence between us.

'Let her stay there,' I said. 'I will not ask her to leave.'

Paddy sighed. After a pause, he said, a little sadly, 'Prof. Seshu has always warned his friends against getting attached to a house, to brick and mortar. But I know Komala Nivas is much more than brick and mortar to you.'

Brick and mortar, Komala Nivas? What did Seshu know?

'Did he ask you to talk to me?' I asked. 'The professor?'

'Well, he phoned from Komala Nivas. He is still there sorting out your father's papers. He needs to do it since your father is . . . well . . . not capable of doing anything now. He asked me what thoughts I had about Komala Nivas, and I agreed with him that . . .'

I cut him short. '. . . I'll give up my Komala Nivas,' I said. 'Bring me whatever paper I have to sign and I will do it.'

Paddy stayed silent; he understood my meaning and we did not speak of the matter again.

That night, I dreamt of Komala Nivas. It was night and there was a huge rain storm raging. There was no electricity. Inga and I were alone in the house. She had lit a hurricane lantern and we sat together in its shadow. Inga was humming a classical melody, a lullaby. I held my arms out to her and she came into them and nestled up to me. I kissed her face, she stopped humming and then I said, Inga, Inga my dearest, I . . . She broke away from me and began to laugh. She laughed and laughed and laughed and I woke up. Sweating.

What did you know about me, Mikhale? Were you not a seer too?

Letter from Inga

Dear Rapa,

There is some bad news. I just heard our Mikhale is missing for some days. I believe he went off somewhere without telling where he was going. After that nobody saw him again. Mikhale's son went here there everywhere but cannot find his father. I am feeling very very bad. Maybe he will still come back one day. But I am not sure.

Sorry.

Inga

Journal

A month later, I was back in hospital. I had become unmindful of the medicines I was to have taken regularly. Paddy looked white and strained as he brought me back to the old room, the same nurses, the same curtain hanging crookedly.

MURDER MOST FOUL
By a staff reporter

The body of a young woman was found yesterday in her house in Station Road. She was allegedly murdered by one or more assailants. Police are suspecting that she was attacked with a heavy kitchen utensil on Thursday afternoon. The woman was working as accounts clerk in the Devi temple on Station Road and used to live alone. On the day of the alleged murder, she left her office early as, according to the temple authorities, she was not feeling well. After that, nobody saw her. Her body was found the next morning by the flower seller who used to give her flowers every day at five in the morning.

Preliminary investigations by the police do not indicate the case to be one of murder for gain. Police sources say that her room had been scrutinized by the killer or killers. There were many papers on the floor, also some account books. The head priest of the temple has reportedly said that the deceased had noticed that there had been tampering with the temple accounts, perhaps by the manager. Police are questioning the manager.

Journal

It was all so easy, Paddy. I put on the slacks and overblouse that Lily had got tailored for me, the dark one, the one you said made me look like a French aristocrat. Of course, your cricket cap did spoil the look but it was really very hot. The nurses were all fast asleep, sprawled out in the verandah and I had to step over them as if they were so many puddles. I crossed the road and waited for the number nine bus. How excited I was. The driver told me where I was to get off. I found myself outside a small temple, its gates firmly shut. There were very few people on the road but one of them, an old woman, said, 'Thambi, come at five o'clock for evening pujai.' I did not know what to do. I looked about uncertainly, feeling a little dizzy, a little sick, extremely disheartened. And then . . .

Then I saw her. She seemed to have come out of nowhere, and now she was walking rapidly away from the temple. Why did she come out then, Paddy? She need not have come out into the afternoon heat like that. But she did. She walked down the road, in that quick way Inga has, wearing a red sari. I followed her. She did not notice me. Why didn't I call out to her even there on the road? I wanted to, I wanted to Paddy, but I didn't.

After about ten minutes of walking through small dirty lanes festooned with washing lines, we came to a broad street with houses hidden by trees and tall shrubs. Inga stopped at a small gate. I waited some distance away, as she unlocked it and went in. She did not lock the gate again. I waited for a few more minutes, my heart was thudding. I walked through the deep shadows of a garden towards a small cottage. The door was ajar and I went in. It was a one-room house. I walked in slowly; I had to stop to take my breath. The living room was bare except for a bedroll in a corner and a writing table with a neat pile of clothes on it. On which lay an open inland letter form. Dear Rapa, Why there are no letters from you for so many days? Are you all right . . .? And then, she was there, Inga was there at the doorway of the kitchen. Inga. My Inga, her face open in astonishment.

I remember walking towards her, holding out my arms. I remember so clearly my words. Inga. I have come. I have come to tell you I love you. I love you Inga. My dearest . . .

Why did she laugh Paddy? Why did Inga laugh? Nothing would have happened if . . . But Paddy she laughed. My arms were still held out but she turned her back on me and went into the kitchen, laughing. I followed her. She was still laughing, saying something I could not understand at first. Then I did. O god. The horror of it. The stench . . .

Why did you say it, Inga? Did you have to? In that way? 'Love?' you said. Amidst the dungfalls of laughter I heard you jeer. 'Love? Like that? I am your sister. You did not know? I am your father's another daughter.'

I snatched up something from the kitchen shelf. It was heavy. I hit him. I hit my father. He was laughing. I hit him in the face. Again and again. I hit my mother, she was laughing too. And Inga's mother. I hit them all. Again and again I hit them. Again and again. She fell. The laughter stopped. Blood pooled across the floor. It was very quiet. I threw down whatever it was I was holding, and went into the front room. I picked up the letter on the table, pushed it into my pocket. I remember how calm I was. I watched myself as I searched the drawers of the table. The first one had a candle, a matchbox and a pen, nothing else. I rummaged through the other; I threw out the ledgers and loose paper which it held. She had not kept any of my letters. Not one.

Afterwards? Afterwards, I went back through the shadowed garden, onto the road. I shut the gate behind me. The road was completely deserted. Everyone was dead. The sun lay all around in enormous clots. I took the same bus back. The driver called me 'thambi' this time and said, young brother, you should go to see a doctor, it may be TB. He was a sharp man. When I reached the hospital, I found the nurses were still asleep. I stepped over them, went into my room and changed my clothes. I took the letter out. I read again the three lines. Then, sitting on the bed, with her voice cupped in my palms, I wept.

Let the day be darkness wherein I was born. Was it Jude who said that? I have fallen into my own darkness. I have no more light. And never will have.

I could have done away with myself that day. Fallen into Inga's pool of blood, she beside me. She and I together.

But I walked away. I left her and walked back to agony. Why?

Was it because of Paddy?

Paddy, the only guardian I ever had.

These pages were once blank, they were my unprospected lands. Here, the streams and hillsides I would have traced, the pathways and streets I would have mapped, here, the pavilioned city I would have built, with its golden domes, its towering spires, its proud, fluttering flags. I will never build it now.

Nor will I ever find that walled garden where the hibiscus blows, with sweet musk roses and eglantine. Where stamens of rain fall on warm, white breasts.

I scribble and scribble on. There is nothing else I can do. There is no mouse hole to disappear into. Only vast mirrors of memories. Regurgitating mirrors. They mock me. How they laugh at me through the long days and nights. Who said life was short?

You remember the green mangoes, Inga? You remember I told you I wanted to write books? You laughed, you remember? You laughed. Were you laughing at me?

Inga I see you. I see you. Can you hear me? Please walk me across the waters Inga. Please. I know you can. Please Inga.

AN AFTERWORD

Now that you have read Rapa's account, you have every right to ask why I did not immediately take her notebook to the police. After all, this was in the nature of a confession, and as a law-abiding citizen and a magistrate, I should have done so. But I could not. She had said I was her only true guardian, I could not break her trust. I would not have her memory besmirched, I would not give up my Rapa to the coarseness of officialdom. Yet this resolve was not easy to live with. Through sleepless nights and lonely, work-heavy days, I argued endlessly with myself. The confessor was no more. What could a police investigation do now? Who was there to be arrested? Who was to stand trial? I told myself that I would act only if the investigation led to a wrong arrest. I made discreet enquiries frequently. Apart from some questioning of officials in the temple where the victim worked, there were no suspects traced. In the absence of any pressure from family members or vote-hungry local politicians, the case was eventually closed.

I know I have done great wrong in keeping the contents of Rapa's journal secret for more than forty years. That has been my ordeal. The world has changed considerably over these years and what could not be told then may be understood now. It is in that hope that I have summoned up the courage to have this published. Over these years, Rapa's presence has been with me always, in every waking moment, and in fitful sleep. This book, I hope, is our expiation, Rapa's and mine.

She died in hospital, eight months after she was diagnosed and treated for Hodgkin's disease, a cancer of the lymph nodes. For a week before that, she asked me to read aloud her favourite poems. She listened, her eyes closed. Now and then she repeated a line softly to herself. That fateful day, as I sat at her bedside, she asked me to read from a volume of Christina Rossetti's poems. As I read, she opened her eyes, smiled and said, clearly and distinctly, 'And if thou wilt, remember, and if thou wilt, forget.'

Those were her last words.

ACKNOWLEDGEMENTS

My fantastic family has walked with me through the briars and thickets of writing – Abhijit, Alo, Ashwin, Anindita, Aditya, Amaya, Raju, Pamposh and Amma. My deepest love.

My very special thanks to Deepthi Talwar and her team at Westland.

and

My profound gratitude to my Guru, Sri M.

www.ingramcontent.com/pod-product-compliance
Lightning Source LLC
Chambersburg PA
CBHW071534200326
41519CB00021BB/6486